# Suffering —
# understanding the love of
# God

Selections from the writings of John Calvin

Compiled and annotated by Joseph A. Hill

 EVANGELICAL PRESS

EVANGELICAL PRESS
Faverdale North Industrial Estate, Darlington, DL3 0PH, England

Evangelical Press USA
P. O. Box 825, Webster, New York 14580, USA

e-mail: sales@evangelicalpress.org

web: http://www.evangelicalpress.org

First published 2005

**British Library Cataloguing in Publication Data available**

ISBN-10 0 85234 607 7                    ISBN-13 978 0 85234 6066 9

# Contents

# *Foreword*

*But Elihu son of Barakel the Buzite, of the family of Ram,
became very angry with Job for justifying himself rather than
God* (Job 32:2, NIV).

A perennial problem for humankind and especially for the
people of God is to reconcile the existence of suffering in a
world created and sustained by a good and gracious God. This
issue casts its shadow over philosophical, theological, and
pastoral engagements, as evidenced in the responses of Job's
interlocutors to Job's plight and as experienced in daily life.
What is the significance of suffering? What does it mean to
suffer and experience pain in light of an omni-benevolent God?
What purposes might suffering serve and to what end is pain
directed? What might one say or how might one pray for one
who suffers? These kinds of questions drive the inquiry into this
perennial problem that vexes the theistic mind.

As I read my colleague and friend's book, *Suffering —
understanding the love of God,* I was impressed with the Elihu-
like treatment of the topic of suffering found in it. Elihu grew
angry with both Job and his interlocutors because neither
considered their arguments as an opportunity to commend and
defend the rightness of the eternal God. Although they struggled
with the meaning of suffering in Job's case, each of the parties
presumed that suffering was only punitive, a punishment for
some infraction of the law of God. None, save Elihu, sought for

a God's-eye view of the subject, and certainly none except the voice from the whirlwind provided a revelatory analysis of its domain. In this book Professor Hill, echoing the voice of the reformer John Calvin, provides such an analysis not with Elihu's anger, but with the Saviour's compassion.

Professor Hill's treatment of suffering and the Christian life reads Midrashically. The reader finds himself taken on a journey through sources and comments on sources related to Calvin's analysis — his justification of God — of suffering. The chapters of the book provide an ongoing dialogue of Calvinian texts (*Institutes*, Commentaries, theological treatises, and letters) with expositions, narrative, prayers, and stories given by Professor Hill. Together these illuminate Calvin's perspective on suffering and his confidence in the divine provision for sanctifying grace for the believer through suffering.

Professor Hill's wise collation of texts illustrates Calvin's concern for a theologically rooted pastoral engagement of the problem of suffering. He begins with the assertion that this question can only be engaged Christianly through the disclosure of God's character known in Scripture. All other attempts will ultimately fail without this God's-eye view. The reader engages the purposes, providence, and goodness of God (theodicy) in a redemptive framework in the early chapters of the text. By this I mean that Professor Hill and Calvin contend that human suffering must be viewed in light of God's suffering love evidenced in and made effectual through the atoning work of Jesus Christ. Discussions of suffering ought to ensue in the *light of the cross*. The middle chapters lead one through the pastoral implications of such a view. Suffering produces godliness, purity, hope, prayer, and patience. Suffering identifies one with other believers and their circumstances throughout history and over the globe. Suffering is the crucible through which faith is tried and tested. Finally, through Job's whirlwind, that marvellous depiction by God of his own glories and grace, the reader is reminded of the necessity of a theologically grounded purview for the problem of suffering.

There is a timeliness to Professor Hill's book for both the church and the society. In an age in which the pastoral and the theological are often presented as conflictual, *Suffering — understanding the love of God* is a faithful reminder of the biblical and Calvinist tradition that weds these while promoting the growth of the covenant elect. It heeds the contention of Dr David Wells that the contemporary church languishes theologically from the 'weightlessness of God' and, as a consequence, is practically barren. The union of a theologically informed discussion with a grace-filled practice found in this text is welcomed for pastors, theologians, and other sufferers on their pilgrimage.

This book is timely in response to two other issues in contemporary culture and emergent from the comments in the previous paragraph. Much of the church today reflects the therapeutic individualism of the larger society. Folks imbibed with the spirit of self-esteem often fail to know the mother of all virtue for Calvin, humility. Patient humility, from the Hill/Calvin perspective, serves as the ground from which godliness is fostered through suffering. Self-esteem, or the idolization of self, is incapable of an Elihu-like response as demonstrated in this book; it is too concerned with self to offer such a defence. Further, there are those in the church and society who manifest a kind of Stoic *apatheia*, a denial of passions. Calvin acknowledges the insipidness of this perspective and treats suffering as real, in and through which one struggles to attain the high hope of glory. Unfortunately, the clear light of Calvin's view is far too often shaded by the dominance of these perspectives.

I first met Professor Reverend Joseph A. Hill over thirty years ago at Geneva College. After a twenty-year separation, I returned to Beaver Falls, Pennsylvania, the home of Geneva College and my home town, to pastor a church that Joe had served as interim pastor. I found that the theological and pastoral integrity and concern I experienced years before continued to vivify Joe's life. The principles and insights contained in this book are the stuff of this Elihu-like advocate of God's grace in the midst of suffering. I, for one, have been blessed by Joe's friendship and honoured to share these reflections.

Dr Robert M. Frazier
Geneva College

# Preface

Planning and preparing a manuscript for publication can be, and usually is, an arduous task, even with modern tools like a computer with its vast capabilities for networking and research. Throughout my preparation of this book I have been guided by the caveat issued by John Calvin in his exposition of Psalm 73:24, a prayer that expresses trust in God: 'You will guide me with your counsel.' Near the beginning of my work I placed in plain sight on my desk Calvin's words, writ large: 'Whoever dares, in a spirit of confident reliance on his own wisdom, to engage in any undertaking will inevitably be involved in confusion and shame for his presumption, since he arrogates to himself what is peculiar to God alone.'

The subject of this book reflects Job's understanding of God's purpose in human suffering — 'When he has tested me, I shall come forth as gold' (Job 23:10). Job's expectation can be shared by everyone who trusts God through the experience of adversity, since affliction and distress, whatever form they may take, contribute, often in mysterious ways, to the believer's salvation and ultimate good. Pain and suffering are the common lot of humankind. Seeing that the church, though protected by God's gracious intervention, is not spared from suffering, Calvin warns that 'The guardianship of God does not secure us from being sometimes exercised with the cross and afflictions, and that therefore the faithful ought not to promise themselves a delicate and easy life in this world, it being enough for them not to be abandoned of God when they stand in need of his help.'

Pain and suffering have meanings which cannot be explained except in the light of Scripture. Even God's revelation in Scripture, however, does not give fully satisfactory answers to all questions concerning human suffering: Why do faithful children of God suffer, sometimes more than 'the wicked'? If God is good and all-powerful, why does he permit tragedy to strike, as a thief in the night, those whom he loves? Does God actually inflict suffering upon his children? Since our Lord promised that whatever we ask in his name will be done for us, why are our prayers for healing and relief from suffering unanswered? Although Scripture does address such issues, we see 'as in a mirror, dimly'. Accordingly, Calvin reminds us repeatedly that the mystery of human suffering remains, since God's ways are incomprehensible — that God has secrets which he does not share with us.

John Calvin's writings — his commentaries on biblical books, his sermons and correspondence, and especially his *Institutes of the Christian religion* — are a rich mine from which I have selected nuggets of divine truth about human suffering, especially as it relates to the sufferings of Christ. I have organized the materials included in this book in terms of the central themes of Calvin's treatment of adversity, suffering, and grief. In general terms, these themes are the purposes of suffering; the providence of God and his infliction of suffering; punishment or chastisement due to sin; the promises of God, which are the foundation of trust; prayer, the sufferer's recourse; the protection which God affords his children even in times of trial; the gift of perseverance, which is the fruit of faith and hope; praise and thanksgiving for God's goodness and mercy; the believer's participation in the sufferings of Christ; the prospect, or hope, of heavenly glory for those who suffer; and pastoral concerns which address those profoundly puzzling questions about God's plan for the Christian's life in this world and, finally, in his heavenly kingdom.

Perhaps the most grievous suffering of recent times is connected with the ongoing war in Iraq. Thousands have faced the terrors of combat, imprisonment, and torture. Families around the world are anguished as they consider the possibility that their loved ones could be killed in combat or captured as prisoners of war; and where such prospects have become realities, the emotional impact is unbearable, apart from divine grace.

Navy Lieutenant Carey H. Cash, a chaplain serving with the US Marines in Iraq, has authored a stirring account of the way in which the Fifth Marine Battalion experienced God's presence amid their fears as they were confronted by the enemy. The first ground force to cross the Iraqi borders at the start of 'Operation Iraqi Freedom', they witnessed the fires of burning oil wells flaring in the night sky, the exploding artillery fire, and a direct hit on an Iraqi tank, causing it to burst into flames, a 'fiery furnace' as Lt Cash calls it in his book, *A table in the presence*.[1] As the Marines and sailors under his pastoral care stared at those awesome flames and artillery tracers piercing the darkness, they asked many questions about faith and salvation and how to draw closer to God. Many of them, faced with danger for the first time, realized their need of God's presence and protection. At home, parents prayed for them and wrote letters telling them of hearts heavy with apprehension and assuring them that the shield of God surrounded them. Much of the story of human suffering during the war in Iraq has yet to be told, but Cash's book reveals the tests of faith in the midst of combat and God's grace that makes faithful men and women 'more than conquerors'.

Human suffering includes all sorts of pain and distress which accompany serious illness, loss of loved ones or friends, natural disasters such as earthquakes, floods, and forest fires; poverty and hunger, accidents, persecution, and many other unfortunate events that touch our lives.

Reading a book about human suffering can be disconcerting and depressing, to be sure; but reading what the Book of books reveals about suffering and about God's promises of deliverance and gracious intervention should be heartening and uplifting — and that is the fundamental purpose of Calvin's commentary upon the subject of faith tested by suffering.

When Augustine published his *Confessions,* he presented a copy to a friend, and on the blank page in the front of the book he wrote these memorable words: 'Behold me [herein], that you may not praise me above what I am ... and if there is anything in me that pleases you, praise with me him whom I wish to be praised.' Calvin would have concurred with Augustine's humble tribute to God's goodness, and so do I.

The idea for this book was prompted by a question put to me by David Clark of Evangelical Press — whether I had in mind another book on Calvin. The idea of another book (besides *Grace and its fruits,* © 2000) appealed to me, and after doing some research in Calvin's writings I settled on human suffering, a subject which is of universal interest. To David Clark, then, I am primarily indebted for the stimulus and subsequent encouragement which he gave. I acknowledge with gratitude also the careful work of Anne Williamson, Senior Editor, and that of Mary MacDonald-Murray, whose skilful editing of the manuscript and modernizing of the excerpts from Calvin give this book a more readable style.

I owe sincere thanks also to others who have helped me with the preparation of this book. Several of my colleagues read portions of the manuscript and made helpful suggestions, namely, Harry Farra, Willard McMillan, Kenneth Smith, and William Teague; Barbara Adams Hill, my wife and 'the excellent companion of my life' (Calvin's encomium in praise of his beloved Idelette), whose forbearance and gracious criticism are deeply appreciated; Linda Hughes, my daughter, whose expertise in English usage was most helpful, and who supplied certain quotations.

To the congregation of Park Presbyterian Church, in Beaver, Pennsylvania, whose gift of a computer enabled me to do the necessary research and typing of the manuscript, I offer my sincere thanks.

The publishers from whose copyrighted works I reproduced certain passages by permission:

Abingdon Press (Nashville)
Baker Book House Company (Grand Rapids, Michigan)
Banner of Truth Trust (Edinburgh, Scotland and Carlisle, Pennsylvania)
Evangelical Press (Darlington, England)
Thomas Nelson, Inc. (Nashville, Tennessee)
Wm B. Eerdmans Publishing Co. (Grand Rapids, Michigan)

All Scripture quotations, unless otherwise indicated, are taken from the New King James Version. Copyright © 1982 by Thomas Nelson, Inc. Used by permission. All rights reserved.

It is a disputed question how far one is justified, when quoting Calvin, in modernizing the spelling of certain words and, in some cases, substituting modern equivalents for archaic words. To retain uniformly the original form of the words is not only inconvenient for many readers, but is sometimes misleading or incomprehensible. We have, accordingly, modified archaic spellings and replaced obsolete words, retaining occasionally, however, archaic forms where such retention appeared to add to the significance.

Joseph A. Hill

*Suffering — understanding
the love of God*

Selections from the writings of John Calvin

---

# Chapter 1

# Living under the cross

---

'Because we are so inclined to put our own comfort
and advantage first and avoid adversity ... Our
most merciful Father comforts us by this teaching:
that he promotes our salvation by inflicting the cross
upon us.'

# I.

# Living under the cross

*God uses suffering to purge sin from our lives, strengthen our commitment to him, force us to depend on grace, bind us together with other believers, produce discernment, foster sensitivity, discipline our minds, spend our time wisely, stretch our hope, cause us to know Christ better, make us long for truth, lead us to repentance of sin, teach us to give thanks in time of sorrow, increase faith, and strengthen character.*

Joni Eareckson Tada

When a three-year old child hunches down on the driveway peering under the family car to pat her furry kitten, and her father, unable to see the child, starts the engine and backs over her, that tragedy has no purpose, as far as anyone can see. The meaning of sorrow and grief over a child's death is never readily discernible and in most cases is impossible to grasp. The same is true of all human suffering: even though we earnestly believe the Bible's claim that God has a purpose in inflicting or permitting suffering, God's purposes remain ultimately incomprehensible — because God himself is incomprehensible.

The Bible nevertheless does shed some light on God's inscrutable purpose: that all suffering endured by God's people serves, in one way or another, to work together for their salvation. Jeremiah 36:3 leaves no doubt about God's beneficent purpose in bringing adversity upon his people: 'It may be that the house of Judah will hear all the adversities which I purpose to bring upon them, that everyone may turn from his evil way, that I may forgive their iniquity and their sin.' In his comment on this verse Calvin states: 'Here God explains the object he had in view: to make another trial whether the Israelites would be healed, so that the teaching of the prophet might be conducive to their salvation.' That much we are permitted to know; beyond that, 'We cannot comprehend God's incomprehensible counsel.'[1]

## God's purposes are many

The Scriptures in many places plainly and distinctly declare that God, for various reasons, uses adversity to test the faithful — sometimes to teach them patience; at other times to subdue the sinful desires of their old natures; sometimes to cleanse and purify them from remnants of their sinful natures; at other times to humble them; or to make them an example to others. Sometimes God uses adversity to stir his people to deeper reflection on the things of heaven.[2]

## Suffering under the cross stimulates prayer

In Psalm 25, the psalmist, by repeating his complaints so frequently, shows that the calamities with which he was assailed were not some trivial evils. We ought to take careful note of this, so that when similar trials and afflictions are measured out to us, we may be enabled to lift up our souls to God in prayer; the Holy Spirit has set this example before our eyes, that our minds may not fail us under the number or weight of afflictions. In seeking relief from his trials, David also prays that his sins may be pardoned, recalling … what he had already stated: that he could not expect to enjoy any divine favour, unless he were first reconciled to God by receiving a free pardon. There are those, demonstrating a lack of spiritual awareness, who are content to be delivered from physical affliction and never search out the sin in their own hearts, preferring rather to remain oblivious to their sins. To find a remedy, therefore, to cares and sorrows, David begins by imploring the remission of his sins, because, so long as God is angry with us, it must necessarily follow that all our affairs will come to an unhappy end; and God always has just ground of displeasure with us so long as our sins continue — that is to say, until he pardons them. And although the Lord has various ends in view in bringing his people under the cross, yet we ought to hold fast the principle, that, as often as God afflicts us, we are called to examine our own hearts and humbly seek reconciliation with him.[3]

God places us in the crucible of suffering intending that we shall give ourselves to prayer, emulating the psalmist: 'I cried out to you, O LORD, and to the LORD I made supplication' (Ps. 30:8):

As the iron which has become rusted is no use until it is heated again in the fire and beaten with the hammer, so, in the same way, when physical security has once more gained mastery, no one can give himself cheerfully to prayer until he has been softened by the cross and thoroughly subdued. And this is the chief advantage of afflictions: that while they make us aware of our wretchedness, they stimulate us again to beg God's favour.

## Living under the cross means trusting in God's power

Because we are so inclined to put our own comfort and advantage first and avoid adversity, Calvin asserts, 'Our most merciful Father comforts us by this teaching: that he promotes our salvation by inflicting the cross upon us.'[4]

> While there are many reasons it is necessary for us to live constantly under the cross, the only thing which made it necessary for our Lord to undertake to bear the cross was to testify and prove his obedience to the Father. As feeble as we are by nature, and as inclined to believe in our own goodness and righteousness, we readily trust in our own ability to stand unimpaired and invincible against all difficulties — unless we are vividly reminded of our weakness. Hence we indulge a stupid and empty confidence in ourselves, and then, trusting to it, we puff ourselves up with pride before the Lord himself — as if our own abilities were sufficient without his grace.
>
> This arrogance is best restrained when the Lord proves to us by experience how great our weakness and our frailty are. Therefore he visits us with disgrace, or poverty, or bereavement, or disease, or other afflictions. Feeling altogether unable to bear these burdens, we immediately ... give way. Humbled in this way, we learn to invoke his strength, which alone can enable us to bear up under a weight of affliction. Even the holiest believers, however well aware that they do not stand in their own strength, but by the grace of God, would feel too secure in their own fortitude and constancy, were they not brought to a more thorough knowledge of themselves by the trial of the cross.[5]

Calvin, in the *Golden booklet of the true Christian life*, reiterates his assertion that adversity brings with it encouragement to trust God for strength and protection. When adversity robs believers of 'foolish confidence' in themselves and they look to God for help, Calvin says, 'They experience the nearness of the divine protection which is to them a strong fortress.'[6] When God divests us of confidence in our own strength, or patience, or endurance, it is then that we 'take refuge in the grace of God'.[7]

> Although in times of tranquillity believers may flatter themselves that they have attained a greater degree of constancy and patience, when they are humbled by adversity they learn how far they have been deceived. Warned by such evidence of their diseased spiritual condition, they make progress in humility and, divesting themselves of their sinful confidence in the flesh, cast themselves on the grace of God. When they have done so, they experience the presence of the divine power, which proves to be ample protection.[8]

## Suffering teaches us patience, hope, and obedience

> When Paul says that tribulation produces patience, and patience, character (Rom. 5:3-4), he is explaining the lessons taught by suffering. God has promised to be with believers during times of trial, and when they feel the truth of the promise, supported by his hand, they endure patiently. They could never do this by their own strength. Patience, therefore, gives believers experiential proof that God does indeed provide the help that he has promised whenever there is need. In this way also, their faith is confirmed, for it would be very ungrateful not to expect that in the future God's truth will be, as they have already seen, firm and constant. We now see what benefits we derive from the cross. As tribulation undermines our false opinions of our own strength and exposes the hypocrisy

of which we are so fond, our trials expel our confidence in ourselves. Humbled in this way, we learn to rely on God alone, which keeps us from sinking under our afflictions. Hope follows victory as the Lord, by performing what he has promised, establishes his truth regarding the future. If these were the only reasons for us to suffer, still they would be sufficient to show how necessary it is for us to bear the cross.[9]

Another purpose that the Lord has in afflicting his people is to test their patience and train them to obedience — not that they can produce obedience to him apart from his enabling them, but because he is pleased to display striking proof of the grace he has conferred upon his saints. He desires evidence of his grace at work in the lives of believers. Accordingly, by demonstrating openly the strength and endurance with which he has provided his servants, he is said to try their patience. Hence God is said to have tempted Abraham (Gen. 21:1, 12), making proof of Abraham's faith by his not declining to sacrifice his only son. Hence, too, Peter tells us that our faith is proved by trials just as gold is tried in a furnace of fire.

In order to prevent the virtues he has conferred upon believers from lurking in obscurity or lying useless and perishing, God does right in supplying the materials and circumstances for exercising those qualities. This is the best reason for the afflictions of the saints, since without those trials, their patience could not exist. I say that they are also trained to obedience by the cross, because in that way they are taught to live not according to their own wishes but by the will or God. Seneca[10] mentions that there was an old proverb, 'Follow God', by which people were exhorted to endure adversity, implying that men only truly submit to God's yoke when they are under his discipline. If it is right that we should in all things prove our obedience to our heavenly Father, certainly we ought not decline any method by which he trains us to obedience.

Still, however, we do not see how necessary that obedience is, unless at the same time we consider how prone we are to shake off God's yoke whenever our old nature has been treated with gentleness or indulgence. We are like unruly horses, that, if kept idle and left to eat for a few days, become unmanageable and no longer recognize the rider whose command they had previously obeyed implicitly. And we invariably become what God complains of in the people of Israel: waxing gross and fat, we kick against him who reared and nursed us (Deut. 32:15). The kindness of God should draw us to ponder and love his goodness, but the rebelliousness of our sinful nature causes us invariably to be corrupted by his generosity; we require his discipline to restrain us from such impudence.

In order that we do not become over-confident in our own wealth, or grow proud and insolent with our own accomplishments, the Lord interferes by means of the cross as he sees fit, subduing and curbing in various ways the arrogance of our natures. As we do not all labour under the same disease, we do not all need the same difficult cure. Hence we see that all do not undergo the same discipline. The heavenly physician treats some gently, while others receive harsher remedies; his purpose is to provide a cure for all. And as all, without a single exception, are diseased with sin, none of us is left free and untouched.[11]

## Suffering is meant to further our salvation

In order to keep us obedient, our merciful Father must not only prevent our weakness but also must often correct our faults. When we suffer trials, we ought to call to mind our recent actions, words, and thoughts, to search out those things that are cause for chastisement. Yet the exhortation to patience in the face of adversity should not be based primarily on the acknowledgement of sin. Scripture supplies a better reason: in adversity, 'We are chastened by the Lord, that we may not be condemned with the world' (1 Cor. 11:32). Therefore, even in the bitterness of suffering, we ought to recognize the kindness and mercy of our Father, since he does not cease to further our salvation. He afflicts us, not in order to ruin or destroy us, but rather to deliver us from the condemnation that the world faces. Let this thought lead us to what Scripture elsewhere teaches: 'My son, do not despise the chastening of the LORD, nor detest his correction; for whom the LORD loves he corrects, just as a father the son in whom he delights' (Prov. 3:11-12). When we become aware of the Father's discipline, should we not behave as obedient children rather than rebelliously imitate desperate men who are hardened in wickedness? God condemns us to destruction if he does not chastise us and call us back when we fall away from him; 'but if you are without chastening ... then you are illegitimate and not sons' (Heb. 12:8). We are most contrary and obstinate if we cannot bear him while he is displaying his goodwill towards us and taking such care for our salvation.[12]

## God's purpose does not conform to a uniform rule

God at times lays upon the faithful the same adversities by which he punishes the ungodly. The psalmist observes this 'inconsistency', yet he also acknowledges the blessings which God bestows upon his servants. He declares accordingly, 'I have been young, and now am old; yet I have not seen the righteous forsaken, nor his descendants begging bread'

(Ps. 37:25). Calvin's comment reinforces God's ample provision for his servants:

> This raises a difficult question ... for certainly many right-eous men have been reduced to begging. David, in Psalm 37:25, refers to Deuteronomy 15:4, where begging is reckoned among the curses of God, from which those who fear and serve God are exempt. What David from his own experience declares in Psalm 37:25 pertains to every era. How then is this consistent — that none of the righteous ever begged for his bread — since Christ places Lazarus among the most abject of beggars (Luke 16:20)?
>
> We must bear in mind ... that no absolute rule can be established with respect to the temporal blessings God confers upon his people. There are various reasons why God does not manifest his favour equally to all the godly in this world. He chastises some while sparing others; he heals some of mysterious ailments while passing by others who do not need that kind of healing; he exercises the patience of some according to the spirit of fortitude he has given them; he punishes others by way of example. In general, he humbles all by the tokens of his anger so that by subtle warnings they may be brought to repentance. He also leads them, by a variety of means, to fix their thoughts on the heavenly life — and yet it is not a vain or imaginary thing that ... God guarantees earthly blessings to his servants as proof of his favour towards them.
>
> An abundance of earthly blessings, sufficient to meet all of their needs, is promised to the godly. However, it must be understood that God will bestow these blessings as he sees fit. Accordingly, the blessing of God may be manifested in the lives of men in general, while for their good some of the godly may live in poverty. If that should happen, those faithful ones should fix their thoughts on heaven, that blessed state in which God will largely rec-

ompense them for all that is lacking in the blessings of this transitory life.

We must also bear in mind that there is no inconsistency if God involves the faithful in the same punishments by which he takes vengeance on the ungodly — seeing them, for example, affected by the same diseases. Although the godly do not despise God, nor devote themselves to wickedness, nor even act according to their own inclinations, yet they are not free from sin or blame. Therefore, it should not surprise us that they are sometimes subjected to punishment. We are, however, certain of this: that God makes provision for his own people, and that, being content with their lot, they will never be in want; as Paul says in Philippians 6:12, by living sparingly, they always have enough.[13]

'Fire is the test of gold; adversity, of strong men.'
Seneca, *On providence,* 5.9

Though the prophet Zechariah, whose prophecies date from 520 to 518 B.C., shared with his contemporaries a zeal for a rebuilt temple and a purified community after Israel's exile, he warned the people that God's purifying would come by their being tested through affliction. God, speaking by the prophet, declares, 'I will bring the one-third of them through the fire, will refine them as silver is refined, and test them as gold is tested. They will call upon my name, and I will answer them. I will say, "This is my people"; and each one will say, "The LORD is my God"' (Zech. 13:9).

Calvin's comment upon the prophet's words focuses on the purification of those whom God brings 'through the fire'. God's purpose is not to consume them, but to purify them for his service:

'He will prove them', he says, 'as silver and gold.' The stubble and the chaff, as John the Baptist teaches us, are indeed cast into the fire (Matt. 3:12), but without any benefit; for the fire consumes the refuse and the chaff and whatever is perishable. But the silver and the gold are put in the fire so that greater purity may be produced and that the preciousness of the metals may become more apparent. Silver, when mined, looks much like the earth from which it comes; gold is similar. But the furnace purifies the dross from the gold and silver so that they attain their value and excellence. So Zechariah says that when God casts his faithful people into the fire, it is according to his paternal purpose: they who once were filthy, in whom dross abounded, become gold and silver.[14]

Calvin observes, moreover, that the church also needs the cleansing fires of affliction:

Though God tries his elect by the fire of afflictions, he does observe moderation: they would faint away if he were to purify them to the core all at once. It is, however, necessary to pass through this trial of which the prophet Zechariah speaks: and thus the state of the church is described — that it ought to be always and continually cleansed, for we are completely unclean. After God has washed us by his Spirit, still many spots of uncleanness remain in us; besides, we contract other pollutions, for we are easily contaminated by those vices which surround us on every side.[15]

## God's purpose is that we might be conformed to his Son

As Peter shows us, our faith is more precious than gold or silver, so it is reasonable that it should be tried. By this means also, our old natures are put to death, that we might not be rooted in our love for this world. More sinful inclinations than we can imagine are corrected as we are taught humility, and our pride, always greater than it ought to be, is brought down. By trials, God also teaches us how much we ought to esteem his Word; if it costs us nothing, we do not understand its value. So he permits us to be afflicted for the sake of his Word, in order to show us how very precious he considers it. Beyond all else, God desires us to be conformed to the image of his Son — as it is fitting that there should be conformity between the head and the members of the body. When we suffer persecution for God's truth, let us not believe that God has forsaken us; rather, let us be assured that he works all things for our greater good. If that idea is repugnant to us, it is because we are always more inclined to seek our rest here below than in the kingdom of heaven. Since our triumph is in heaven, we must be prepared for combat while we live here upon the earth.[16]

The figure of the church's being tried by fire as in a crucible is very graphic, as Calvin's comment on Psalm 66:10 reveals: 'For you, O God, have tested us; you have refined us as silver is refined.' Calvin's remarks emphasize God's benevolent purpose in afflicting the faithful: when testing their faith and obedience, God always intends suffering for their good.

When faced with affliction, it is of great importance that we should consider it as coming from God and as expressly intended for our good. It is in reference to this that the psalmist speaks of their having been *proved and tried.*

While he speaks clearly of God's trying his children with a view to purging away their sin, as dross is expelled from the silver by fire, he would imply, also, that trial had been made of their patience. The figure implies that their probation had been severe; for silver is cast repeatedly into the furnace. God's children express themselves thankful to God that, while proved with affliction, they had not been destroyed by it, although their affliction was both varied and severe...[17]

## Faith is more precious than gold

Our faith is tested in the crucible of suffering and is thus purified. The fire of affliction also reveals the quality of our faith:

If we prize a perishable metal like gold so much that, to prove its value, we test it with fire, is it any wonder that God should want to test our faith, which he prizes so much more highly, in the same way? Peter compares faith to gold so as to present faith as the more precious of the two, and to imply that it is worth the trial to which God subjects it. He may have been speaking of a double testing of gold with fire: once when it is purified of its dross, and then again when it is tested for judging its quality. Both of these tests apply to faith as well. Much of the impurity of unbelief remains in us. When we are, as it were, purified in God's furnace or crucible by various afflictions, the dross of unbelief is purged, and faith becomes pure and clean before God. At the same time, it is tested to show whether it is a true or a false faith. It is the same with gold as with silver; for since silver is worthless before it is purified, so also our faith receives the honour of a crown before God, when it is purified in the proper way.[18]

## Sorrow and joy are mingled together

When Christians must endure affliction, they can by faith 'exult'
in the hope of heaven. They rejoice even while they sorrow.

> Peter exhorts rather than praises them, for his object was
> to show the fruit that was to come from the hope of salva-
> tion — even spiritual joy, by which not only the bitterness
> of all evil might be mitigated, but also all sorrow over-
> come... It seems somewhat inconsistent when he says
> that the faithful, who exulted with joy, were at the same
> time sorrowful, for these are contrary feelings. But the
> faithful know by experience how these things can exist
> together... Faithful believers are not logs of wood, nor
> have they divested themselves of human feelings, but
> they are affected by sorrow, fear, and danger, and feel
> poverty as an evil and persecutions as hard and difficult
> to be borne. Hence they experience sorrow from evils,
> but it is so mitigated by faith that they do not cease at the
> same time to rejoice... Though joy overcomes sorrow, it
> does not put an end to it, for it does not divest us of hu-
> manity... All those who regard their troubles as necessary
> trials for their salvation not only rise above them, but also
> turn them into an occasion of joy.[19]

## Christian joy centres in Christ

Joy, a fruit of the Holy Spirit's indwelling, differs from happiness
or momentary elation over one's good fortune. It is a sustained
mood of exultation which issues from the assurance of God's
favour and the hope of an inheritance in the heavenly kingdom.
Christian hope centres in Jesus Christ; it is an eschatological joy
related to the expectation of the return of Christ. Peter speaks of
an incorruptible inheritance that is reserved in heaven for

believers: '… salvation ready to be revealed in the last time. In this you greatly rejoice' (1 Peter 1:4-7), even though your faith is being tested, tried as it were by fire.

The 'various trials' by which the 'pilgrims' of the early church were grieved had a noble purpose. God intended by means of trials to prove their faith: 'that the genuineness of [their] faith, being much more precious than gold that perishes, though it is tested by fire, may be found to praise, honour, and glory at the revelation of Jesus Christ' (1 Peter 1:7). Calvin understood the Christians' ability to 'rejoice with joy inexpressible' amid trials as eschatological joy, issuing from their genuine faith in Christ:

> This phrase, 'the revelation of Jesus Christ', is added that the faithful might learn to hold on courageously to the last day. For our life is now hidden in Christ, and will remain hidden and, as it were, buried, until Christ appears from heaven. The whole course of our life leads to the destruction of the external man, and all the things we suffer are, as it were, the preludes to death. It is therefore necessary that we should fix our own eyes on Christ if we wish in our afflictions to behold glory and render praise. Trials, though to us full of reproach and shame, become glorious in Christ; but that glory is not yet plainly seen, for the day of resurrection is not yet come.[20]

In a similar vein, the apostle James exhorts the Jews who were 'scattered abroad' to rejoice while suffering the trial of their faith: 'Count it all joy when you fall into various trials, knowing that the testing of your faith produces patience…' (James 1:2-3).

Calvin's exposition of James's exhortations would encourage the persecuted church in the Sudan, Iran, Afghanistan, China, and other countries today:

> James's first exhortation is to bear trials with a cheerful mind. It was especially necessary at that time to comfort

the Jews, almost overwhelmed as they were with troubles. The very name of the nation was so infamous that
they were hated and despised by all people wherever
they went; and their condition as Christians rendered
them even more miserable because they regarded some
of their own nation as their most inveterate enemies. At
the same time, this consolation was not suited only to one
time, but it is always useful to believers, whose life is a
constant warfare on earth.

We must understand *temptations* or *trials* as including
all adverse things; and they are so-called because they
are the tests of our obedience to God. He bids the faithful, when faced with these, to rejoice, not only when they
fall into temptation, but also into many trials of various
kinds. And, since these adversities serve to put to death
our sinful natures, and as the vices of the flesh continually
shoot up in us, so trials must necessarily be repeated.
Besides, we labour under various diseases, so it is no
wonder that different remedies are applied to them. The
Lord afflicts us in various ways because ambition, greed,
envy, gluttony, intemperance, excessive love of the world,
and the innumerable lusts with which we struggle cannot
all be cured by the same medicine.

When James bids us to 'count it all joy', he means that
we should so view temptations as opportunities for
growth as to regard them as occasions of joy … for there
is nothing in afflictions which ought to disturb our joy.
And thus, he not only commands us to bear adversities
calmly and with an even mind, but also shows us that this
is a reason why the faithful should rejoice even when
pressed down by them.

Certainly, all aspects of our nature are so formed that
every trial produces in us grief and sorrow, and not one
of us can so completely divest himself of his nature as not
to grieve and sorrow when faced with trials. But by the
guidance of the Spirit, the children of God can rise above

the sorrow of their natures, and so it is that they continue
to rejoice even in the midst of trouble.

We now see why James calls adversities *trials* ... because they serve to try our faith... It might ... be ob-
jected: 'How can we judge as sweet that which is bitter to
the senses?' He then shows ... that we ought to rejoice in
afflictions because they produce fruit that ought to be
highly valued — that is, patience... We certainly dread
diseases and poverty and exile and prison and reproach
and death, because we regard them as evils, but when we
understand that they are turned through God's guidance
into helps and aids to our salvation, it is ingratitude to
complain and not willingly to submit to such trials.[21]

## Suffering is often mingled with blessing

In one of the many letters that Calvin wrote in order to console
his friends who suffered dishonour and reproach, he expresses
his conviction that suffering for the faith has a divine purpose:
that God might shed his blessings on his suffering children.

It is consoling to recognize that God not only tries our
faith, but also that, in withdrawing us from the allure-
ments and delights of the world, which deceive us, he lets
us taste his bounty and feel his aid by gathering us, as it
were, under his wings, that we may say with David that
our highest good is to cling to him. Indeed, when it goes
well with us, it is difficult to prevent our minds, in their
rebelliousness, from going astray, and it is a rare miracle
when those who have long basked in prosperity hold on
to their fear of the Lord. And that is the reason why, to
keep his children in restraint, he sends them various afflictions.

Though we no doubt feel that what we call adversities
are common to us and unbelievers alike and to profane

people who give themselves up entirely to the world, God nevertheless blesses those afflictions which we have to suffer, turning them to such account that we have always reason for consolation and rejoicing in our sorrows. You cannot help but recognize also that he has been pleased to spare you, for you know how much more harshly he deals with many others, who do not have ... any mitigation in their afflictions.[22]

## Suffering leads to life on a higher plane

The sufferings of Jesus serve as a paradigm that imparts meaning to all suffering. In his sufferings and death, Jesus shows that suffering for his sake, though unjust and seemingly meaningless, can transform life by producing virtues such as patience and perseverance and hope. In his classic statement in Romans 5:1-5, Paul states that he not only endures many kinds of suffering, but also he glories in them — because, as one who had been 'crucified with Christ', he would ultimately be glorified with him. Such an outcome was not reserved only for Paul, but also for all who bear the cross. The faithful may be 'harassed and distressed in this life', but Paul 'declares that their calamities, far from preventing their happiness, even promote their glorying.'[23]

Calvin would not have agreed with W. Somerset Maugham, who said, 'It is not true that suffering ennobles the character; happiness does that sometimes, but suffering, for the most part, makes men petty and vindictive' (*The Moon and Sixpence*). Calvin, to the contrary, viewed suffering as redemptive and life ennobling.

God, in answer to the believer's prayers, grants his all-sufficient grace and imparts his strength, so that through his or her suffering the Christian is strengthened in spirit, though weak in body, and is made more trusting, patient,

humble, compassionate, and thankful. Paul at last concludes that all the sorrows we endure contribute to our
salvation and final good.

By saying that the saints glory in tribulations, he is not
to be understood as saying that they did not dread them
or seek to avoid adversities, or that they were not distressed with the bitterness of the trials when they happened (for there is no patience when there is no feeling of
bitterness). Rather, Paul means that in their grief and sorrow they are not without great consolation. Because they
regard whatever they bear as being dispensed to them for
their good by the hand of a most generous Father, they
are said to glory: for whenever salvation is promoted,
there is no lack of a reason for glorying.

We are then taught here ... the design of our tribulations, if indeed we would prove ourselves to be the children of God. Tribulations ought to form in us the habit of
patience. If they do not accomplish this end, it is our sinfulness obstructing the Lord's work, for how does he
prove that adversities do not hinder the glorying of the
faithful, except that by their patience in enduring them
they feel the help of God which nourishes and confirms
their hope?

According to Romans 5:1-5, we only grow in patience
as we should when we regard both the patience and the
growth as evidence of God's power working in us. In this
way, we have hope for the future, trusting that God's favour, which has always supplied our needs, will never be
lacking from us.

Hope does not disappoint; that is, it regards salvation
as most certain. It appears, then, that the Lord tries us by
adversities for this end — that our salvation may by these
trials be gradually advanced. Those evils then, which do
in a sense promote our happiness, cannot render us miserable. And in this way it is proved ... that the godly have
reasons for glorying in the midst of their afflictions.

Referring to the whole passage (Rom. 5:1-5), I ... would say that trials stimulate patience in us, and that patience — as evidence of divine help — encourages us to entertain hope. However much we may be pressed and feel nearly consumed, still we feel God's favour towards us, which provides the richest consolation — much more abundant than when all things are prospering. That prosperity and happiness, which only appear to be so, are misery itself when God is displeased with us. But when God is favourably disposed towards us, even calamities will be turned to a prosperous and joyful issue.

Seeing that all things must serve the will of the Creator, who, according to his paternal favour towards us ... overrules all the trials of the cross for our salvation, the knowledge of God's love towards us [vs. 5] is instilled into our hearts by the Spirit of God; for the good things which God has prepared for his servants are hidden from the ears and the eyes and the minds of men, and the Spirit alone can reveal them. And when Paul says that God's love is 'poured out in our hearts', he means that the revelation of divine love towards us is so abounding that it fills our hearts. Being in this way spread through every part of our being, it not only mitigates sorrow during adversities, but also, like a sweet seasoning, it renders tribulations into something we can actually love.[24]

## Affliction is meant to humble us

Paul speaks of having been 'caught up to the third heaven', probably in a night-vision (2 Cor. 12:2). Such a unique experience of heavenly glory might make one boastful, and to prevent Paul from being 'exalted above measure by the abundance of the revelations' entrusted to him, 'a thorn in the flesh' was given to him, which Paul calls 'a messenger of Satan'. Whatever malady that thorn was, Paul, says Calvin, was kept back from pride and learned humility. Calvin sees in Paul's 'poison-dipt' thorn a lesson for all the faithful, when experiencing pain and suffering:

> Whatever the infirmity is under which we labour, let us bear in mind that we are, as it were, buffeted by the Lord, with the intent of making us ashamed, and, in this way, of teaching us humility. Those who are mature in the faith, whose lives display much spiritual fruit, should be especially careful to reflect on this if they are persecuted by those who hate and revile them: these things are not merely rods of the heavenly Master but buffetings, intended to humble them and beat down all presumption and pride. [25]

Calvin cites a sermon by Augustine, in which he shows 'how dangerous a thing the "poison of pride" is... "inasmuch as it cannot be cured except by poison"'. Calvin would have 'all the pious take notice of this', namely, that God's purpose in sending affliction is that we might learn to be humble.

## Suffering is not all bad

Paul assures us that 'All things work together for good to those who love God' (Rom. 8:28), and he includes suffering among those things. Suffering is not good in itself, but God has his own purposes which he accomplishes through suffering. The writer of Psalm 119 viewed his own suffering as having a favourable outcome: 'It is good for me that I have been afflicted, that I may learn your statutes' (v. 71). Calvin answers the question, 'Is suffering ever good?' in the affirmative. When the psalmist declares that through adversity he had learned obedience to God's commands, Calvin states:

He here confirms the sentiment ... that it was profitable to him to be subdued by God's discipline, that he might more and more be brought back and softened to obedience. By these words he confesses that he was not exempt from the perverse obstinacy with which all mankind are infected. Had it been otherwise with him, the profit of which he speaks, when he says that his submission was due to his being brought low, would have been mere pretence — even as none of us willingly submits his neck to God until he softens our natural hardness by the strokes of a hammer. It is good for us to continually taste the fruit which comes from God's corrections, that they may become sweet to us, and that in this way we, who are so rebellious and wayward, may permit ourselves to be brought into submission.[26]

The church, which is called 'the communion of saints', is exhorted to 'Bear one another's burdens' in obedience to our Lord's command: 'Love one another as I have loved you' (Gal. 6:2; John 13:34). It sometimes happens, however, that no one will come forward to render aid or support to one of the members who is suffering. In such a situation — often as a last resort — the suffering one looks to God for help, since no human help is forthcoming. Painful and disappointing as it may be to be forsaken by friends in a time of need, it was God's purpose for David to be abandoned, in order that God's mercy might be manifested in an extraordinary manner. David in his time of trouble poured out his complaint before God: 'Look on my right hand and see, for there is no one who acknowledges me; refuge has failed me; no one cares for my soul' (Ps. 142:4). There is a valuable lesson to be learned from this, as Calvin points out:

David shows that there was good cause for the dreadful sufferings he experienced, since no human aid or comfort was to be expected, and destruction seemed inevitable.

When he speaks of having looked and yet perceived not
a single friend among men, he does not mean that he
had turned his thoughts to earthly helps in forgetfulness of
God, but that he had made such inquiry as was justifiable
regarding someone on earth who might assist him. Had
any person of the kind presented himself, David would
no doubt have recognized him as an instrument of God's
mercy; but it was God's purpose that he should be abandoned of all assistance from man, and that his deliverance from destruction should thus appear more extraordinary.[27]

## Suffering trains us to seek God's help

The prophet Isaiah knew the pain of poverty but also the
goodness of God, who turns his face towards those who call
upon him. Isaiah anticipated our Lord's beatitude: 'Blessed are
you poor, for yours is the kingdom of God' (Luke 6:20). Isaiah
praised God for his faithfulness, truth, and goodness: 'For you
have been a strength to the poor, a strength to the needy in his
distress…' (Isa. 25:4). Calvin writes:

> We see in the prophet's words the fruit of conversion,
> namely, that the Lord raises from the dead, and brings
> us, as it were, out of the grave, stretching out his hand to
> us from heaven to rescue us even from hell. This is our
> first access to him, for it is only in our poverty that he
> finds the means of exercising his kindness. To us in our
> turn, therefore, it is necessary that we be poor and needy,
> so that we may obtain assistance from him; and we must
> lay aside all reliance and confidence in ourselves before
> he displays his power in our behalf. This is the reason
> why he visits us with chastisements and with the cross, by
> which he trains us, so that we may be able to receive his
> assistance and grace.[28]

Much as we prefer prosperity to poverty, security to danger, and health to affliction, we in fact live, as Calvin puts it, 'in the midst of death'. It is God's purpose that we should 'have one foot in the grave', that we might seek God's help and trust in his grace. The Lord's goodness to the faithful is the theme of the psalmist's praise of God in Psalm 138: 'Though I walk in the midst of trouble, you will revive me; you will stretch out your hand against the wrath of my enemies, and your right hand will save me' (v. 7). Although Calvin's comments on this verse are not altogether comforting, they nevertheless encourage us to trust God in the midst of trouble:

By nature we are so delicately averse to suffering as to wish that we might all live safely beyond range of its arrows and shrink from close contact with the fear of death, as something altogether intolerable. On the slightest approach of danger we are immoderately afraid, as if our emergencies precluded the hope of divine deliverance. This is faith's true office: to see life in the midst of death and to trust in the mercy of God — not as that which will procure us universal exemption from evil, but as that which will restore us to life in the midst of death every moment of our lives. God humbles his children under various trials, that his defence of them may be the more remarkable, and that he may show himself to be their deliverer as well as their preserver. In the world believers are constantly exposed to enemies, and David asserts that he will be safe under God's protection from all their machinations. He declares his hope of life to lie in this, that the hand of God was stretched out for his help — that hand which he knew to be invincible and victorious over every foe. And from this we are taught that it is God's method to exercise his children with a continual conflict, so that having one foot, as it were, in the grave they may flee with alarm to hide themselves under his wings, where they may abide in peace.[29]

## Suffering bids us to pity those who suffer

In his sermon on Hebrews 10:31 — 'It is a fearful thing to fall
into the hands of the living God' — Calvin exhorted his congregation to 'Pity those who are in distress', even if they are
suffering for their own misdeeds:

> Someone may say, 'Are we not resisting God when we
> are sorry for those who are punished for their sins? Is this
> not striving against God's justice?' No, for we may recog-
> nize God's justice and praise and glorify him for what he
> does, and yet nevertheless be sorry for those who are
> punished, because we ourselves may have deserved as
> much or more. We ought to seek the welfare of all men,
> especially those who are nearest to us. And when God
> has established any bond between those who suffer and
> us, we must pity them. At the same time, we recognize
> civil justice, which is a little mirror of God's justice, and
> yet we do not cease to have pity on the offender.
>     When a criminal is punished, men do not say that he
> has been wronged, or that the judge is cruel. But they say
> that those who are in the place of justice do their duty
> and render an acceptable sacrifice to God when they put
> an offender to death. Yet, in the meantime, we do not
> cease to pity the poor creature who will suffer for his evil
> deeds. If we are not touched by this, there is no humanity
> in us. If we grant this with respect to earthly justice, which
> is a little spark of God's justice, then when we come to
> the sovereign seat of justice on high, ought we not first to
> glorify God for all that he does, assuring ourselves that he
> is just and upright in all respects? And yet this should not
> hinder us from pitying those who suffer punishment, to
> comfort them and aid them, and when we are unable to
> do them any good, to wish for their salvation, praying
> God to make their corrections profitable in drawing them

home, and not to allow them to become hardhearted and to strive at his hand.

## Suffering prepares us for eternal glory

Believers should accustom themselves to a level of contempt of the present life that does not generate either hatred of life or ingratitude towards God. For this life, though it is filled with innumerable miseries, is yet deservedly reckoned among the divine blessings which must not be despised... To believers especially, this life should be a testimony to the divine benevolence, since the whole of it is destined to the advancement of their salvation. For before he openly reveals to them the inheritance of eternal glory, God intends to reveal himself as our Father in inferior instances, and those are the benefits which he daily confers on us...

It is a far superior reason for gratitude if we consider that here we are in some measure prepared for the glory of the heavenly kingdom. But the Lord has ordained that those who are to be hereafter crowned in heaven must first engage in conflicts on earth, so that they may not triumph without having surmounted the difficulties of warfare and obtained the victory...[30]

When, because God's purpose in human suffering is not always evident, we cry from the depths of our misery, 'Why? Why *me?*' we acknowledge, perhaps tacitly, that we are facing the mystery of God's incomprehensible ways: 'Oh, the depth of the riches both of the wisdom and knowledge of God! How unsearchable are his judgments and his ways past finding out! "For who has known the mind of the LORD? Or who has become his counsellor?"' (Rom. 11:33-34).

Herman Bavinck poses a series of questions that reflect the apostle Paul's awe of God's majesty, wisdom and glory:

God as the object of human knowledge — who can
fathom that? How can man know God, the infinite and
incomprehensible, who can be measured by neither time
nor eternity, in whose presence angels cover their faces
with their wings, who lives in unapproachable light, and
whom no man has seen nor can see? ...What does [a
man] know of things in their origin, essence and purpose?
Is he not ringed round with mystery on every hand? Is he
not always standing on the boundaries of the unknown?
And is it to be supposed that such a man, poor, weak,
erring, and benighted, should know God, the high, holy,
alone-wise, and almighty God?[31]

For the Christian especially, suffering is not meaningless,
even though we may not in this life discover the meaning or
purpose of an affliction. From the perspective of eternity we
can, through faith in God's goodness, be assured, as Paul was,
that 'Our light affliction, which is but for a moment, is working
for us a far more exceeding and eternal weight of glory, while
we do not look at the things which are seen, but at the things
which are not seen. For the things which are seen are temporary, but the things which are not seen are eternal' (2 Cor. 4:17-
18).

The answer of Scripture to the suffering of God's children is
summed up in one of the hymns of the church:

How firm a foundation, you saints of the Lord,
is laid for your faith in his excellent Word!
What more can he say than to you he has said,
to you who for refuge to Jesus have fled?

Fear not, I am with you; O be not dismayed,
for I am your God and will still give you aid;
I'll strengthen you, help you, and cause you to stand,
upheld by my righteous, omnipotent hand.

When through the deep waters I call you to go,
the rivers of sorrow shall not overflow;
for I will be with you in trouble to bless,
and sanctify to you your deepest distress.

When through fiery trials your pathway shall lie,
My grace all-sufficient shall be your supply;
the flame shall not hurt you; I only design
your dross to consume and your gold to refine.

The soul that on Jesus has leaned for repose
I will not, I will not desert to its foes;
that soul, though all hell should endeavour to shake,
I'll never, no never, no never forsake![32]

*Suffering — understanding
the love of God*

Selections from the writings of John Calvin

---

## Chapter 2

## Treasuring up bright designs

---

'Whenever any doubt may arise in our minds regarding the providence of God, we should strengthen ... ourselves with this consideration: that God, who provides food for the beasts of the field ... can never cease to take care of the human race.'

# 2.

# Treasuring up bright designs

*When we ask about the basis of our faith in providence, we are asking simply for an analysis of faith itself, of that faith which rests in God's revelation of his providence, and of that faith which finds in that revelation its complete confidence.*

G. C. Berkouwer

Anyone who is going through a time of sickness and pain is likely to have questions, not only about the purpose of suffering, but also whether God takes notice of those who suffer. 'If God is all-powerful, why does God allow human suffering to occur?' they ask. 'If God is good, why does he let bad things happen to good people?' Questions like these are very difficult for those who believe that God is good and that he not only governs the universe which he created but cares about people who suffer.

A rather common belief is that when God created the world he turned it over to natural forces and let the world run itself — implying that bad things just happen. This theory sounds plausible because it exonerates God for the bad things that occur in the world. The problem with this line of reasoning is that if God is not in some sense responsible for bad things, then he is not responsible for good things, either. If we do not 'blame' God for death, then we should not praise God for life. We cannot have it both ways. Either God is immanently involved in the world, or God simply leaves to chance everything that happens, the good and the bad.

Most Christians have some sense of God's providential involvement in the world, but many have only a vague understanding of what Scripture teaches regarding divine providence.

One of Calvin's contemporaries, Guido de Brès, a preacher of the Reformed churches of the Netherlands, died as a martyr in 1567. De Brès had been the principal author of the *Belgic Confession of Faith,* which contains a declaration of belief regarding divine providence. This article of faith was drawn from the holy Scriptures and is entitled 'The providence of God and his government of all things'. The text of this article follows:

We believe that this good God, after he had created all things, did not abandon them or give them up to fortune or chance, but that he rules and governs them according to his holy will, so that nothing happens in this world without his orderly arrangement. Yet God is neither the author of, nor can he be charged with, the sin that occurs. For his power and goodness are so great and incomprehensible that he orders and does his work in the most excellent and just manner, even when the devils and wicked men act unjustly. We will not curiously inquire into what he does that surpasses human understanding and is beyond our ability to comprehend. But with the greatest humility and reverence we adore the righteous judgments of God, which are hidden from us, being content to be Christ's disciples, in order to learn only those things which he has revealed to us in his Word, without inquiring beyond those limits.

This doctrine affords us unspeakable consolation, since it teaches us that nothing can happen by chance, but by the arrangement of our most gracious heavenly Father, who watches over us with fatherly care, keeping all creatures under his control, so that not one hair of our head (for they are all numbered) nor even a sparrow can fall to the ground without the will of our Father, in whom we put our entire trust, being persuaded that he so restrains the devil and all our enemies, that they cannot hurt us without his permission and will.[1]

## God governs all things at all times

God controls everything in the natural world, including floods, tornadoes, hurricanes, and all other natural forces, however violent. An example of this is noted in Psalm 29:10-12: 'The LORD sits enthroned over the flood; the LORD is enthroned as King forever.' Calvin writes:

> Some think that David here alludes to that memorable instance of God's vengeance, when he drowned the world at once by the flood in the time of Noah and thus testified to all ages that he is the judge of mankind. In my opinion ... he is reminding us that those floods which still threaten destruction to the earth are controlled by the providence of God in such a way as to make it evident that it is God alone who governs all things at all times. David therefore mentions this among other proofs of God's power, so that even when the elements appear to be mingled and confounded together by the utmost fury of the weather, God controls and moderates these commotions from his throne in heaven.[2]
>
> It is base ingratitude ... not to perceive God's providence and government in the whole course of nature, but it is detestable foolishness to believe that his unusual and extraordinary works, which compel even wild beasts to obey him, will not teach us wisdom.[3]
>
> But when once the light of divine providence has illumined the believer's soul, he is relieved and set free, not only from the extreme fear and anxiety which formerly oppressed him, but also from all care. For as he justly shudders at the idea of chance, so he can confidently commit himself to God. This, I say, is his comfort, that his

heavenly Father so embraces all things under his power — so governs them at will by his nod and regulates them by his wisdom — that nothing takes place except according to his appointment. It is the believer's comfort to know that, having been received into God's favour and entrusted to the care of his angels, neither fire, nor water, nor sword can do him harm, except in so far as God their master is pleased to permit. For thus sings the psalm: 'Surely he shall deliver you from the snare of the fowler and from the perilous pestilence. He shall cover you with his feathers, and under his wings you shall take refuge. His truth shall be your shield and buckler. You shall not be afraid of the terror by night, nor of the arrow that flies by day, nor of the pestilence that walks in darkness, nor of the destruction that lays waste at noonday' (Ps. 91:3-6). Hence the exulting confidence of the saints: 'The LORD is on my side; I will not fear. What can man do to me?' (Ps. 118:6). 'Though an army may encamp against me, my heart shall not fear' (Ps. 27:3). 'Yea, though I walk through the valley of the shadow of death, I will fear no evil' (Ps. 23:4).[4]

'All men acknowledge that the world is governed by the providence of God, but when there comes some sad confusion of things which disturbs their ease and involves them in difficulty, there are few who retain in their minds the firm persuasion of this truth of divine providence.'[5] Calvin's statement certainly applies to the recent devastating attacks by terrorists in the United States and other countries. Few people, when discussing these calamities, mention the providence of God as being in some way behind those disasters. Some, in fact, attribute all tragedy to 'bad luck' or chance. Calvin, on the other hand, insists that there is no such thing as fortune or chance:

We must consider that the providence of God, as taught in Scripture, is opposed to fortune and fortuitous causes.

By an erroneous opinion prevailing in all ages — an opinion almost universally prevailing in our own day — namely, that all things happen by chance, the true doctrine of providence has not only been obscured, but almost buried. If one falls among robbers or ravenous beasts; if a sudden gust of wind at sea causes shipwreck; if one is struck down by the fall of a house or a tree; if another, when wandering through desert paths meets with deliverance, or after being tossed by the waves arrives in port and makes some wondrous hair's breadth escape from death, all of these occurrences — prosperous as well as adverse — will be attributed by worldly sense to fortune. But those who have learned from the mouth of Christ that all the hairs of their heads are numbered (Matt. 10:30) will look farther for the cause and hold that all events whatsoever are governed by the secret counsel of God.[6]

Psalm 113 comforts us with the assurance that, even though God is exalted above all nations and above even the heavens, he cares for his servants, especially the poor and needy: 'The LORD is high above all nations, his glory above the heavens. Who is like the LORD our God, who dwells on high, who humbles himself to behold the things that are in the heavens and on the earth? He raises the poor out of the dust, and lifts the needy out of the ash heap, that he may sit with princes — with the princes of his people. He grants the barren woman a home, like a joyful mother of children' (vv. 4-9).

Calvin's expansion of these thoughts in his commentary on Psalm 113 should encourage those who are struggling to make ends meet or to succeed in life:

In this passage (Ps. 113:5-9), the psalmist praises God's providential care in relation to those varied changes which men are inclined to regard as accidental. He declares that it is solely by God's direction that things un-

dergo changes far beyond what we anticipate. If the
course of events were always uniform, men would ascribe
it merely to natural causes, whereas the unexpected
changes which take place teach us that all things are regu-
lated in accordance with the secret counsel of God. Often, on the other hand, struck with astonishment at the
events which have happened contrary to our expectation,
we instantly ascribe them to chance. And as we are so apt
to view things from a point opposite to that of recognizing
God's superintending care, the prophet urges us to ad-
mire God's providence in matters of marvellous or unusual occurrence.

## God is exalted and glorious but cares about his people

The theology of John Calvin begins and ends with 'the vision of
God and his glory'. The Calvinist, states Benjamin B. Warfield,
is one 'who has seen God in his glory, is filled, on the one hand,
with a sense of his unworthiness to stand in God's sight as a
creature, much more as a sinner, and on the other hand, with
adoring wonder that nevertheless this God is a God who
receives sinners'.[7]

The glory of God is a central element in Calvin's thought.
Equally important for Calvin, however, is the condescending
grace of God. Psalm 113, he says, highlights the majesty and
condescension of God:

In this psalm the providence of God provides reason for
praising him. Though his excellence is far above the
heavens, nevertheless he deigns to cast his eyes upon the
earth to take notice of mankind. And as not a few are
disconcerted by the unexpected turns of event which they
observe occurring in the world, the psalmist takes occasion, from these sudden and unlooked-for changes, to
warn us to attend expressly to God's providence, so that

we may be certain beyond all doubt that all things are governed according to his will.

Verses 4-7 of the psalm focus on both the majesty and the condescension of God: Here the psalmist encourages us to acknowledge God's care of the faithful who suffer — even though God is exalted above all: 'The LORD is high above all nations, his glory above the heavens. Who is like the LORD our God, who dwells on high, who humbles himself to behold the things that are in the heavens and in the earth? He raises the poor out of the dust, and lifts the needy out of the ash heap.' Calvin comments:

The meaning of verses 4-7 is that though God's glory is far above the heavens, the distance at which he is placed does not prevent his governing the world by his providence. God is highly exalted, but he sees clearly from a long distance away, so that he need not change places when he would condescend to take care of us. We on our part are poor and lowly, but our wretched condition is no reason why God will not concern himself about us. While we view with admiration the immensity of God's glory as raised above all heavens, we must not disbelieve his willingness to foster us under his fatherly care. The two things are, with great propriety, conjoined here by David: on the one hand, when we think of God's majesty, we should not be terrified into a forgetfulness of his goodness and benevolence. Nor, on the other hand, should we lose our reverence for his majesty in contemplating the condescension of his mercy.[8]

## God takes notice of his people in their times of trouble

In a time of great distress, persecuted by enemies and harassed by false witnesses, David is sure that God knows what is going on. In Psalm 35 he asks, 'LORD, how long will you look on? This you have seen, O LORD; do not keep silence. O LORD, do not be far from me' (vv. 17, 22). Calvin understands God's observation of the affairs of mankind as an aspect of divine providence:

> If we desire to strengthen ourselves against the scoffing and derision of our enemies, the best means which we can employ for this end is to overlook them and to elevate our thoughts to God. In the confidence of his fatherly care over us, we should ask him earnestly to show us that our troubles are known to him, and that, the more he sees the wicked eagerly watching every opportunity to accomplish our ruin, the more quickly he would come to our aid... David was fully persuaded that God looks upon the poor and afflicted and marks all the wrongs which are done to them. If, therefore, we would properly frame our requests, a clear conviction and persuasion of the providence of God must shine in our hearts...[9]
>
> If God graciously condescends to extend his providential care even to the irrational creation, much more does he provide for the needs of men. And, indeed, whenever any doubt may arise in our minds regarding the providence of God, we should strengthen and encourage ourselves with this consideration: God, who provides food for the beasts of the field and maintains them in their present state, can never cease to take care of the human race.[10]

David reiterates, in Psalm 37, his persuasion that God sees and knows the needs of his faithful ones: 'The LORD knows the days of the upright, and their inheritance shall be forever. They shall not be ashamed in the evil time, and in the days of famine they shall be satisfied' (vv. 18-19). Calvin shares this conviction:

Nothing is more profitable for us than to have our eyes
continually set upon the providence of God, which alone
can best provide for us everything we need. David says
that ... God is not ignorant of the dangers to which we
are exposed and the help which we need. We ought to
employ this doctrine as a source of consolation under
every unexpected change which may seem to threaten us
with destruction. We may be harassed in various ways
and distracted by many dangers which every moment
threaten us with death; but this consideration ought to
prove to be a sufficient ground of comfort for us — that
not only are our days numbered by God, but that he
knows all the vicissitudes of our lot on earth. Since God
then so carefully watches over us for the maintenance of
our welfare, we ought to enjoy, in this our pilgrimage on
earth, as much peace and satisfaction as if we were put in
full possession of our paternal inheritance and home.
Because God looks upon us with favour, David concludes that our inheritance is everlasting. Moreover, in
declaring that God protects those who are upright, he
exhorts us to the sincere pursuit of truth and uprightness
... if we desire to be placed in safety under the protection
of God...[11]

If God reigns in heaven, and if his throne is erected
there, it follows that he must necessarily attend to the
affairs of men... But it is the glory of our faith that God,
the Creator of the world, does not disregard or abandon
the order which he himself at first established. And when
he suspends his judgements for a time, it is appropriate
for us to lean upon this one truth — that God beholds all
things from heaven — in the same way that David contented himself with this consolatory consideration alone:
God rules over mankind and observes whatever is trans-
acted in the world, although his knowledge and the exercise of his jurisdiction are not at first apparent.[12]

Were it not for God's 'fatherly care and providence', we would have no security and peace: 'So numerous are the dangers which surround us that we could not stand a single moment, if his eye did not watch over our preservation. But the true security for a happy life lies in being persuaded that we are under divine governing.'[13]

Calvin emphasizes 'the immeasurable greatness of the divine being' who, nevertheless, is actively involved everywhere in the universe.

> God not only founded heaven and earth but also governs all things according to his power. To acknowledge that God made the world, but maintain that he sits idle in heaven and has no concern in the management of it, is to cast disrespectful and irreverent aspersions upon his power; and yet the idea, absurd as it is, obtains wide currency among men. They would not say, perhaps, in so many words, that they believed that God slept in heaven, but in imagining, as they do, that he gives over the reins to chance or fortune, they leave him the mere shadow of power … whereas Scripture teaches us that it is a real practical power by which he governs the whole world as it pleases him. The psalmist, when declaring, 'Whatever the LORD pleases he does, in heaven and in earth' (Ps. 135:6), expressly asserts that every part of the world is under the divine care, and that nothing takes place by chance or without God's determination.[14]

God governs all things in the heavens and on the earth, Calvin insists. Though he saw the universe from a sixteenth-century perspective, Calvin's portrayal of the heavenly bodies is surprisingly 'modern'. 'Surely the world is established, so that it cannot be moved', declares the psalmist. 'Your throne is established from of old; you are from everlasting to everlasting' (Ps. 93:1-2). Calvin comments:

The psalmist proves — from the fact that God created the world — that God will not neglect it. A simple survey of the world should of itself suffice to attest to a divine providence. The heavens revolve daily and, immense as is their fabric and inconceivable the rapidity of their revolutions, we experience no concussion, no disturbance in the harmony of their motion. The sun, though varying in its course every diurnal revolution, returns annually to the same point. The planets, in their wanderings, maintain their respective positions. How could the earth hang suspended in the air if it were not upheld by God's hand? By what means could it maintain itself unmoved, while the heavens above are in constant, rapid motion, if its divine maker did not fix and establish it?[15]

'The LORD is in his holy temple, the LORD'S throne is in heaven; his eyes behold, his eyelids test the sons of men' (Ps. 11:4). Calvin reiterates the psalmist's conviction that, despite appearances, God rules over all and takes notice of the actions of humankind:

The psalmist does not simply say that God dwells in heaven, but that he reigns there, in a royal palace, as it were, and has his throne of judgement there. Nor do we ... render to him the honour which is his due, unless we are fully persuaded that his judgement seat is a sacred sanctuary for all who are in affliction and unrighteously oppressed. When, therefore, deceit, craft, treachery, cruelty, violence, and extortion reign in the world — in short, when all things are thrown into disorder and darkness by injustice and wickedness — let faith serve as a lamp to enable us to behold God's heavenly throne, and let that sight suffice to make us wait in patience for the restoration of things to a better state.[16]

## God is always the supreme cause of all that happens

God normally acts through others, including evil persons, but God is always the supreme cause of things that happen to us, as Calvin points out in the *Institutes*, I.17.6:

> The mind of a Christian, when it is certainly persuaded that all things happen by the ordination of God and that nothing happens by fortune or chance, will always direct his views to God as the supreme cause of all things, and will also consider secondary causes in their proper order. He will not doubt that the particular providence of God is watchful for his preservation, never permitting any event which it will not overrule for the Christian's advantage and safety.

God, says Calvin, permits evil persons to do us wrong, but holds them in check and overrules their attempts to destroy us. In the *Institutes*, I.17.7, 8, he cites several examples from Scripture of God's providential overruling of plots against those whom he would protect:

> Sometimes, when God has permitted our enemies to attempt what their rage and passion prompted, he opportunely breaks their course of action and does not allow them to proceed to the accomplishment of their designs. In this way he prematurely defeated the counsel of Ahithophel, which would have been fatal to David (2 Sam. 17:7-14). In this way he also takes care to govern all his creatures for the benefit and safety of his people. He governs even the devil himself, who did not dare to attempt anything against Job without God's permission and command (Job 1:12). The necessary consequences of knowing this are gratitude in prosperity, patience in adversity, and a wonderful security respecting the future. Every prosperous and pleasing event, therefore, the de-

vout man will ascribe entirely to God... If any adversity befalls him, he will immediately lift up his heart to God, whose hand is most capable of impressing us with patience and peace of mind. If Joseph had dwelt on a review of the deceitful treachery of his brothers, he never could have recovered his fraternal affection for them. But as he turned his mind to the Lord he forgot his injuries and was so inclined to mildness and clemency as even voluntarily to administer consolation to them, saying, 'It was not you that sent me here, but God sent me before you to save your lives' (Gen. 45:5, 7-8).

Although God does employ secondary causes and human agents in implementing his will and secret counsel, he does not turn everything over to other causes, but, rather, acts through them to accomplish his purposes. God, says Calvin, is the primary cause of all that happens, the bad as well as the good — though he is not the 'author' of sin.

Calvin and his associate, William Farel, had been expelled from Geneva in 1538. From Strasbourg, Calvin, in that same year, wrote a letter to his 'beloved brethren in our Lord who are the remnant of the dispersal of the church of Geneva'. In those days, epidemics, particularly the plague, decimated the church, and many Christians were hunted down and persecuted. Calvin acknowledged that evil and suffering were used by God to test the servants of God. Calvin wrote, 'The punishments he sends are for your good and salvation', and he added, 'You must not think that these things happened to you without the dispensation of the Lord, who also acts through the unrighteous, according to the counsel of his own will.'[17]

It is the opinion of many that God's providence 'amounts to no more than a certain maintenance of order in the world'. God, in other words, governs in a general sense, but particular events occur 'without his due counsel'. Calvin insists, to the contrary, that 'There is a special providence exerted in the government of the various parts of the world; that there is no

such thing as chance and what appears to be fortuitous is in
reality ordered by God's secret wisdom.' It is Calvin's fixed
opinion that 'Nothing happens without the divine will and
decree.' God's will 'may be mysterious', Calvin acknowledges,
'but it is to be regarded with reverence, as the fountain of all
justice and righteousness…'[18]

Sometimes it happens, however, that faithful Christians are
tempted to doubt that God cares about them, especially when
they see evil persons prospering, while they, though godly, are
suffering. Even the psalmist, in Psalm 73, confesses, 'I was
envious … when I saw the prosperity of the wicked' (v. 3).
Calvin sees this way of looking at suffering as playing into the
hands of the devil:

> Experience shows how small a view we have of the provi-
> dence of God. We no doubt all agree that the world is
> governed by the hand of God, but if this truth were
> deeply rooted in our hearts, then our faith would be dis-
> tinguished by far greater steadiness and perseverance in
> overcoming the temptations with which we are assailed in
> times of adversity. But when the smallest temptation
> which we meet dislodges this doctrine from our minds, it
> is clear that we have not yet been truly and in good ear-
> nest convinced of its truth.
>
> Besides, Satan has numerous clever devices by which
> he dazzles our eyes and bewilders our minds; and then
> the confusion of things which prevails in the world pro-
> duces so thick a fog as to render it difficult for us to see
> through it and to conclude that God governs and extends
> his care to things here below. The ungodly for the most
> part triumph; and although they deliberately stir God's
> anger and provoke his vengeance, yet from his sparing
> them trouble, it seems as if they had done nothing wrong
> in deriding him, and that they will never be called to ac-
> count for it. On the other hand, the righteous, pinched by
> poverty, oppressed with many troubles, harassed by in-

creased wrongs and covered with shame and reproach,
groan and sigh in proportion to the earnestness with
which they endeavour to do good to all men... When
such is the state of matters, where shall we find that person who is not sometimes tempted and seduced by the
unholy suggestion that the affairs of the world roll on at
random and, as we say, are governed by chance? This
unhallowed belief has doubtless obtained complete possession of the minds of unbelieving persons, who are not
illuminated by the Spirit of God... Accordingly, we see
the reason Solomon declares that, since 'All things come
alike to all: one event happens to the righteous and the
wicked' (Eccles. 9:2), the hearts of men are full of irreverence and contempt for God; they do not consider that
things apparently so disordered are under the direction of
God.[19]

This knowledge — that all things are under the direction of God — is necessarily followed by gratitude in
prosperity, patience in adversity, and incredible security
for the time to come. Everything that prospers and turns
out according to his wish, the Christian will ascribe entirely to God, whether he has experienced God's generosity through the instrumentality of men, or has been
aided by inanimate creatures. He will reason that it was
the Lord who caused people to be favourably disposed
towards him, making them the instruments of God's
kindness to him. In an abundant harvest, the Christian
will think that it is the Lord who listens to heaven, that the
heaven may listen to the earth, and the earth herself to
her own offspring; in other cases, he will have no doubt
that he owes all his prosperity to the divine blessing, and,
admonished by so many circumstances, will feel it impossible to be ungrateful.[20]

Even when we are aided by inanimate objects, such as electricity or a motor vehicle or medicine, we must consider that it is God who energizes them:

> With regard to inanimate objects, we must hold that though each is possessed of its particular properties, yet all of them exert their force only in so far as directed by the immediate hand of God. Hence they are merely instruments into which God constantly infuses what energy he considers suitable, turning them to any purpose at his pleasure.[21]

Knowing that God controls all things also keeps us from becoming despondent and impatient when troubles arise. Calvin writes,

> Why is it that God's servants' confidence never fails? Why is it that, though the earth apparently revolves at random, they know that God is everywhere at work and feel assured that his work will be their safety? When assailed by wicked men, they would become despondent if they were not consoled by remembering and meditating on providence. The godly have ample sources of consolation when they call to mind that the hand of God restrains the devil — and the whole train of the ungodly — in all directions, as with a bridle. The forces of evil can neither conceive any mischief, nor plan what they have conceived, nor, however much they have planned, move a single finger to perpetrate, except so far as God permits — no, except in so far as he commands. They are not only bound by fetters, but also are even forced to do God service. As it belongs to the Lord to activate the fury of such foes and turn and govern it according to his pleasure, so also it is God's prerogative to determine the measure and the end, so as to prevent those adversaries from breaking loose and wandering as they please... Pay attention to

God's control, even of the ungodly, and you will at once perceive that ignorance of divine providence is the greatest of all miseries, and the knowledge of it the greatest happiness.[22]

Certainty about God's providence helps us in all adversities. Since God is the supreme cause of all that happens to us, we should rest content, knowing that God wills all things for our advantage. David is an example of patient submission to God's will — as he says in Psalm 39:9, 'I was mute; I did not open my mouth, because it was you who did it.'

There is no more effective remedy for anger and impatience than meditation on divine providence. The one who cannot bring to mind this thought — the Lord willed it; it must therefore be borne, not only because it is not right to struggle with God, but also because God wills nothing that is unjust or inappropriate — has grown very little. The whole matter comes to this: when we are unjustly assailed by men, we must overlook their malice (which only aggravates our grief and whets our minds for vengeance) and remember to ascend to God and hold firmly to the knowledge that whatever an enemy has wickedly committed against us was permitted and sent by God's righteous indignation.[23]

## Good people suffer, too

Is sickness a consequence of sin and health a reward for virtue? Not at all; we must avoid oversimplification of Calvin's views. Concerning this question he maintained an ambivalent position. Like most of his contemporaries, he viewed epidemics, persecution, and martyrdom as appeals to faithfulness. But this did not imply that the faithful prosper and that the reprobates suffer poverty. The experience of Job shows that godly people do not necessarily have good fortune or success. On this point Calvin observes, 'These two things can very well go together; that is, the good may be under a curse, as Job was, so that their lives are subject to many evils; and the wicked may make merry, be prosperous, triumph, and have everything they want.'[24]

Calvin himself, however, seems to have oversimplified the respective life situations of the godly and the wicked. For example, his introduction to his commentary on Psalm 37 appears to be unrealistic and contrary to the experience of many who are faithful and good people:

> However great the prosperity which the wicked enjoy for a time, the psalmist declares their happiness to be transient and evanescent, and that, therefore, they are miserable — the happiness of which they boast is cursed. On the other hand, the pious and devoted servants of God never cease to be happy, even in the midst of their greatest calamities, because God takes care of them and comes to their aid in due time. This, indeed, is paradoxical and wholly repugnant to human reason. Good men often suffer extreme poverty, grow weak under many troubles, and bear reproaches and wrongs, while the wicked and profligate triumph and are regaled with pleasures. Do we then suppose that God does not care for the things that are done on earth? It is on this account that ... the teaching of this psalm is so much more profitable. Withdrawing our thoughts from the present state of things, it instructs us to confide in the providence of God until he stretches out his hand to help those who are his servants and demands of the ungodly a strict account of their lives, as thieves and robbers who have abused his bounty and fatherly goodness.

When we see evildoers enjoying everything their hearts could desire — great houses, several motor cars (including two

Jaguars), and all the amenities that give pleasure, as well as good health — we are admonished not to fret about our more modest lifestyle or become envious; this we are advised in Psalm 37:1:

> David lays this down as a general principle: the prosperity of the wicked, in which they greatly rejoice, should by no means trouble the children of God, because it will soon fade away. On the other hand, although the people of God may be afflicted for a time, they still will have every reason to be contented with their lot. All this depends on the providence of God, for unless we are convinced that he governs the world in righteousness and truth, our minds will soon stagger and at length completely fail us.[25]

Although God's servants share the same adversities as the ungodly, God makes it up to his servants in due time, so that 'They shall not be ashamed in the evil time, and in the days of famine they shall be satisfied' (Ps. 37:19). Calvin writes:

> This verse shows us that the faithful have no right to expect such exemption from affliction and trial as they might desire, but they are assured of deliverance in the end — which, though it eventually will be obtained, yet is of such a nature that it can be realized only by faith. We must regard these two things as inseparably connected: as the faithful are mingled with the wicked in this world, so hunger and adversity are common to both. The only difference between them is that God stretches out his hand towards his own people in their time of need, while he abandons the ungodly and takes no care of them. It could be argued that the wicked often gratify their desires and fare sumptuously in time of famine, while the faithful are oppressed with poverty and deprivation. The fulness spoken of here in Psalm 37:19 refers more to this: as the faithful live sparingly and often labour hard to subsist,

they are fed by God as surely as if they had far more of this world's abundance than the ungodly, who greedily devour the good things of this life in all their variety and abundance, yet are never satisfied. Besides, these temporal blessings are not always seen flowing in one uniform course. The hand of God is indeed always open, but we are distressed by hardship and limited in our desires, so that our own unbelief is no small hindrance to God's liberality. Moreover, as our corrupt nature would soon break forth into excess, God deals with us more sparingly; and, so that he might not corrupt us by too much indulgence, he trains us to be frugal by bestowing with a sparing hand what he was ready otherwise to lavish upon us in full abundance. And indeed, whoever considers how addicted we are to sensuality and pleasure will not be surprised that God should exercise his own people with poverty and deprivation. But although God may not bestow upon us all that is necessary for our gratification, yet, unless our own ingratitude prevents us, we will experience, even in famine and deprivation, God's gracious and generous nourishment of us.[26]

Calvin summarizes the matter of suffering endured by the faithful in this way:

The miseries of the godly are so tempered with God's fatherly mercy that they do not fail under their burden, and even when they fall they do not sink into destruction... The godly, although they serve God sincerely and try to lead a blameless life, are not allowed to continue unmoved and always in the same condition, but are often afflicted and cast down by various trials.[27]

## Does God inflict suffering on his people?

Calvin explicitly attributes suffering to God's providential permission. He insists that whether we are afflicted with poverty or disease or bereavement or any similar calamity, we do well to remember that none of these things happen without the will and providence of God. Calvin is quick to point out that nothing, including human suffering, happens by chance; it is God's hand that smites us. Although this is not a particularly comforting thought, it teaches us to find our consolation in God's unfailing grace, as the psalmist did: 'You have laid me in the lowest pit, in darkness, in the depths. Your wrath lies heavy upon me, and you have afflicted me with all your waves... My eye wastes away because of affliction. LORD, I have called daily upon you; I have stretched out my hands to you' (Ps. 88:6-7, 9). Calvin takes up the psalmist's lament with open acknowledgment of God's providential ordering of human suffering:

> The psalmist acknowledges ... that whatever adversities he endured proceeded from the divine hand. No one will seek relief from God without the established belief that it is God's hand that strikes him and that nothing happens by chance. It is clear that the psalmist's grief grows more bitter, the nearer he comes to God, for nothing is more dreadful than God's judgement.[28]

Though God may smite us with his hand, he also at the same time upholds us with his hand. Psalm 37:23-24 says, 'The steps of a good man are ordered by the LORD, and he delights in his way. Though he fall, he shall not be utterly cast down; for the LORD upholds him with his hand.' Calvin cites a parallel statement in Proverbs 24:16, which assures us that 'A righteous man may fall seven times and rise again.'

By these words we are taught that the godly are not only subjected to frequent afflictions in this life, but that they are visited with daily trials, and yet are never forsaken by the Lord. We must ... observe that even the slightest fall would be enough to destroy us, if God did not uphold us by his hand.[29]

Life may be a struggle, but our Lord Jesus Christ will be a Saviour in the midst of our troubles. Calvin assures us of God's ever-present mercy and provision:

We can patiently pass through this life with its misery, hunger, cold, contempt, reproaches, and other troubles — content with this one thing: that our King will never leave us destitute, but will provide for our needs until, our warfare ended, we are called to triumph. Such is the nature of his rule, that he shares with us all that he has received from the Father.[30]

David's lament in Psalm 39 acknowledges that the persecution he had to endure was God's doing: 'I was mute, I did not open my mouth [to complain], because it was you who did it' (v. 9). Calvin writes:

We have here a very profitable and instructive lesson. Nothing is better able to restrain violent paroxysms of grief than the realization that we deal with God and not with mortal man. God will always maintain his own righteousness, even in the face of everything men may say against him in their complaints and accusations... Some, then, ascribe their miseries to fate or fortune, others to other people, and others account for their troubles from a variety of causes suggested by their own imaginations. Scarcely one in a hundred recognizes in his troubles the hand of God. So men allow themselves to indulge in bitter complaints without ever thinking that they offend God in doing so. David, on the contrary, seeking to subdue every unholy desire and sinful excess, returns to God and resolves to keep silence, because the affliction which he is now suffering proceeded from God. As David, who was afflicted with the severest trials, resolved nevertheless to keep silence, let us learn from this that it is one of the chief exercises of our faith to humble ourselves under the mighty hand of God and to submit to his judgements without murmuring or complaining... David regards the secret judgements of God with such reverence and wonder that, satisfied with God's will alone, he considers it sinful to open his mouth to utter a single word against him.[31]

The author of Psalm 71 likewise attributes his troubles to God's providential dealings with him; but the psalmist also acknowledges God's gracious deliverance: 'You, who have shown me great and severe troubles, shall revive me again, and bring me up from the depths of the earth. You shall increase my greatness, and comfort me on every side' (vv. 20-21).

'When David complains that calamities had been *shown* him', says Calvin, 'he means that he had suffered them. And as he attributes to God ... the deliverance which he had obtained, so he acknowledges that whatever adversities he had endured were inflicted on him according to the counsel and will of God.' If David had always enjoyed a life of prosperity, 'He would not have experienced what it is to be delivered from destruction by the stupendous power of God.'[32] So it is also with us:

We must be brought down even to the gates of death before we can see God as our deliverer. As we are born without thought or understanding, our minds, during the earlier part of our life, are not sufficiently impressed with a sense of the author of our existence; but when God comes to our help as we are lying in a state of despair, this resurrection is to us a bright mirror from which we see

his grace reflected. In this way David amplifies the goodness of God, as he declares that, though he was plunged
into a bottomless pit, he was nevertheless drawn out by
the divine hand and restored to the light. And he boasts
not only of having been preserved perfectly safe by the
grace of God, but also of having been advanced to higher
honour — a change which was, as it were, the crowning
of his restoration. It was as if he had been lifted out of
hell, even up to heaven. His commendation of divine
providence is intended to convey his conviction that no
adversity happened to him by chance, as was evident
from the fact that his condition was reversed as soon as
the favour of God shone upon him.[33]

The problem of God's involvement in suffering emerges also
in Calvin's sermons on Job. God is not portrayed as the author
of evil or of sin, but God mysteriously decides to test his servant
Job, who is regarded as a righteous man. Calvin writes:

Let us take … the example of Job, for there as in a mirror
we can contemplate how God acts, and the devil on the
other side. For all the afflictions that come to Job were
not simply by the permission of God, but God willed
them to test the patience of his servant. It is therefore God
who afflicted Job. Now, by whose hand was Job afflicted? We see that the devil was the agent of all this, and
that still he can do nothing except in so far as God commands him. And Job, when he was thus beaten down,
knew well that it was with God that he had a dispute.[34]

The first-century Christians who suffered persecution were
given a new perspective on their distress, if not comfort, by the
thought that they were suffering in accordance with God's will,
as Peter reminded them: 'For it is better, if it is the will of God,
to suffer for doing good than for doing evil' (1 Peter 3:17).

Calvin's comment on this statement declares God's will to be the primary cause of suffering for the sake of the truth:

> In these words — 'if it is the will of God' — Peter reminds us that if we suffer justly it is not by chance, but according to the divine will; and he assumes that whatever God wills or appoints is only for the best reason. So the faithful always have this comfort in their miseries: they know that they have God as their witness, and they know also that they are led by him to the conflict in order that they may, under his protection, give proof of their faith.[35]

## God's providence cannot be fully grasped

We see as in a mirror, dimly, writes Paul, and we know in part (1 Cor. 13:12). Calvin, in his comments on Psalm 91:8 — 'Only with your eyes shall you look, and see the reward of the wicked' — frankly acknowledges the limits of our understanding of God's providence:

> Though there is much in this world that appears dark, the psalmist hints that, even amid all the confusion that reigns, we may see from God's judgements that he does not disappoint the expectations of his believing people. The psalmist, however, was addressing those who have eyes to see, who are privileged with the true light of faith, who are fully awake to the consideration of the divine judgements, and who wait patiently and quietly till the proper time arrives. Most people confuse their minds on the subject of God's judgements by starting to draw conclusions, and they are prevented from discovering the providence of God by judging according to sense. It is fitting for us, as was the case with the psalmist, to be satisfied with apprehending the judgements of God only in

some imperfect measure while we remain on earth, and leaving God to defer the fuller discovery of them to the day of complete revelation.[36]

Calvin makes much of the mystery of God's will, which is ultimately incomprehensible. God's judgements are like 'a great and bottomless abyss', according to Psalm 36:6. The psalmist is generally understood to mean that 'The judgements of God far exceed our limited capacity and are too mysterious for our being able to understand them.' Calvin, however, understands the psalmist's declaration 'in a much more extensive sense and as meaning that, however great the depth of wickedness which there is among men — although it seems like a flood which breaks forth and overflows the whole earth — yet greater still is the depth of God's providence, by which he disposes and governs all things'.[37]

Whenever our faith is shaken by the confusion and disorder in human affairs, and when we are unable to explain the reasons for this disorder and confusion, let us remember that the judgements of God in the government of the world are with the highest propriety compared to a great depth which fills heaven and earth, so that the consideration of its infinite greatness may overwhelm our minds with admiration, swallow up all our cares, and dispel all our sorrows. When the psalmist adds, 'O LORD, you preserve man and beast', the meaning is to this effect: since God graciously condescends to extend his providential care even to the irrational creation, much more does he provide for the needs of men. And indeed, whenever any doubt may arise in our minds regarding the providence of God, we should strengthen and encourage ourselves with this consideration: that God, who provides food for the beasts of the field and maintains them in their present state, can never cease to take care of the human race.[38]

Sorrow may blind us and prevent our seeing God's hand in our experiences, so that we fall into despair. In Alan Paton's novel, *Cry, the Beloved Country,* a chronicle of suffering in South Africa during the days of apartheid, Father Vincent says desperately to his friend, Stephen Kumalo, "'No one can comprehend the ways of God." Kumalo looked at him, not bitterly or accusingly or reproachfully. "It seems that God has turned from me", he said. "That may seem to happen", said Father Vincent. "But it does not happen, never, never, does it happen."'[39]

Like Stephen Kumalo, a psalmist in the time of Israel's despondency laments before God his plight. I am like a dead man, he says, 'whom you remember no more' (Ps. 88:5). Calvin would have admonished the psalmist not to let pessimism 'overmaster' him:

> Although faith in the truth that God extends his care both to the living and the dead is deeply rooted in the hearts of all his genuine servants, yet sorrow often so clouds their minds as to exclude from them all remembrance of his providence. From perusing the complaints of Job, we may perceive that when the minds of the godly are pre-occupied with sorrow, they are not immediately pierced by the consideration of the secret providence of God ... the truth of which they bear engraved on their hearts. Although the psalmist, then, was persuaded that the dead also are under the divine protection, yet, in the first par-oxysm of grief he spoke less advisedly than he ought to have done; for the light of faith was, as it were, extinguished in him, although ... it soon afterwards shone forth. This is particularly useful to observe — that should we be at any time weakened by temptation, we may, nevertheless, be kept from falling into despondency or despair.[40]

Although we cannot fully comprehend God's providence in our lives, especially in our personal adversities, sorrow, and distress, we can take courage knowing that God is not only sovereign over all things and events, but also infinitely gracious, and that in due time 'He will make it plain.' William Cowper's great hymn, composed in 1774, encourages us to trust in God's never-failing mercy:

> O God, in a mysterious way
> Great wonders you perform;
> You plant your footsteps in the sea
> And ride upon the storm.
>
> Deep in unfathomable mines
> Of never-failing skill
> You treasure up your bright designs,
> And work your sovereign will.
>
> O fearful saints, fresh courage take;
> The clouds you so much dread
> Are big with mercy and shall break
> In blessings on your head.
>
> Our unbelief is sure to err
> And scan your work in vain;
> You are your own interpreter,
> And you will make it plain. [41]

When sorrow or distress or pain press hard upon us, we can take comfort in the Lord's promise to Joshua, 'I will not leave you nor forsake you' (Josh. 1:5), and in the assurance that God not only regards our sorrows but keeps them in remembrance. God does not forget our sorrows, the psalmist assures us, recalling David's grief when, according to the title of Psalm 56, he was captured by the Philistines in Gath. David prays that God will always remember his sorrows: 'You number my wanderings; put my tears in your bottle; are they not in your book?' (Ps. 56:8). Calvin writes:

> It would appear from this passage (Psalm 56) that the prayers of David proceeded upon faith in the providence of God, who watches our every step, and by whom (to use an expression of Christ) 'the very hairs of our head are numbered' (Matt. 10:30). Unless we are persuaded in our minds that God takes special notice of each affliction which we endure, it is impossible for us ever to gain such confidence as to pray that God would put our tears into his bottle, with a view to regarding them and being induced by them to interpose in our behalf... David enlivens his hope by the consideration that all his tears were written in the book of God and would therefore certainly be remembered. And we may surely believe that if God bestows such honour upon the tears of his saints, he must number every drop of their blood which is shed. Tyrants may burn their flesh and their bones, but their blood remains to cry aloud for vengeance; and intervening ages can never erase what has been written in the register of God's remembrance.[42]

How then can we know and believe that God rules over all things at all times, that he takes notice of us in our times of trouble and cares about us, and, when we are afflicted by his hand, that he does so only in order to promote our salvation? The answer is that if indeed our faith rests in the revelation that God has given, then it rests in Jesus Christ. G. C. Berkouwer insists emphatically that 'No one can believe in the providence of God without knowing the way to God through Jesus Christ. Paul underscores this thought in Romans 8 in his hymn to God's providence. Nothing forms an absolute menace any longer: neither oppression nor fear; persecution, hunger, nor sword; life nor death; present nor future. This faith is no general, vague notion of providence. It has a concrete focus: "If God is

for us, who is against us? He that spared not his own Son, but
delivered him up for us all, how shall he not also with him freely
give us all things?" (Rom. 8:31-32). All dangers are relativized,
contained by his love: the love of God in Christ Jesus our Lord.
There is no purer expression than this of the depth of man's
faith in God's providence.'[43]

# Suffering — understanding the love of God

Selections from the writings of John Calvin

---

## Chapter 3

## Suffering and God's goodness

---

'In the very bitterness of tribulation we ought to recognize the kindness and mercy of our Father, since even then he does not cease to further our salvation.'

# 3.
# Suffering and God's goodness

*It is everywhere evident that God's wrath is not the whim of demonic power. The wrathful God maintains his righteousness, but in this jealous preservation he gives his Son for the redemption of the world.*

G. C. Berkouwer

We have seen, in chapters one and two, that God's incomprehensible rule over human affairs raises many questions about the meaning and purpose of God's activity in the world and in human life. God's goodness and mercy, one might think, would preclude his inflicting suffering on people in every part of the world. All sorts of doubts and criticisms are either quietly entertained or openly expressed concerning the goodness and justice of God: Why is this happening to me? What have I done to deserve God's punishment? If God is love, he wouldn't make people suffer the way they sometimes do!

When we think of the many disasters that have caused enormous misery to thousands of people around the world, we can understand the puzzlement that surrounds these events. Human suffering, tragedy and sorrow, untimely death, natural disasters, and all the shocking events which almost daily bewilder us — how is it possible to reconcile those painful realities of life with the omnipotence and goodness of God?

Seeking answers to such concerns is the problem of theodicy — an attempt to justify or vindicate God's providential rule — to 'prove that, in spite of all enigmas and all criticisms, God's governing of the world is holy, good, and just' and to 'bring certainty out of doubt, confidence out of suspicion...' Theodicy, meaning 'justification of God', seeks 'to defend God against all complaints or accusations by demonstrating the meaningfulness and purposefulness of God's activity in the world and in human life'.[1]

Catastrophic events have always raised questions about God's rule and God's goodness. Consider the horrendous disaster in Southeast Asia on 26 December 2004. An underwater earthquake — the strongest in thirty years — sent a titanic tsunami over costal areas of Indonesia, Sri Lanka, India and Thailand. Mike Griffiths, an Indonesia-based British conservationist, said the devastation caused by the immense ocean wave was like that of a nuclear blast. The death toll reached over 150,000 and the homes of nearly a million people were destroyed. Entire villages were levelled; billions of dollars will be needed to rebuild the stricken areas.

On All Souls' Day, 1 November 1755, a terrifying earthquake struck Lisbon, Portugal. The destruction and loss of life were awesome. Hundreds of buildings and houses collapsed, killing those inside and many on the streets. The violent quake set off a tsunami whose rebounding waves rolled over the city at a height of fifty feet. Lamps were upset and domestic fires spread their flames, igniting a conflagration that burned for three days and completed the destruction of the city. More than 60,000 people died in the disaster in Lisbon, and thousands more died in the surrounding areas.

The survivors of the Lisbon catastrophe believed that the earthquake was sent by an angry God as punishment for the sins of Lisbon's 250,000 souls. But they could not explain why *their* city was destroyed while others, just as 'sinful', were spared.

More recently, a devastating earthquake struck south-eastern Iran on 26 December 2003. Rescue workers shivered in near-freezing temperatures and worked in total darkness, searching for anyone buried alive in the rubble. Government officials estimated that more than 20,000 died; more than 30,000 were injured in the ancient Silk Road city of Bam, which was eighty-percent destroyed by the quake. The less fortunate survivors must have wondered, 'Is God good?'

On 6 March 2000, a flood in southern Africa left hundreds dead and around 1.5 million homeless — the worst flood in living history. Crops and village granaries were washed away, destroying food supplies, and roads, bridges, and dams were destroyed. An estimated $10 billion worth of damage was caused to crops, livestock, infrastructure, and property. The government warned that thousands of people would face starvation because food distribution was virtually impossible in some areas. Hundreds of children were separated from their parents; some of them saw their parents and siblings swept away by the rising waters, and many children were orphaned. Anguished victims in flood-stricken Zimbabwe and Mozambique must have cried, 'Is God angry with us?'

On a quiet morning in September 2001, tragedy struck in New York City when hijacked airplanes rammed the twin towers of the World Trade Center, killing 3,000 occupants. On that same morning, two other aircraft were hijacked by terror-ists; one crashed into the Pentagon in Washington, killing all passengers and killing or injuring a number of Pentagon em-ployees; the other, bound for a strike on the United States Capitol, went down in a field in Pennsylvania, killing all aboard. In the days following those disasters, uncommon courage and valour were shown by firemen and police and other rescue workers. 'Where was God on 9/11?' many were asking.

The perplexity that was so troubling after those disasters prompted pastors to console their congregations with the assertion that God was present in the midst of the smoke and rubble, and that God was suffering along with the distraught families of the victims. But such answers to the enigma of God's involvement in tragedy raise still other questions: When disaster occurs, is it our responsibility to defend God against complaints

and criticisms? Has God entrusted to us the duty of justifying
him? Must we not rather find answers to our doubts and distress
in the comforting teaching of the gospel, that the ungodly are
justified by his grace?[2]


## Sometimes God does get angry

It is indeed unsettling to think that God is angry with anyone
except the most depraved individuals. But does not Scripture
teach that God punishes those who are disobedient and those
who worship and serve other gods?

Jeremiah delivered a stinging warning to the Jews who had
fled to Egypt thinking they would escape the wrath of Nebu-
chadnezzar:

> Thus says the LORD of hosts, the God of Israel: 'You have
> seen all the calamity that I have brought on Jerusalem
> and on the cities of Judah; and behold, this day they are
> a desolation, and no one dwells in them, because of the
> wickedness which they have committed to provoke me to
> anger, in that they went to burn incense and to serve
> other gods...' Therefore thus says the LORD of hosts, the
> God of Israel: 'Behold, I will set my face against you for
> catastrophe and for cutting off all Judah. And I will take
> the remnant of Judah who have set their faces to go to
> the land of Egypt, and they shall all be consumed ... by
> the sword and by famine; and they shall be an oath, an
> astonishment, a curse, and a reproach! For I will punish
> those who dwell in the land of Egypt, as I have punished
> Jerusalem, by the sword, by famine, and by pestilence'
> (Jer. 44:2-3, 11-13).

Calvin goes so far as to denominate God's punishment of the Jews living in Egypt as *vengeance*. His comment reveals the detestable nature of the Jews' idolatry:

> The Lord declared that he would take vengeance on impiety, as he had done previously. The Jews in Judah, when they were intoxicated by their prosperity, had been visited by great calamity. As God shakes them from their lethargy, the prophet reminds them of what they had suffered: 'As I visited Jerusalem then, so will I visit those who dwell in Egypt...' It was madness for the Jews to hope to be safe in Egypt when they had not been safe in the holy land, God's sanctuary... Jeremiah's purpose was to remind them of the ruin of Jerusalem and the land of Judah, so that they would know they could not escape the hand of God by going to Egypt against God's command; God would judge them more severely in Egypt than he had in Judah.[3]

There are times when our circumstances incline us to doubt God's goodness and to question the value of faith. In the face of personal tragedy, we are prone to wonder whether God cares enough to spare us from pain and suffering — especially when others around us are carefree and happy. And when the church is under attack by enemies of Christ, the problem of theodicy is especially acute. 'Why do the nations rage?' the psalmist asks (Ps. 2:1). Why does God permit evil kings to launch attacks even against 'his Anointed'?

The same complaint is heard from the mouth of the prophet Habakkuk: 'Why do you look on those who deal treacherously, and hold your tongue when the wicked devours a person more righteous than he?' (Hab. 1:13). Again, it is the problem of theodicy — justification of the ways of God — that Habakkuk is dealing with. A contemporary of Jeremiah, he anticipates the imminent invasion of Judah by the Chaldeans. In this time of national crisis the prophet is confronting honestly the pro-

foundly disturbing enigma: why a just and powerful God sits
idly by and allows a wicked people to swallow up his own
'more righteous' people. To this nagging question God gives his
own answer, which is eternally valid: God is sovereign, as ever,
and in his own way and at the proper time he will deal with the
wicked. The righteous person, in the meantime, 'shall live by his
faith' (Hab. 2:4).

Calvin does not attempt to solve the problem of theodicy,
that is, to justify God's punishment of his people. His comments
on the dialogue between the prophet and God simply reiterate
what Habakkuk already knows, that God sees the way of the
wicked and looks after the righteous with fatherly care:

> The prophet here does not divest God of his power, but
> speaks in doubt, and does not contend so much with
> God as with himself. A profane man would have said,
> 'There is no God, there is no providence', or, 'He does
> not care for the world; he takes his pleasure in heaven.'
> But the prophet says, 'Lord, you see.' He ascribes to God
> what particularly belongs to him — that he does not ne-
> glect the world which he has created. At the same time,
> the prophet here inclines two ways, and alternates: 'Why
> do you look on … when the wicked devours a person
> more righteous than he?' Habakkuk does not say that the
> world revolves by chance, nor that God takes his delight
> and ease in heaven … but he confesses that God sees the
> world and that he exercises care over the affairs of men.
> Nevertheless, as he could not see his way clearly in a
> state of things so confused, he argues the point rather
> with himself than with God.[4]

That of course is the way of wisdom, for, as Paul would say
to a gainsayer, 'Who are you to reply against God?'
(Rom. 9:20). In those times of trouble when we ask, 'Where is
God now? Why does he not show mercy?' the answer must be:
God is with us in the deepest valley of suffering. God is sover-

eign, but the throne from which he rules over the events that affect our lives is a throne of grace. Thus, the glory of his majesty and power is not a terrifying thing to which silent resignation is the only fitting response. Rather, it prompts us to sing a hymn of praise like Habakkuk's:

> Though the fig tree may not blossom,
> Nor fruit be on the vines;
> Though the labour of the olive may fail,
> And the fields yield no food;
> Though the flock may be cut off from the field,
> And there be no herd in the stalls —
> Yet I will rejoice in the Lord,
> I will joy in the God of my salvation.[5]

God's anger is the effect of his holiness and is expressed in his punishment of sin. The reality of God's anger and wrath is apparent in both Old and New Testaments. The confidence of the psalmist in God's love and mercy is linked together with the acknowledgement of human sinfulness: 'For we have been consumed by your anger, and by your wrath we are terrified' (Ps. 90:7). Likewise Paul, after quoting from Habakkuk — 'The just shall live by faith' — sounds a stern warning: 'For the wrath of God is revealed from heaven against all ungodliness and unrighteousness of men, who suppress the truth in unrighteousness' (Rom. 1:17-18).

If it is not comforting to contemplate the dark side of God's acts, neither is it comforting to know that wrongdoing is often followed by suffering the consequences. This truth was laid down as an axiom by Elihu Root in a lecture which he delivered at Princeton University: 'We all know, of course, that we cannot abolish all the evils in this world by statute or by the enforcement of statutes, nor can we prevent the inexorable law of nature which decrees that suffering shall follow vice and all the evil passions of mankind.'[6]

Calvin would have agreed that suffering inexorably follows vice. He observed that certain diseases are not only a result of immoral practices but also God's punishment for sin. He writes:

> After fifty years, is it not clear that God has raised up new illnesses connected with fornication? From where do they come, these foul diseases that do not need to be listed? From where do these things come, if God has not deployed punishments that were previously unknown? The world was astounded, and people were terrified for a time, but they have not, to this day, observed the hand of God. Today we are accustomed to seeing those who despise God, lead dissolute lives, and abandon themselves to every form of sin. And if God strikes them with some sort of dreadful disease, so that they are ravaged by cancer or other illness, they continue in their course of action and do nothing but jeer.[7]

The issue of AIDS is currently in the headlines. In the two decades since the outbreak of the disease, HIV has infected more than sixty million people, and AIDS has caused the death of twenty million people. The pandemic has ravaged countless lives and left families destitute. More than fourteen million children have been orphaned by the disease, and that number is expected to triple by 2010.[8]

HIV/AIDS is often transmitted sexually, though not all infected persons have contracted the disease through sexual contact. It is well known that promiscuous sexual activity, particularly — in North America and Western Europe — male homosexual activity, puts at risk those who engage in it. The question of whether in such cases AIDS is punishment for 'immoral' or 'unnatural' sexual contact has been debated back and forth, and often it is said that 'It is just one of those things that happens.' The Scriptures, however, include homosexual activity among punishable sexual sins: Leviticus 18:22 states, 'You shall not lie with a male as with a woman. It is an abomi-

nation'. And Romans 1:24-27 describes homosexual acts as
'uncleanness' and 'lust'. 'Women exchanged the natural use for
what is against nature. Likewise also the men ... burned in their
lust for one another, men with men committing what is shame-
ful and receiving in themselves the penalty which was due.'

Archbishop Desmond Tutu, in an interview on the ABC
Television news program *Nightline,* discussed the vast epidemic
of AIDS in South Africa. He was asked whether AIDS is punishment for sin, specifically as regards young children whose
emaciated bodies are slowly wasting away toward certain
death. The cleric said that he could not believe in a 'sadistic
God' who would punish children with AIDS. If AIDS is punishment, then 'I am more just than God', he said; but he added, 'I
am not more just than God.'

Calvin on the other hand addresses the issue of homosexual
behaviour, presumably as regards adults. Paul, in Romans 1:24-27, states that 'The wrath of God is revealed against
all ungodliness and unrighteousness of men', because, turning
away from the true God, they began to worship idols, and as a
consequence God 'gave them up' to uncleanness and lusts.
This judicial abandonment resulted in their giving in to the 'lusts
of their hearts' and practising 'unnatural' acts, which Calvin
considers the exercise of God's wrath upon the ungodly:

> Paul does not let these offenders evade the issue. Though
> their irreverence and turning away from God may not be
> outwardly apparent, they cannot escape God's just con-
> demnation. The consequences of their rebellion against
> God can only be viewed as clear evidence of the Lord's
> wrath. Because God's wrath is always just, it logically fol-
> lows that the sin that exposed them to condemnation
> must have preceded the condemnation itself. The apos-
> tasy and defection of men is demonstrated by this: the
> Lord punishes those who alienate themselves from his
> goodness by casting them headlong into various courses
> that lead to perdition and ruin (a homosexual lifestyle is

but one example). By comparing these vices of which
they were guilty to irreverence — of which Paul had previously accused them — Paul shows that they suffered
punishment through the just judgement of God. Nothing
is dearer to us than our own honour, and it reveals extreme blindness when we do not fear to bring disgrace
upon ourselves. That disgrace and shame also is the most
suitable punishment for a reproach done to the divine
majesty.[9]

Calvin's view is that God's judicial abandonment of the
ungodly for their religious apostasy did not occur merely by
God's permission:

It is certain that God not only permits men to fall into sin
by secretly allowing them to do so, but that he also, by his
equitable judgement, so arranges things that they are led
and carried into that sin by their own lusts, as well as by
the devil. Paul therefore uses the phrase 'God gave them
up' to their sin. Some distort the meaning of the phrase to
mean that we are led into sin only by God's permission;
as Satan administers God's wrath and is, as it were, the
one who executes God's wrath, so Satan is armed against
us by the command of his judge, not by secretly allowing
sin. This does not mean, however, that God is cruel or
that we are innocent. Paul plainly shows that we are only
delivered into Satan's power when we deserve such a
punishment. It must be emphasized that the cause of sin
is not from God, since the roots of sin always abide in the
sinner himself.[10]

'Sinners in the hands of an angry God' is not the central
theme of Romans, of course. It is the prelude to the theme of
grace and the revelation of the righteousness of God
(Rom. 3:21). Sovereign grace is the believer's hope, since the
righteousness of God was revealed in Christ. We should note

well that God's righteousness is not merely moral rectitude, the righteousness of the law, but one which dynamically accomplished salvation through the work of Christ.

## God's punishment is chastisement for his people

The words 'vengeance', 'punishment', and 'chastisement' appear in the same context, in Calvin's commentary on Psalm 6. David's plea, in the first verse, is one of deep pathos: 'O LORD, do not rebuke me in your anger, nor chasten me in your displeasure.' Despite the sternness of Calvin's pronouncement that God is angry with sinners, the passage has a pastoral tone:

> The calamity David was experiencing had, perhaps, been inflicted by men, but David wisely considers that he has to deal with God. Those who undergo affliction miss the point if they do not immediately look closely and clearly at their sins, to be convicted that they have deserved God's wrath. Yet we see most people's reaction to trouble: they complain that they are afflicted and miserable, but scarcely one in a hundred looks to the hand that strikes. Since we do not of our own accord anticipate God's judgement, let us learn, whatever form our afflictions take, to turn our thoughts immediately to God and to acknowledge him as the judge who summons us as guilty before his court.
>
> We should notice that David does not simply ascribe to God the afflictions under which he suffers, but, rather, he acknowledges his troubles to be the just compensation for his sin. This is unlike the attitude of many, who, when they come to realize that God is angry with them, often indulge in irreverent complaining rather than finding fault with themselves and their own sins.

David does not take God to task, as if God were an enemy treating him cruelly without any just cause. Rather, David yields to God the right to rebuke and chasten and desires and prays only that God will limit the punishment. By this he declares God to be a just judge in taking vengeance on the sins of men. But as soon as David confesses that he is rightly being chastised, he earnestly begs God not to deal with him in strict justice or according to the utmost extent of the law. He does not altogether refuse punishment, for that would be unreasonable, and he judges that a lack of punishment would be more harmful to him than beneficial. What David feared was the wrath of God, which threatens sinners with complete destruction. In the face of God's anger and indignation, David proposes gentle, fatherly chastisement, which he was willing to bear.

We have a similar plea in the words of Jeremiah (Jer. 10:24): 'O LORD, correct me, but with justice; not in your anger, lest you bring me to nothing.' God is indeed angry with sinners when he punishes them, but mixed with his anger is the sweetness of his grace to mitigate their sorrow. He also shows himself to be favourably disposed towards them as he moderates their punishment and mercifully draws back his hand. But we should be terrified to see God as the avenger of wickedness, and it is not without cause that David ... is afraid of God's anger and indignation. The meaning is this: I do confess, O Lord, that I deserve to be destroyed and brought to nothing. But as I would not be able to bear the severity of your wrath, do not deal with me as I deserve, but rather pardon my sins, by which I have provoked your anger against me.

As often, then, as we are pressed down by adversity, let us learn from the example of David to turn to prayerful confession, in order that we may be brought into a state of peace with God. It is not to be expected that it can be well and prosperous with us if we are not interested in his favour. Thus it follows that we shall never be without a load of evils until God forgives our sins.[11]

It is, admittedly, unpleasant to contemplate the wrath of God and the punishment that is an expression of his wrath; but in the Scriptures we are faced with the reality of God's holy reaction to human sin and the suffering which God sometimes does inflict upon those who are disobedient. The Scriptures plainly teach that godly people are not exempt from God's punishment, which is always just. In his exposition of Psalm 66:10-12, Calvin speaks of the afflictions of God's people, again referring to them as both 'punishment' and 'chastisement': 'It is noticeable that the psalmist speaks of all the cruelties which they had most unjustly suffered from the hands of their enemies as *punishment*.' In the same context, he states that after 'God had exercised his people with every form of calamity', he brought them 'into a fruitful place'. 'The truth conveyed', states Calvin, 'is that God, although he visits his children with temporary *chastisements* of a severe description, will ultimately crown them with joy and prosperity.'[12]

'When visited by affliction, it is of great importance that we should consider it as coming from God and as expressly intended for our good.'[13] One surmises that a cancer patient would not find this statement very helpful; but for the faithful sufferer, affliction does have a chastening effect. A psalmist, contemplating God's awesome works, praises God, even though, as he says, 'You laid affliction on our backs' (Ps. 66:11). Alluding to the purifying effect of Israel's suffering, he says, 'You, O God, have tested us; you have refined us as silver is refined' (Ps. 66:10). 'God tests his children with a view to purging away their sin, as dross is expelled from the silver by the fire...'[14]

## God administers chastisement in love

'O God … why does your anger smoke against the sheep of
your pasture?' (Ps. 74:1). Calvin answers that God is not angry
with his elect; nevertheless, he does chastise them, intending to
cause them to reflect on the seriousness of their sins:

> The adversities we undergo are not the arrows of fortune
> thrown at us at random. They are the means of punish-
> ment that God, in his mysterious providence, uses to dis-
> cipline us for our sins… Properly speaking, God is not
> angry with his elect, though he sometimes uses bitter
> medicine to deal with their sinfulness. Because the chas-
> tisement that we experience powerfully tends to produce
> in us some comprehension of God's wrath, the Holy
> Spirit, by the word *anger*, admonishes the faithful to ac-
> knowledge their guilt in the presence of infinite purity.
> Therefore, when God disciplines and chastens us, it is our
> duty to reflect upon what we deserve and to consider this:
> although God is not subject to the emotions of anger, it is
> not because of us — who have grievously offended him
> by our sins — that his anger is not kindled against us.
> God's people plead for mercy in fleeing to the remem-
> brance of the covenant by which they were adopted to be
> his children.[15]

Although God's wrath is exercised against the ungodly, his
chastisement of the faithful proceeds 'rather from love than
from wrath', since, according to God's plan, all things must
work together for our salvation — even when we are painfully
disturbed by our sins:

> Our minds are clouded by profound ignorance, which
> must involve much doubt and trepidation, especially as
> our hearts are, by a kind of natural instinct, inclined to

unbelief. Above all, our own conscience, oppressed by its incumbent load of sin, sometimes complains and groans within itself, sometimes accuses us, sometimes murmurs in secret, and sometimes is openly disturbed... To sustain these attacks, faith arms and defends itself with the Word of the Lord. And when temptation such as this assails us — that God is our enemy because he is angry with us — faith objects: he is merciful even when he afflicts, because chastisement proceeds rather from love than from wrath... Thus the devoutly religious mind, however strangely it may be agitated and harassed, rises at length superior to all these difficulties and never permits its confidence in the divine mercy to be shaken.[16]

It is difficult for us to understand how persecution could do us good, yet that is the conclusion drawn by the anonymous author of Hebrews and by Calvin as well. Addressing Christians whose faith in Christ was weakened by the prospect of persecution, Calvin says:

The apostle teaches us that the persecutions which we endure for the gospel's sake are ... useful to us, because they are remedies to destroy sin. In this way God keeps us under the yoke of discipline, lest our flesh should become wanton. In this way he also sometimes checks the impetuous and sometimes punishes our sins, in order that we may in the future be more cautious. With this honour indeed the Son of God favours us: that he by no means regards what we suffer for his gospel as punishment for sin.[17]

When we have the entire text of Hebrews 12:4-11 before us, we can begin to understand how persecution could have a salutary purpose:

You have not yet resisted to bloodshed, striving against sin. And you have forgotten the exhortation which speaks to you as sons: 'My son, do not despise the chastening of the LORD, nor be discouraged when you are rebuked by him; for whom the LORD loves he chastens, and scourges every son whom he receives.' If you endure chastening, God deals with you as with sons; for what son is there whom a father does not chasten? But if you are without chastening, of which all have become partakers, then you are illegitimate and not sons. Furthermore, we have had human fathers who corrected us, and we paid them respect. Shall we not much more readily be in subjection to the Father of spirits and live? For they indeed for a few days chastened us as seemed best to them, but he for our profit, that we may be partakers of his holiness. Now no chastening seems to be joyful for the present, but painful; nevertheless, afterward it yields the peaceable fruit of righteousness to those who have been trained by it.

When God chastises the godly, he has 'no other end in view as to the elect, but to promote their salvation; it is a demonstration of his paternal love'. Calvin reminds us that we cannot experience God's love under chastisements unless we are convinced that 'They are fatherly scourges by which he chastises us for our sins.' Calvin says, furthermore:

Everyone who knows and is persuaded that he is chastised by God must immediately be led to this thought, that he is chastised because he is loved by God. For when the faithful see that God interposes in their punishment, they perceive a sure pledge of his love, for unless he loved them he would not be solicitous about their salvation. Hence the apostle concludes that God is offered as the Father to all who endure correction... In a word, he teaches us that God's corrections are then only paternal when we obediently submit to him.[18]

Our aversion to parental discipline goes back to childhood, when we were made to stand in a corner of the bedroom until we repented and dried our tears. The punishment we detested was not so much our having to stand in a corner, but the feeling that our parent was angry with us. But it was for our good, nevertheless. Calvin's comments on Hebrews 12:11: 'No chastening seems to be joyful for the moment, but painful' exhibit a paternal point of view:

> The author of Hebrews adds this to prevent our measuring God's chastisements by our present feelings. He shows us that we are like children who dread the rod and shun it as much as they can, for, owing to their age, they cannot yet judge how useful it may be to them. The object, then, of this admonition is that chastisements cannot be judged rightly if evaluated by what we feel under them, and, therefore, that we must fix our eyes on the end: in this way we will receive the *peaceable fruit of righteousness,* meaning the fear of the Lord and a godly and holy life, of which the cross is the teacher. He calls it 'peaceable' because in adversities we are alarmed and disquieted, being tempted by impatience, which is always noisy and restless. Being chastened, we acknowledge with a resigned mind that what seemed bitter and grievous to us has become profitable.[19]

Many of us find comfort, as well as instruction, by reading the Psalms. Sometimes, a confession is drawn out by the psalmist's example. This might occur while coming across Psalm 119:67: 'Before I was afflicted I went astray, but now I keep your word.' Calvin's comment on this verse is instructive:

> Since even a prophet of God was required to have his rebellion forcibly corrected, this kind of discipline is certainly necessary for us. The first step in obedience is the putting to death of our old sin nature, towards which

none are naturally inclined, so it should not surprise us
that God uses many and various troubles to remind us of
our task. As our old nature is sometimes obstreperous —
even when it seems to be tamed — it is no wonder to find
God repeatedly subjecting us to discipline. He does this in
different ways. Some are humbled by poverty, some by
shame. Some are brought low by disease, some by troubles at home, and some by hard and painful labour. In
this way, according to the diversity of sin to which we are
prone, he applies to each its appropriate remedy. It is
obvious how profitable a truth this confession contains.[20]

## What is a faithful response to chastisement?

Our persistent effort to exonerate ourselves is in stark contrast to
the biblical message of sin and judgement. The Scriptures never
explain suffering apart from the connection between sin and
judgement. God made this connection clear even before the
Fall, and the theme recurs again and again throughout Scripture. But Scripture also instructs us to respond to God's judgements with humility and faith. This instruction applies not only
to individuals but also to the church, which often needs to feel
God's chastening rod. God's people in exile felt the sting of
God's indignation; the psalmist, in Psalm 102, speaks for the
nation when he acknowledges that the enemies' reproach and
his grief and weeping were punishments which God adminis-
tered in his indignation and wrath (vv. 8-10).

Calvin applies the anguished complaint to the individual
psalmist himself and, in a pastoral way, to us:

The psalmist's reason for begging God's pardon with such
passion was the uneasiness and anxiety that his sins
caused him, which could only be relieved by obtaining
reconciliation with God. This proves that his prayer did

not proceed from seeking to conceal his own thoughts, as many who highly commend the grace of God in reality care little about it. David, on the contrary, declares that his own sin subjects him to constant anguish of mind, and it is this that imparts such earnestness to his supplications.

From David's example, we learn that it is those whose consciences have been wounded with a sense of their sinfulness and who can find no rest until they have obtained assurance of God's mercy who can be said to seek reconciliation with God in a proper manner. We will never seriously apply to God for pardon until we have obtained such a view of our sins as affects us with fear. The more easily satisfied we are under our sins the more we provoke God to punish them with severity, and if we really desire absolution from his hand, we must do more than confess our guilt in words; we must institute a rigid and formidable scrutiny into the character of our transgressions... The psalmist acknowledges his transgression, including, besides adultery, treachery and cruelty; nor was it one man only whom he had betrayed, but the whole army which had been summoned to the field in defence of the church of God.[21]

Psalm 38 is also a model for all who experience God's rebuke and are chastened by his rod. David has set an example of what our response to God's harsh dealing with us should be when he pleads, 'O LORD, do not rebuke me in your wrath, nor chasten me in your hot displeasure' (v. 1).

David does not expressly ask that his afflictions should be removed, but only that God would moderate the severity of his chastisements. Hence we may infer that David did not give loose reins to the desires of the flesh, but offered up his earnest prayer in a duly chastened spirit of devotion... David is content with a divine mitigation of his affliction, as if he had said, 'Lord, I am not unwilling to be

chastened by you, but I beg you, meanwhile, not to afflict
me beyond what I am able to bear, but to temper the
fierceness of your indignation according to the measure
of my infirmity, lest the severity of the affliction should
entirely overwhelm me...' David does not secretly indulge a fretful and discontented spirit, but spreads his
complaint before God; and he does this, not in the way
of sinful complaining, but of humble prayer and un-
feigned confession accompanied by the hope of obtaining forgiveness... As every chastisement of God should
remind us of his judgement, the true wisdom of the
saints ... is to 'turn to him who strikes them'.[22]

David, as soon as he recognized his affliction as coming from God, turns to his own sin as the cause of the
divine displeasure. He had already been fully satisfied in
his own mind that God is not like a tyrant who exercises
cruelty needlessly and at random, but a righteous judge
who never manifests his displeasure by inflicting judgements except when he is grievously offended. If, then, we
would render to God the praise which is due to him, let
us learn by the example of David to connect our sins with
his wrath.[23]

The wrong way to respond to the chastisements with which
God afflicts us, Calvin states, is to 'obstinately rebel against God
and refuse to bow in humble submission'. He cites 1 Peter 5:6:
'Humble yourselves under the mighty hand of God, that he
may exalt you in due time', and follows with his own exhortation: 'Let us therefore learn that there is no other way by which
we can obtain consolation in our afflictions than by laying aside
all stubbornness and pride and humbly submitting to the
chastisement of God.'[24]

Tears that are shed in a time of affliction are rarely tears of
penitence, but more likely they are shed out of self-pity and
pain or sorrow. When God's people were in exile in Babylon,
they wept when they remembered how they had once wor-

shipped God in his temple, and, hanging their harps on the willow trees, they suspended their songs of praise. Still, says Calvin, 'They were not so entirely overwhelmed by their calamities as not to recognize in them the deserved chastisement of God, and that they could be charged with obstinately struggling against him; for their tears were the expression of humility and penitence as well as of distress.'[25]

From the depths of misery and despair a psalmist cries to God in behalf of the whole nation that was suffering at God's hand (Ps. 130:1). The writer of the psalm, writes Calvin, 'acknowledges that although grievously afflicted he had justly deserved such punishment as had been inflicted on him'; and Calvin appends this pastoral note:

> Since by his example he gives a rule which the whole church ought to observe, let no one presume to intrude into the presence of God, except to humbly seek to appease his wrath. Particularly when God exercises severity in his dealings towards us, let us know that we are required to make the same confession which is written here: 'If you, LORD, should mark iniquities, O LORD, who could stand?' (v. 3). Whoever flatters himself or buries his sins by inattention to them deserves to pine away in his miseries — at least he is unworthy of obtaining from God the smallest alleviation of his affliction.[26]

## Suffering is not always punishment

If Calvin's view of affliction and suffering seems unduly harsh and pitiless, we may find some consolation in knowing that not all suffering is punishment. It may help us to gain a clearer perspective if we consider, for example, the case of Job. This servant of God suffered great calamities and afflictions, even though he was 'blameless' (Job 1:1). The Lord informed Satan twice that Job was 'a blameless and upright man, one who fears

God and shuns evil' (Job 1:8; 2:3). So why did God lay such heavy suffering on Job? Calvin addresses this question in his comments regarding the man who was blind from his birth (John 9:1-11). God, he says, has different reasons for inflicting suffering on people:

> Sometimes he does not look at their sins, but only tests their obedience, or trains them to patience, as we see that holy Job — a righteous man and one who fears God — is miserable beyond all other men; and yet it is not on account of his sins that he is sore distressed. The design of God was that his piety might be more fully ascertained even in adversity. Those who say that all afflictions, without any distinction, are sent on account of sins are false interpreters — as if the measure of punishments were equal, or as if God looked to nothing else in punishing men than what every man deserves.[27]

The problem of suffering is not simple: Peter seeks to comfort the persecuted faithful by reminding them that it is better 'to suffer for doing good than for doing evil' (1 Peter 3:17). Calvin's comments on this verse raise the question once again: 'Does not God chastise the faithful whenever he allows them to be afflicted?' Calvin says, 'To this I answer that it indeed often happens that God punishes them according to what they deserve. Peter does not deny this, but he reminds us what a comfort it is to have our cause connected with God, and how God does not punish sins in those who endure persecution for the sake of righteousness, since in one sense they are innocent.'[28]

The case of the man who was born blind was the occasion for a similar question: Why does an innocent person suffer? Is the affliction a means of chastisement for some sin that has been committed, perhaps in the past?

The writer of the Gospel of John, recounts an encounter which Jesus had with the unfortunate man. This gave the disciples occasion to ask a question that had long been debated among the Jews: 'Who sinned, this man or his parents?' Behind this question were the assumption that all suffering is punishment and the inference that, since, according to the Decalogue God visits the iniquities of the parents upon their descendants, the Lord might have punished, in the son, some crime of his parents.

To the disciples' question Jesus replied, 'Neither this man nor his parents sinned.' Calvin clarifies Jesus' statement:

> Christ does not absolutely say that the blind man and his parents were free from *all* blame; but he declares that we ought not to seek the cause of blindness in sin... God sometimes has another object in view than to punish the sins of men when he sends afflictions to them. Consequently, when the causes of afflictions are concealed, we ought to restrain curiosity, so that we may neither dishonour God nor be malicious towards other people. Therefore Christ assigns another reason. This man, he says, was born blind so that 'The works of God should be revealed in him' (John 9:3)... So long as he was blind, there was exhibited in him a proof of the severity of God, from which others might learn to fear and humble themselves. It was afterwards followed by the benefit of his cure and deliverance, in which the astonishing goodness of God was strikingly displayed.[29]

Joni Eareckson Tada had a serious accident while swimming at low tide, leaving her paralyzed and virtually helpless. Her robust faith in Christ, however, enabled her to rise above her permanent disability and to go on living. Looking back from a distance at her unfortunate accident, she wrote, 'People with disabilities, more than most, look for answers to the questions of "Who's in charge?" and "Why did this happen?" And a disabled person is only pushed farther into hopelessness and despair if he thinks that his multiple sclerosis or spinal cord injury, birth defect or hearing impairment is all a result of chance or random acts of others.' As this wounded young woman studied the Scriptures, she began to recognize God's sovereignty in her suffering, and this prompted her to write, 'A disability can be God's way of reaching down and stretching our heart's capacity not only for himself, but for others. People with disabilities are a vivid reminder to us that God, in his holy and sovereign will, uses suffering to achieve his ultimate end in our lives: to conform us to the image of his Son (Rom. 8:28-29).'

With Joni's positive and faithful attitude she became a witness to the grace of God in Christ and a helper to other people with disabilities, as Lausanne senior associate for disabled.[30] Her experience of suffering, though different from Calvin's, taught her that God's grace sustains the sufferer in the darkest hour. Calvin writes:

> It is true that when the heart is in perplexity and doubt, or rather is tossed hither and thither, faith seems to be swallowed up. But experience teaches us that faith, while it fluctuates amidst these agitations, continues to rise again from time to time, so as not to be overwhelmed. If at any time it is at the point of being stifled, it is nevertheless sheltered and cherished, for though the tempests may become ever so violent, it shields itself from them by reflecting that God continues faithful, and never forsakes his children.[31]

When God makes suffering people 'instruments of his glory', as in the case of the blind man and of Joni Eareckson Tada, we are assured that even crippling affliction can be seen by faith to 'work together for good to those who love God'. In some unexpected ways, tragedy can, by God's unfailing grace, draw families closer to God; and often, after grace and time have healed their wounds, they experience a deepening of their faith and the forging of new links with the eternal.

## Chastisement is mingled with grace

Psalm 103 affirms God's goodness to those who suffer: God 'heals all your diseases' and 'redeems your life from destruction'. (vv. 3-4). Such optimism may provide little comfort for a terminal cancer patient as life ebbs away. But 'There is a balm in Gilead to make the wounded whole', and the psalmist, unflinching in his optimism, discovers that in the midst of his afflictions God is still gracious to him. Calvin explains:

> The psalmist teaches us that the incomparable grace of God shines forth in the very commencement of our salvation, as well as in its whole progress. To enhance the commendation of this grace, he adds the words 'tender mercies' in the plural number. He asserts that we are *surrounded* with them — as if he had said, 'Before, behind, on all sides, above and beneath, the grace of God presents itself to us in immeasurable abundance, so that there is no place devoid of it.'[32]

God's tender mercies never fail, even when we feel the sting of his chastisements. Calvin reminds us that 'Temporary punishments are the fatherly chastisements of God, and the consideration that they are temporary alleviates sorrow.'

> If, therefore, we also would find reason for patience and consolation when we are under the chastening hand of God, let us learn to fix our eyes on this moderation on the part of God, by which he encourages us to entertain good hope. From seeing this moderation, let us rest assured that, although he is angry, yet he does not cease to be a father. The correction which brings deliverance does not inflict unmitigated grief; the sadness which it produces is mingled with joy.[33]

The joy we experience amidst our afflictions is the deep-down joy that comes from our assurance that says, 'All is well with my soul', for — to quote Calvin — 'Although God may chastise us, yet he does not immediately cast us off, but, on the contrary, he testifies that our salvation is the object of his care.'[34]

So that we will not be overwhelmed with the weight of chastisement, God restrains his hand and makes consid-erable allowance for our weakness. In this way the prom-ise is fulfilled: He does not withdraw his loving-kindness from his people, even when he is angry with them, for while he is correcting them for their profit and salvation, he does not cease to love them. Thus we may depend on God always to treat us with fatherly love, for he says, 'I will not "allow my faithfulness to fail, [and] my covenant I will not break"' (Ps, 89:33-34).[35]

Calvin frequently speaks of 'chastisement with moderation', as in his comments on Psalm 98:30: Even though God will not allow the disobedient to escape unpunished, 'He promises that in his chastisements he will exercise a fatherly moderation and will not execute vengeance upon them to the full extent which their sins deserve.'[36]

God's moderation, Calvin assures us, issues from God's goodness towards his exiled people, and towards us also, as he emphasizes in his comment upon Isaiah 48:9:

That the Lord spares us, that he mitigates or remits pun-ishment, and, in a word, that he pays any attention to us — all this is entirely the result of his grace, so that we ought not to ascribe it to any merits or fulfilled obligations of men... Isaiah declares that remission is made by free grace 'for God's name's sake', for he speaks of punish-ment which he might justly have inflicted on the Jews. He had the most just cause for destroying the nation, if he had not determined to defend his glory.[37]

When faith prevails, experience as well as Scripture tells us that God's grace never fails. Calvin's *Institutes* has much to say about God's grace in the midst of suffering. In a section on 'The cross as fatherly chastisement', Calvin says:

> In the very bitterness of tribulation we ought to recognize the kindness and mercy of our Father, since even then he does not cease to further our salvation. God afflicts us, not in order to ruin or destroy us, but rather to deliver us from the condemnation of the world. Let this thought lead us to what Scripture elsewhere teaches: 'My son, do not despise the chastening of the Lord, nor detest his correction; for whom the LORD loves he corrects, just as a father the son in whom he delights' (Prov. 3:11-12). We are most contrary if we cannot bear him while he is demonstrating his goodwill to us and the care which he takes of our salvation.[38]

Were it not for God's sovereign grace, his leniency in dealing with us, and his compassion towards us when we are racked with pain, or are 'down on our luck' or without the means to make ends meet, our being reminded that our misfortune is God's way of chastising us would be rather depressing. It is in our experience of suffering that the problem of theodicy becomes a very personal matter: How can God be love when he doesn't give me relief from this torturous pain? But the problem of theodicy is not with God. Man in his guiltiness is the problem. And God has solved *that* problem by giving his Son for our redemption. It is we, after all, and not God, who need to be justified. And it is in the acknowledgement of our guilt that it becomes possible to honour God's incomprehensible governing of the world and of our lives. When we know Christ, who was sent from the heart of God to reveal him to us, we know of God's holiness and mercy, of his righteousness and grace.[39]

And in the knowledge of Christ it is possible in this 'vale of tears' to sing a doxology:

Great and marvelous are your works,
Lord God Almighty!
Just and true are your ways,
O King of the saints![40]

The doxologies of Scripture are not uttered in circumstances of security or prosperity. They are, perhaps, best exemplified in the sublime exclamation of Psalm 22:3: 'But you are holy, enthroned in the praises of Israel.' Psalm 22 begins with an agonizing 'Why?'—'My God, my God, why have you forsaken me? Why are you so far from helping me, and from the words of my groaning? O my God, I cry in the daytime, but you do not hear; and in the night season, and am not silent.' This is a psalm of abject suffering and a psalm of trust in God's mercy; a psalm of struggle and also of faith and thanksgiving. In the midst of terrible trouble, the psalmist can utter a rapturous eulogy: You are enthroned in the praises of Israel! [41]

The 'Why?' of *our* anxious hearts is answered finally in Christ's agonizing hours on the cross. As the shadow of death darkened his spirit, he cried out, 'My God, my God, why have you forsaken me?' And it is his agony that provides our salvation.

*Suffering — understanding*
*the love of God*

Selections from the writings of John Calvin

---

## Chapter 4

## Standing on the promises

---

'If we do not want our faith to tremble or waver, we must support it with the promise of salvation, which is voluntarily and liberally offered to us by the Lord, in consideration of our misery rather than from respect for our worthiness.'

# 4.
# Standing on the promises

*The words of Jehovah are pure words: silver melted in an excellent crucible of earth, purified seven times.*

John Calvin, translation of Psalm 12:6

The foundation of our Christian faith is the absolute trustworthiness of God's promise that he will protect us and keep us safe, even in the midst of adversity and suffering. Calvin's comments on Psalm 12:6 (the epigraph of this chapter) are both instructive and comforting:

> The psalmist declares that God is sure, faithful and steadfast in his promises. But ... the word of God would be of no purpose if he had not called himself and other believers to meditate on God's promises in their afflictions... After telling us how God gives to his servants the hope of speedy deliverance, even in their deepest distresses, the psalmist now adds, to support their faith and hope, the assurance that God promises nothing in vain or for the purpose of disappointing us.
>
> There is no truth which is more generally received ... than that God is true; but there are few who openly give him credit for this when they are in adversity. It is, therefore, highly necessary for us to cut off the occasion of our distrust; and whenever any doubt respecting the faithfulness of God's promises steals in upon us, we ought im-

mediately to lift up against it this shield: the words of the
Lord are pure. The imagery of *silver,* which the psalmist
employs, is indeed far below the dignity and excellence of
so great a subject as God's Word; but it is very well
adapted to the measure of our limited understanding.
Silver, if thoroughly refined, is valued at a high price
among us. But when we compare it to refined silver, we
are far from showing the true price of the Word of God, a
price which is inestimable — and its purity is of less account with us than that of corruptible metal.[1]

## The promise of God is the foundation of our faith

A few excerpts from Book III, chapter 2 of the *Institutes* will
suffice to show Calvin's emphasis on the promise of God as the
foundation of our faith:

> Paul, after an enumeration of all possible adversities
> (Rom. 8:39), glories that they can never separate us from
> the love of God; and in his prayers, he always begins with
> the grace of God, from which all prosperity proceeds.
> David likewise establishes only the divine favour as a de-
> fence against all the terrors which disturb us: 'Though I
> walk through the valley of the shadow of death, I will fear
> no evil; for you are with me' (Ps. 23:4).[2]
>     We view this promise, which we have done nothing to
> deserve, as the foundation of faith, for faith rightly rests
> on the promise of God. Faith admits God's truthfulness in
> all things — whether he commands or prohibits, whether
> he promises or threatens. Though faith obediently re-
> ceives God's injunctions, carefully observes his prohibi-
> tions, and attends to his threatening, faith properly begins
> with the promise of God, on which it stands and in which
> it ends. Faith seeks in God for life, which is found not in

precepts or in denunciations of punishments, but in the promise of undeserved mercy. A conditional promise, which sends us back to our own works, promises life to us only if we find it in ourselves. Therefore, if we do not want our faith to tremble or waver, we must support it with the promise of salvation, which is voluntarily and liberally offered to us by the Lord, in consideration of our misery rather than from respect for our worthiness. For that reason, Paul in Romans 10:8 calls the gospel the 'word of faith', a description he does not apply to the precepts and promises of the Law, since there is nothing that can establish faith but the generous message by which God reconciles the world to himself.[3]

When pain and suffering strike, our faith is well founded if it is standing on the promises of God. For all of God's promises have strong confirmation in Christ, as 2 Corinthians 1:20 informs us, 'All the promises of God in him are Yes, and in him Amen.' The reason for this is plain, says Calvin: 'For, if God promises anything, he gives a proof of his benevolence, so that there is no promise of his which is not a testimony of his love… Every promise is an attestation of divine love for us, and it is beyond all controversy that no one is loved by God except in Christ.'[4]

Calvin encourages us, moreover, to 'Keep in view this general doctrine: all the promises of God rest upon Christ alone as their support … and it is only in Christ that the Father is propitious to us. Since the promises are testimonies of his fatherly kindness towards us, it follows that it is in Christ alone that they are fulfilled.'[5]

Calvin concludes that 'The nature of faith could not be better or more clearly expressed than by the substance of the promise, which is the proper foundation on which it rests.' He cites Hebrews 11:1, 'Faith is the substance of things hoped for, the evidence of things not seen.' *Substance,* Calvin explains, refers to a 'prop … on which the pious mind rests and reclines'. Faith, resting on the firm foundation, 'is a certain and secure possession of those things which are promised to us by God'.[6]

When we are standing on the secure foundation of God's grace in Christ, the light of God's grace clears away the clouds of doubt, since 'The LORD is my light and my salvation' (Ps. 27:1). 'Oh, send out your light and your truth! Let them lead me' (Ps. 43:3). Calvin comments:

> The term *light* is to be understood as denoting favour. As adversities not only obscure the face of God but also overcast the heavens, as it were, with clouds and fogs, so also, when we enjoy the divine blessing which makes us rich, it is like the cheerful light of a serene day shining around us; or rather the light of life, dispelling all that thick obscurity which overwhelmed us in sorrow... The psalmist adds *truth,* because he expected this light only from the promises of God... David rests with confidence in this: God, who is true and cannot deceive anyone, has promised to assist his servants. We must therefore explain the sentence in this way: LORD, send forth your light, that it may be a token and testimony of your truth, or that it may really and effectually prove that you are faithful and free from all deceit in your promises. The knowledge of the divine favour, it is true, must be sought for in the Word of God; nor has faith any other foundation on which it can rest with security than his Word; but when God stretches out his hand to help us, the experience of this is no small confirmation both of the Word and of faith.[7]

Calvin knew from his own experience that when we suffer or are troubled, we are likely to become disheartened, but if we take refuge in God, he says, 'We shall gather new hope, for when the Lord fulfils his promises he confirms his truth for the future.'[8]

## Faith in God's promises sometimes falters

In times of trouble and suffering, faith in the promises of God is often overshadowed by doubt and overcome by temptations. Even the greatest saints are affected by these weaknesses, but God's grace ultimately prevails, and those who 'wait upon the Lord' will not simply give up and fall away. This is Calvin's strong opinion. After showing that assurance is linked with faith, he writes:

> But it will be said that this differs widely from the experience of believers, who, though they recognize the grace of God towards them, not only feel disquietude (this often happens), but also sometimes tremble, overcome with terror, so violent were the temptations which assail their minds. This scarcely seems consistent with the certainty of faith. It is necessary to solve this difficulty in order to maintain the doctrine that is laid down above. When we say that faith must be certain and secure, we certainly do not speak of an assurance which is never affected by doubt, nor of a security which anxiety never assails; rather, we maintain that believers have a perpetual struggle with their own distrust, and are far from thinking that their consciences possess placid quiet, uninterrupted by perturbation. On the other hand, whatever is the mode in which they are assailed, we deny that they fall off and abandon that sure confidence which they have formed in the mercy of God.
>
> Scripture does not set before us a brighter or more memorable example of faith than David, especially if one has regard to the constant tenor of his life. And yet how far his mind was from being always at peace is declared by innumerable complaints… 'Why are you cast down, O my soul? And why are you disquieted within me?' (Ps. 42:5). His alarm was undoubtedly an obvious sign of distrust, as if he had thought that the Lord had forsaken

him. In another passage we have a fuller confession: 'For
I said in my haste, "I am cut off from before your eyes"'
(Ps. 31:22). In another passage, in anxious and wretched
perplexity he debates with himself; no, he raises a question as to the nature of God: 'Has God forgotten to be
gracious? Has he in anger shut up his tender mercies?'
(Ps. 77:9). What follows is harsher still: 'And I said, "This
is my anguish; but I will remember the years of the right
hand of the Most High."' As if desperate, he considers
himself to be destroyed. He not only confesses that he is
agitated by doubt, but, as if he had fallen in the contest,
leaves himself nothing in reserve — God having deserted
him and made the hand which was accustomed to help
him the instrument of destruction. Consequently, after
being tossed among tumultuous waves … he exhorts his
soul to return to her quiet rest (Ps. 116:7). And yet,
strangely, amid those commotions, faith sustains the believer's heart and truly acts the part of the palm tree,
which supports any weights laid upon it and rises above
them. Thus David, when he seemed to be overwhelmed,
did not cease to ascend to God by urging himself forward. But when the one who is anxiously contending
with his own infirmity has recourse to faith, he is already
in a great measure victorious. We may infer this from the
following passage and others similar to it: 'Wait on the
LORD; be of good courage, and he shall strengthen your
heart; wait, I say, on the LORD!' (PS. 27:14).[9]

There are times in everyone's life when discouragement sets
in, or fears torment, or our patience seems to be running out.
Such negative mental states usually occur when we are suffering
some disease or other special difficulty; and it is in such times
that faith seems to be failing us. Calvin addresses these difficulties in his comments on Psalm 42:5: 'Why are you cast down, O
my soul? And why are you disquieted within me? Hope in God;

for I shall yet praise him, the help of my countenance and my God.' Calvin comments:

> Whenever our infirmities rise up in vast array and, like the waves of the sea, are ready to overwhelm us, our faith seems to us to fail. Consequently, we are so overcome by mere fear that we lack courage and are afraid to enter into the conflict. Whenever such a state of indifference and faintheartedness seizes us, let us remember that to govern and subdue the desires of their hearts, and especially to contend against the feelings of distrust which are natural to all, is a conflict to which the godly are frequently called. There are two evils specified, which — however apparently different — yet assail our hearts at the same time. One is *discouragement* and the other *disquietude*. When we are quite downcast, we are not free of a feeling of disquietude, which leads us to grumble and complain. The remedy for both of them is here added: 'hope in God', which alone inspires our minds … with confidence in the midst of the greatest troubles; and secondly, the exercise of patience preserves our minds in peace… David, relying upon the promises of God, not only encourages himself to cherish good hope, but also promises himself certain deliverance.[10]

## God's promises are solid and sure

God is the number-one promise keeper, and 'if we rely on God alone' and persevere through 'the trials of the cross', we will 'experience the certainty of his promises'.[11] This proves true for all who trust God, who hears us when we pray. He is not far off in the lofty heights of heaven, but in Christ he has drawn near to us. Psalm 145:18 reassures us when we feel abandoned:

'The LORD is near to all who call upon him, to all who call upon him in truth.'

> This truth is principally applicable to believers, to whom God gives the singular privilege of drawing near to him, promising that he will be favourable to their prayers. Faith, there is no doubt, lies idle and even dead without prayer, in which the spirit of adoption shows and exercises itself and by which we show evidence of our trust that we consider all his promises to be stable and sure. The inestimable grace of God ... towards believers appears in this: He exhibits himself to them as a Father. As many doubts steal upon us when we pray to God, and as we either approach him with trembling or fail by becoming discouraged and lifeless, David declares it to be true without exception, that God hears all who call upon him.[12]

In the crucible of experience, we sometimes feel the intense heat of suffering and then, perhaps, the psalmist's grief comes to mind: 'My soul melts from heaviness' (Ps. 119:28).

> The psalmist assures himself of a remedy for his extreme sorrow, provided God would stretch out his hand towards him. Formerly, when almost lifeless, he entertained the expectation of a revival through the grace of God. Now also, by the same means, he cherishes the hope of being restored to renovated and complete vigour, notwithstanding that he had been nearly consumed. He adds the petition, 'Strengthen me according to your word' because, apart from his Word, God's power would afford us little comfort. But when God comes to our aid, even if our courage and strength fail us, his promise is abundantly efficacious to fortify us.[13]

If our faith supports us in times of trouble, it is only because faith is founded on the promises of God; without faith in God's promises, we become distressed and discouraged beyond measure. This was David's experience: 'I would have lost heart, unless I had believed...' (Ps. 27:13).

David intimates that he was supported solely by faith; otherwise he would have perished a hundred times... David's meaning is: 'Had I not relied on the promise of God and been assuredly persuaded that he would safely preserve me, and had I not continued firm in this persuasion, I would have utterly perished.' There was no other remedy.[14]

Let us learn, therefore, to put such a value on God's power to protect us as to put to flight all our fears. The minds of the faithful — because of the infirmity of the flesh — cannot be at all times entirely devoid of fear; but, immediately recovering courage, let us, from the high tower of our confidence, look down upon all our dangers with contempt... With the promises of God before our eyes, and the grace which they offer, our unbelief does him grievous wrong if we do not with unshrinking courage set God against all our adversities.

When God, therefore, kindly allures us to himself and assures us that he will take care of our safety, since we have embraced his promises, or because we believe him to be faithful, it is fitting that we highly extol his power, and that it may consume our hearts with admiration of him... Moreover, we must extend this confidence still farther, in order to banish all fears from our consciences — like Paul, who, when speaking of his eternal salvation, boldly exclaims, 'If God is for us, who can be against us?' (Rom. 8:31).[15]

It is of no little importance to be rid of your self-love and made fully conscious of your weakness — so impressed with a sense of your weakness as to learn to distrust yourself. Learn to distrust yourself so as to transfer your confidence to God, reclining on him with such heartfelt confidence as to trust in his aid, and continue invincible to the end, standing by his grace so as to perceive that he is true to his promises, and so assured of the certainty of his promises as to be strong in hope.[16]

## We must rest on the promise of God

David, in a time of great distress — the time of his persecution by Saul — resisted the temptation to hide himself in a mountain wilderness. It appeared that 'There remained for him no hope of life, unless he should relinquish his kingdom, which had been promised to him...'[17] But facing his advisors he said, 'In the LORD I put my trust; how can you say to my soul, "Flee as a bird to your mountain?"' (Ps. 11:1).

David stood firmly on the foundation of his faith — the promise of God to deliver him. To those who advised him to flee to a place of concealment he replied, 'If the foundations are destroyed, what can the righteous do?' (Ps. 11:3). Calvin comments,

Psalm 11:1 teaches us that, however much the world may hate and persecute us, we ought nevertheless to continue steadfast at our post, so that we may not deprive ourselves of a right to lay claim to the promises of God, and so that these promises may not slip away from us. However much and however long we may be harassed, we ought always to continue firm and unwavering in the faith of our having the call of God.[18]

Another of Israel's psalmists cried out to God in his distress, 'I am afflicted very much; revive me, O LORD, according to your word' (Ps. 119:107). Calvin encourages us to pray as that psalmist prayed:

> His prayer to be 'quickened', or revived, implies that he was on the point of death. He, however, shows ... that though he was besieged by death he did not faint because he leaned on God. This is a point worthy of our notice, for, though at the beginning we may call upon God with much promptness, yet when the trial increases in severity, our hearts quail, and in the extremity of fear our confidence is extinguished. Yet the psalmist implores God for grace, not in order that his life be preserved in safety, but in order that he might recover the life he had lost — which indicates both the low condition to which he was reduced and his continued confidence in God. We must also observe attentively the last part of the clause, 'according to your word'. We will pray coldly, or rather we will not pray at all, if God's promise does not inspire us with courage in our sorrow and distress. In a word, as we have said elsewhere, it is indispensably necessary that we should have this key at hand, in order to our having free access to the throne of grace.[19]

In the time of Israel's great distress, facing virtual annihilation and prolonged exile, God's prophet Habakkuk, who was active during the last quarter of the seventh century B.C., consoled his people with the thought that their faith would see them through the calamity and that it is possible to experience joy in the midst of suffering. Calvin applies the prophet's message to all believers:

> During the time when poverty or famine or any other affliction is to be borne, God will render us joyful with this one consolation: relying on his promises, we look to him as the God of our salvation. In this way, Habakkuk sets on one side the desolation of the land and on the other

the inward joy which the faithful never fail to possess, for they are upheld by the perpetual favour of God... The inward joy which faith brings to us can overcome all fears, terrors, sorrows, and anxieties.[20]

## Fulfilment of promises is sometimes deferred

When we are suffering affliction, we become agitated and impatient if our prayers for recovery are not answered speedily. Calvin takes Psalm 62:1 to be the believer's model for submissive waiting for God's promise to be fulfilled: 'Truly my soul silently waits for God; from him comes my salvation.'

The resolution to wait silently when experiencing affliction implies a meek and submissive endurance of the cross. It expresses the opposite of that heat of spirit which would put us in a posture of resistance to God. The silent waiting of one who trusts God in affliction is that of composed submission ... in the exercise of which he acquiesces in the promises of God, gives place to his Word, bows to his sovereignty, and suppresses every inward murmur of dissatisfaction.[21]

When God does not immediately answer our prayers for deliverance from affliction, we tend to look elsewhere for relief. That was the psalmist's experience, and sometimes it is ours. The pathos of his prayer must touch the heart of God: 'How long, O LORD? Will you forget me forever? How long will you hide your face from me? How long shall I take counsel in my soul, having sorrow in my heart daily?' (Ps.13:1-2).

As in severe sickness those having a disease desire to change their position every moment — and the more acute the pains which afflict them are, the more fitful and

eager they are to shift and change — so when sorrow
seizes upon the hearts of men, its miserable victims are
violently agitated within, and they find it more tolerable to
torment themselves without obtaining relief, than to endure their afflictions with composed and tranquil minds.
The Lord, indeed, promises to give to the faithful 'the
Spirit of counsel' (Isa. 11:2), but he does not always give
it to them at the very beginning of any matter in which
they are interested. He sometimes permits them for a
time to be embarrassed by long deliberation without
coming to a firm decision, or to be perplexed, as if they
were entangled among thorns, not knowing where to
turn.[22]

When suffering goes on and on and we grow weary and
impatient, it may be helpful to read Psalm 37 with its star-
promise: 'Delight yourself also in the LORD, and he shall give
you the desires of your heart' (v. 4). David refers not to 'the
vain and fickle joys with which the world is deluded, but the
true repose enjoyed by the godly...' Calvin continues:

> For whether all things smile upon us, or whether the Lord
> exercises us with adversities, we ought always to hold fast
> this principle: The Lord is the portion of our inheritance;
> our lot has fallen in pleasant places (Ps. 16:5-6). We must
> therefore constantly recall to our minds this truth, that it
> can never be well with us except to the extent that God is
> gracious to us, so that the joy we derive from his paternal
> favour towards us may surpass all the pleasures of the
> world. To this injunction a promise is added, assuring us
> that if we are satisfied in the enjoyment of God alone, he
> will liberally bestow upon us all that we shall desire...
> This does not imply that the godly immediately obtain
> whatever their imagination may suggest to them; nor
> would it be for their profit that God should grant them all
> their vain desires. The meaning simply is that if we stay

our minds wholly upon God, instead of allowing our
imaginations, like others, to roam after idle and frivolous
fancies, all other things will be bestowed upon us in due
season.[23]

David with his infectious optimism utters a sweeping prophecy — that those who wait on the Lord shall inherit the earth
(Ps. 37:9). Waiting for such an inheritance requires patience
and perseverance, for the realization of the promise may be
long delayed. Waiting implies that God's people 'are exercised
by a severe conflict for the trial of their faith', and that 'They
groaned under the burden of the cross.'[24]

The possession of the earth which he promises to the
children of God is not always realized to them, because it
is the will of the Lord that they should live as strangers
and pilgrims in it. Neither does the Lord permit them to
have any fixed abode in it, but rather tries them with frequent troubles, so that they may desire with greater alac-
rity the everlasting dwelling place of heaven. The flesh is
always seeking to build its nest here for all time; and if we
were not tossed hither and thither and not allowed to rest,
we would by and by forget heaven and the everlasting
inheritance. Yet, in the midst of this disquietude, the possession of the earth ... is not taken away from the children of God; for they know most certainly that they are
the rightful heirs of the world. Hence it is that they can eat
their bread with a quiet conscience, and although they
suffer want, yet God provides for their necessities in due
season. Finally, although the ungodly labour to effect
their destruction and consider them unworthy to live
upon the earth, yet God stretches forth his hand and protects them; no, he so upholds them by his power that
they live more securely in a state of exile than the wicked
do in their nests to which they are attached. And thus the
blessing of which David speaks is in part secret and hid-

den, because our reason is so dull that we cannot comprehend what it is to possess the earth; and yet the faithful truly feel and understand that this promise is not made
to them in vain, since, having fixed the anchor of their
faith in God, they pass their life every day in peace, while
God makes it evident in their experience that the shadow
of his hand is sufficient to protect them.[25]

The fullness of the inheritance which is promised lies in the
future, beyond our death. This thought can be quite depressing,
for death is, according to Paul, an 'enemy'. The prospect of
death's being destroyed at last (1 Cor. 15:26) is small consolation to those who have terminal illness, and to their families. It is
true nevertheless that death, eventually, shall be no more. John
Donne (1573–1631), an English poet and theologian, looked
death in the eye and derided her:

Death, be not proud, though some have called thee
Mighty and dreadful, for thou art not so;
For those whom thou think'st thou dost overthrow,
Die not, poor Death, nor yet canst thou kill me.
From rest and sleep, which but thy pictures be,
Much pleasure; then from thee much more must flow,
And soonest our best men with thee do go,
Rest of their bones, and soul's delivery.
Thou art slave to fate, chance, kings, and desperate men,
And dost with poison, war, and sickness dwell;
And poppy or charms can make us sleep as well
And better than thy stroke; why swell'st thou then?
One short sleep past, we wake eternally,
And death shall be no more; Death, thou shalt die.[26]

We may languish in despair, but God is none the less
faithful, kind, and good. Calvin, commenting on Hosea 13:14,
states that whatever our condition may be, God remains the
same. His power to deliver us is not diminished, 'Nor is his

purpose changed, so as not to be always ready to help.' Calvin continues:

> From the prophet Hosea we may learn that the power of God is not to be measured by our rule: were we lost a hundred times, let God be still regarded as a saviour. If then despair at any time should so cast us down that we cannot lay hold on any of his promises, let this passage come to our minds, which says that God is death's 'plagues' and the grave's 'destruction'. 'But death is near to us; what then can we hope for any more?' That implies that God is not superior to death. But when death claims so much power over men, how much more is the power that God has over death itself! Let us then feel assured that God is the destruction of death, which means that death can no longer destroy — that death is deprived of that power by which men are naturally destroyed, and that though we may lie in the grave God is yet the destruction of the grave itself.[27]

## A closing prayer by John Calvin

In the midst of the severest trials, both for God's people and for himself, the prophet Habakkuk exults in God's continued goodness and mercy. Despite his anticipation of famine and other hardships, the prophet exclaims, 'Yet I will rejoice in the LORD, I will joy in the God of my salvation' (Hab. 3:18). Calvin echoes the prophet's plight, expressing both pathos and hope in the prayer with which he concludes his lecture on the passage:

> Grant, Almighty God, that as we cease not daily to provoke thy wrath against us, and as the hardness and obstinacy of our flesh is so great that it is necessary for us to be in various ways afflicted — O grant that we may patiently

bear thy chastisements and under a deep feeling of sorrow flee to thy mercy. May we in the meantime persevere in the hope of thy mercy, which thou hast promised, and which has been once exhibited towards us in Christ, so that we may not depend on the earthly blessings of this perishable life, but, relying on thy Word, may proceed in the course of our calling, until we shall at length be gathered into that blessed rest which is laid up for us in heaven; through Christ our Lord. Amen.

*Suffering — understanding
the love of God*

Selections from the writings of John Calvin

---

## Chapter 5

## Pour out your heart

---

'When we are so shut up by grief as
to shun the light and presence of men,
that ... is the most proper season for
engaging in prayer.'

# 5.
# Pour out your heart

*Lord, hearken and pity, O Lord my God, light of the blind and strength of the weak; yea also light of those that see, and the strength of the weak; yea also light of those that see, and strength of the strong; hearken unto my soul, and hear it crying out of the depths. For if thine ears hear us not in the depths also, whither shall we go? To whom shall we cry?*

Augustine[1]

How does God want us to pray so that he will listen to us? This question may seem elementary, but when we think about what prayer is — a serious act of worship — we will understand the need for instruction. In case anyone should imagine that prayer is only casual chatting with God, Paul, who knew the anguish of a heavy heart, instructed those who were suffering and had lost hope, telling them that although 'We do not know what to pray for as we ought ... the Spirit himself makes intercession for us with groanings which cannot be uttered' (Rom. 8:26).

In Calvin's time much thought was given by the Reformers to the question of how believers should pray, and the well-known catechism of the German church at that time included basic instruction on the subject of prayer. How does God want us to pray so that he will listen to us?

The *Heidelberg catechism* (A.D. 1563) asks that question and gives the following answer:

> First, we must from the heart call upon the one true God only, who has revealed himself in his Word, for all that he has commanded us to pray. Second, we must thoroughly know our need and misery, so that we may humble ourselves before God. Third, we must rest on this firm foundation, that although we do not deserve it, God will certainly hear our prayer for the sake of Christ our Lord, as he has promised us in his Word.[2]

This brief guide to acceptable prayer, being drawn from the teaching of Scripture, reflects Calvin's frequent encouragements to prayer. His model for earnest and effectual prayer is David, the 'sweet singer of Israel'. Consider for example the introduction to Calvin's commentary on Psalm 113:

> David, being afflicted, not only with the deepest distress, but also feeling overwhelmed by a long succession of calamities and multiplied afflictions, implores the aid and succour of God, the only remedy which remained for him; and ... taking courage he entertains the assured hope of life from the promise of God, even amid the terrors of death.

No one can fully understand the hopelessness of the heart that sorrows daily, except one who has experienced it. Calvin knew the misery of prolonged affliction and sorrow, and he was able to identify with David:

> It seemed to David, so far as could be judged from beholding the actual state of his affairs, that he was forsaken by God. At the same time, however, the eyes of his mind, guided by the light of faith, penetrated even to the grace of God, although it was hidden in darkness. When he did

not see even a single ray of good hope in whatever direction he turned, so far as human reason could judge, con-
strained by grief he cries out that God did not notice him.
Yet by this very complaint he gives evidence that faith
enabled him to rise higher and to conclude, contrary to
the judgement of the flesh, that his welfare was secure in
the hand of God. Had it been otherwise, how could he
direct his groanings and prayers to God? Following this
example, we must so wrestle against temptations as to be
assured by faith, even in the very midst of the conflict,
that the calamities which urge us to despair must be overcome, just as we see that the infirmity of the flesh could
not hinder David from seeking God and having recourse
to him. In this way he has united, very beautifully, affections which are apparently contrary to each other.[3]

## 'Pour out your heart before him.'

The full text of Psalm 62:8 is 'Trust in him at all times, you
people; pour out your heart before him; God is a refuge for us.'
Prayer can easily become a recourse only in times of trouble, a
last resort after we have tried every other means of relief.
Trusting in God 'at all times', Calvin says, 'means both in
prosperity and adversity'. The psalmist's admonition implies
'the blameworthiness of those who waver and succumb under
every variation in their outward circumstances'. Calvin continues:

God tests his children with afflictions, but here they are
taught ... to abide them with constancy and courage. We
are bound to honour his name by remembering, in our
greatest extremities, that to him belong the issues of life
and death. And as we are all inclined at such times to
shut up our affliction in our hearts — a circumstance

which can only aggravate the trouble and embitter the
mind against God — David could not have suggested a
better remedy than that of turning over our cares to God.
We always find that when the heart is pressed under a
load of distress, there is no freedom in prayer. Under trying circumstances we must comfort ourselves by reflecting
that God will extend relief, provided we just freely roll our
burdens over upon him.[4]

David's prayers are frequently cries for help. His agonizing
pleas are filled with pathos as he pours out his heart before
God. Consider Psalm 25: 'The troubles of my heart have
enlarged; bring me out of my distresses! Look on my affliction
and my pain, and forgive all my sins' (vv. 17-18). But David,
despite his suffering, never lost sight of God's covenant mercies.
In this same psalm he offers encouragement to all who pray for
relief from pain and distress. God's covenant love is the ground
of our assurance that God will hear our cry for help: 'The secret
of the LORD [the 'friendship of the LORD', NRSV] is with those
who fear him, and he will show them his covenant' (v. 14).
Calvin's heart swells with sympathy towards those who can
identify with David in his distress, and at the same time he
reminds them that God's mercy never fails:

> David, by having recourse to the mercy or compassion
> and goodness of God, testifies that he does not trust to
> his own merit as any ground of hope. He who derives
> everything from the fountain of divine mercy alone finds
> nothing in himself that is entitled to recompense in the
> sight of God... Although God, who from his very nature
> is merciful, may withdraw himself and cease for a time to
> manifest his power, yet he cannot deny himself. That is to
> say, he cannot divest himself of the feeling of mercy
> which is natural to him and which can no more cease
> than his eternal existence can. But we must firmly main-
> tain this doctrine: God has been merciful even from the

beginning, so that if at any time he seems to act with severity towards us and to reject our prayers, we must not imagine that he acts contrary to his real character, or that he has changed his purpose. From this we learn what the Scriptures everywhere inform us: that in all ages God has looked upon his servants with a benign eye and extended his mercy towards them. This, at least, we ought to regard as a fixed and settled point, that although the goodness of God may sometimes be hidden and, as it were, buried out of sight, it can never be extinguished.[5]

Calvin himself found solace in prayer. He was no stranger to grief, yet he never ceased pouring out his wounded heart at the throne of grace, and he encouraged others in their distress to do the same:

When we are so shut up by grief as to shun the light and presence of men, the gate is so far from being shut against our prayers, that then in truth is the most proper season for engaging in prayer; for it is a singular alleviation of our sorrows when we have opportunity freely to pour out our hearts before God.[6]

To anyone who would hesitate, when suffering intensely, to sob and complain and 'let it all out' before God, Calvin has this to say:

When God permits us to lay open before him our infirmities without reserve and patiently bears with our 'foolishness', he deals in great tenderness towards us. To pour out our complaints before him after the manner of little children would certainly be to treat his majesty with very little reverence, were it not that he has been pleased to allow us such freedom. I purposely make use of this illustration, so that the weak, who are afraid to draw near to God, may understand that they are invited to him with such gentleness as that nothing may hinder them from familiarly and confidently approaching him.[7]

Many of the psalms contain anguished cries for help and despairing laments. People who have suffered a spinal injury that left them paralyzed, or parents whose child must face life with spina bifida (a congenital defect in which part of the spinal cord is exposed and can cause mental impairment) — to name only two afflictions — can surely identify with those cries and laments.

Psalm 22 may be the most desolate of David's prayers. From the heart-wrenching 'Why' of verse 1 to his plea for help in verse 19, there is nothing but sadness and gloom. But David would not have cried out as he did, had he not trusted God to hear and answer his cry: 'O LORD, do not be far from me; O my strength, hasten to help me' (v. 19). Calvin writes:

> As David's miseries had reached their utmost height, and as he did not see even a single ray of hope to encourage him to expect deliverance, it is a wonderful instance of the power of faith that he not only endured his afflictions patiently, but that from the abyss of despair he arose to call upon God. Let us notice particularly that David did not pour out his lamentations thinking them to be in vain and of no effect, as people who are in perplexity often pour forth their groanings at random. The prayers which he offered show sufficiently that he hoped for such a result as he desired... He does not pray in a doubting manner, but promises himself the assistance which the eye of sense did not yet perceive.[8]

The eye of faith, however, did perceive God's faithfulness to his covenant, and David, believing that God's grace would ultimately extend far beyond Israel, poured out his heart in praise and prophecy: 'All ends of the world shall remember and turn to the LORD' (Ps. 22:27).

Calvin further notes that David 'not only ... had to contend outwardly with his enemies, but ... was also afflicted inwardly with sorrow and anguish of heart.' The troubles of his heart had 'enlarged', implying that

> The weight and number of his trials had accumulated to such an extent that they filled his whole heart, even as a flood of water bursting every barrier and extending far and wide covers a whole country. Now, when we see that the heart of David had sometimes been wholly filled with anguish, we need no longer wonder if at times the violence of temptations overwhelms us. But let us ask with David, even while we are at the point of despair, that God would give us help.[9]

Thomas Moore (1779–1852) composed a wonderfully comforting hymn, 'Come, you disconsolate', which invites all who suffer to

> Come to the mercy seat; fervently kneel:
> Here bring your wounded hearts; here tell your anguish;
> Earth has no sorrows that heaven cannot heal.

This old hymn echoes the call to prayer and trust that is found in many of the psalms. A few of the psalms, however, seem devoid of all such encouragement. Psalm 88, for example, is surely one of the most doleful prayers in all Scripture. The psalmist pours out his heart before God in a gloomy lament: 'Let my prayer come before you; incline your ear to my cry. For my soul is full of troubles, and my life draws near to the grave... But to you I have cried out, O LORD, and in the morning my prayer comes before you. LORD, why do you cast off my soul? Why do you hide your face from me? ... I suffer your terrors; I am distraught' (vv. 13-15).

There is not a single note of hope in this psalm. It is a lament from the abyss of suffering, an outcry of grief without consolation. And yet, it is by all accounts a prayer. There are times when we ourselves might be overshadowed by hopelessness and despair; but it is then that we should pray most fervently, even if mournfully and disconsolately, seeking help at heaven's mercy seat. The faithful know in their heart of hearts, even when things seem hopeless, that God's ears are open to their cries. Calvin sees Psalm 88 in a similar light:

> The psalmist does not proudly enter into debate with God, but mournfully desires some remedy for his calamities. This kind of complaint justly deserves to be reckoned among the unutterable groanings which Paul mentions in Romans 8:26. Had the psalmist thought himself to be rejected and abhorred by God, he certainly would not have persevered in prayer. But here he sets forth the judgement of the flesh, against which he strenuously and magnanimously struggles, that it might at length be evident from the result that he had not prayed in vain.
>
> Although, therefore, this psalm does not end with thanksgiving but with a mournful complaint, as if there remained no place for mercy, yet it is so much the more useful as a means of keeping us in the duty of prayer. The psalmist, in heaving these sighs and discharging them, as it were, into the bosom of God, doubtless did not cease to hope for the salvation of which he could see no signs by the eye of sense. He did not call God, at the beginning of the psalm, 'the God of my salvation' and then bid farewell to all hope of help from God.[10]

When David was being pursued by Saul he took refuge in a cave (1 Sam. 22:1), where he sought protection and fortified himself against the temptation to kill Saul. He prayed earnestly for God's intervention. Psalm 142:1-4 describes his distress and lonely prayer vigil in the cave of Adullam:

I cry unto the LORD with my voice;

With my voice to the LORD I make my supplication.
I pour out my complaint before him;
I declare before him my trouble.
When my spirit was overwhelmed within me,
Then you knew my path.
In the way in which I walk
They have secretly set a snare for me.
Look on my right hand and see,
For there is no one who acknowledges me;
Refuge has failed me;
No one cares for my soul.

What is important for us to observe, according to Calvin, is that David did not pour out self-pity to the people around him, but passionately made known his complaint to God, with submission and confidence in God's mercy:

David states clearly that he laid his fears upon God. To pour out one's thoughts and tell over his afflictions implies the reverse of those perplexing anxieties which people brood over inwardly to their own distress, and by which they torture themselves and are chafed by their afflictions rather than led to God. It also implies the reverse of those frantic exclamations to which others give voice who find no comfort in the superintending providence and care of God. In short, we are left to infer that while David did not give way before men to loud and senseless lamentations, neither did he permit himself to be tormented by inward and suppressed cares, but made known his grief with unsuspecting confidence to the Lord.[11]

When troubles come, it is often easier to complain to sympathetic friends than to God. We may feel that complaining does not belong in our prayers; that prayer should consist only of supplication, confession, and thanksgiving. Besides, you may think, God knows my problem anyway, and complaining will only make me feel worse. But David's prayers reveal that we should open our hearts before God, even though God already knows what we are going through. David prays, 'LORD, all my desire is before you; and my sighing is not hidden from you. My heart pants, my strength fails me; as for the light of my eyes, it also has gone from me' (Ps. 38:9-10). Of course God knew all about David's 'plague'; after all, God himself had inflicted him with 'foul and festering' wounds, so that he might be chastened and renewed in spirit. David nevertheless did complain to God, but he also humbly begged God for mercy: 'Make haste to help me, O LORD, my salvation!'(v. 22).

> David in Psalm 38 declares that he had discharged all his sorrows into the bosom of God. The reason why most people derive no profit from complaining grievously in their sorrow is that they do not direct their prayers and sighs to God. David, then, in order to encourage himself in the assured conviction that God will be his deliverer, says that God had always been a witness to his sorrows and was well acquainted with them. He had neither indulged in a fretful spirit, nor poured out into the air his complaints and howlings as the unbelieving are accustomed to do, but spread out before God himself all the desires of his heart.[12]

As we have seen, the prophet Habakkuk complained bitterly about the Chaldeans' assault on God's chosen people, because, he reasoned, the Chaldeans deserved to be punished more than the community of the elect. Calvin writes:

> We now see that the prophet can be justly excused, though he expostulates here with God, for God does not condemn this freedom of our prayers. On the contrary, the end of praying, as it is said in the psalms, is that every one of us should pour out his heart before God. As, then,

we communicate our cares and sorrows to God, it is no wonder that the prophet, according to the manner of men, says, 'Why do you show me iniquity and make me see trouble?'[13]

Calvin continues,

Why do we pray, except that each of us may unburden his cares, his grief, and anxieties by pouring them into the bosom of God? Since, then, God allows us to deal so familiarly with him, nothing wrong ought to be ascribed to our prayers when we freely pour out our feelings — provided the bridle of obedience keeps us within due limits, as was the case with the prophet Habakkuk.[14]

## The gate of prayer is always open

What assurances do we have that our prayers are heard? Surely we must go beyond the pious slogan, 'Prayer changes things', if we are to pray with confidence and hope. In truth, it is *God* who changes things in answer to prayer. In the midst of our struggles and troubles we would not pray at all if we doubted that God hears our complaints and requests. Our assurance that God's ears are open to our cries comes not only from personal experience of answered prayer, or from the inner feeling of being in God's presence when we pray — although such experiences do reinforce our confidence in prayer — but chiefly from the Holy Spirit's testimony in holy Scripture. This testimony includes the prayers of the saints, the declarations of Jesus and the apostles, the intercession of Christ, and the intercession of the Holy Spirit.

## *The prayers of the saints*

David, when describing the happiness of those who trust in the Lord, mentions their access to God in prayer as one of their blessings. God keeps a close lookout for the righteous, he says, 'and his ears are open to their cry' (Ps. 34:15). 'The righteous cry out, and the LORD hears, and delivers them out of their troubles' (v. 17). God is not in some lofty realm beyond our reach; on the contrary, 'The LORD is near to those who have a broken heart' (v. 18). The psalmist's meaning, says Calvin, is that:

> They are heard as often as they cry. This is a doctrine applicable to all times; and David does not merely relate what God has done once or twice, but what he is accustomed to do. It is also a confirmation of verse 15, where he had said that the ears of the Lord are open to the cry of the righteous; he now demonstrates the effect — that God is not deaf when we lay our complaints and groanings before him. By the word *cry* we are taught that although God defends the righteous they are not exempt from adversity. He regulates the protection which he affords them in such a wonderful manner that he exercises them by various trials. In like manner, when we see that deliverance is promised only to those who call upon God, this ought to prove no small encouragement to us to pray to him. It is not his will that the godly should so regard his providence as to indulge in idleness, but rather, being firmly persuaded that he is the guardian of their safety, that they should direct their prayers and supplications to him.[15]

One of the great and marvellous answers to a prayer of one of God's saints is that offered by Hannah. Being childless, she complained that 'The LORD had closed her womb... And she was in bitterness of soul, and prayed to the LORD and wept in anguish' (1 Sam. 1:6, 10). God heard her anguished prayer: 'So it came to pass in the process of time that Hannah conceived and bore a son, and she called his name Samuel, saying, "Because I have asked for him from the LORD"' (v. 20). The name Samuel, in Hebrew, literally means 'heard by God' and is a reminder that the Lord's ears are open to the cries of his saints.

## The declarations of Jesus and the apostles

In one of his final discourses to the disciples, Jesus encouraged them to pray, promising to answer all their requests: 'Whatever you ask in my name, that will I do, that the Father may be glorified in the Son. If you ask anything in my name, I will do it' (John 14:13-14). Since Christ is the mediator through whom we offer prayer to the Father, we have confidence that our prayers will be heard — and answered. Calvin comments:

> All see and feel that they are unworthy to approach God; and yet most men burst forward, as if they were out of their senses, and rashly and haughtily address God. Afterwards, when that unworthiness of which I have spoken comes to their recollection, every man contrives for himself various expedients. On the other hand, when God invites us to himself, he holds out to us one mediator only, by whom he is willing to be appeased and reconciled. But here again the wickedness of the human mind breaks out, for most do not cease to forsake the road and to stray into many other paths. The reason why they do so is that they have a poor and slender perception of the power and goodness of God in Christ. To this is added a second error: we do not consider that we are justly excluded from approaching God, until he calls us, and that we are called only through the Son. And if our Lord's promise has not sufficient weight with us, let us know that when Christ repeats, a second time, that we must pray to

the Father in his name, he lays his hand on us, as it were,
that we may not lose our pains by fruitlessly seeking other
intercessors.[16]

The author of 1 John, who calls himself 'the elder', wrote to
late first-century Christians, in order to deepen their spiritual life
and to encourage them to pray more earnestly. He instructs
them that they must, however, 'Continue to believe in the name
of the Son of God' (1 John 5:13); and they must always pray in
his name and for things agreeable to his will. 'Now this is the
confidence that we have in him, that if we ask anything according to his will, he hears us' (1 John 5:14). Calvin, following
John's statement, says that 'The godly dare confidently to call
upon God'; and he links John's confidence with that of Paul in
Ephesians 3:12 — 'We have by faith access to God with
confidence' — and in Romans 8:15: 'The Spirit gives us a
mouth to cry "Abba, Father"'. Calvin continues:

> And doubtless, if we were driven away from an access to
> God, nothing could make us more miserable. On the
> other hand, provided this asylum is open to us, we
> should be happy even in extreme evils. No, this one thing
> renders our troubles blessed, because we surely know
> that God will be our deliverer and, relying on his paternal
> love towards us, we flee to him.[17]

One of Calvin's chief desires is that the children of God pray
unceasingly and passionately, that God may supply all their
wants in accordance with God's will. He writes,

> This, then, is an application of the general doctrine to the
> special and private benefit of everyone, lest the faithful
> should doubt that God is favourable to prayers of each
> individual. With quiet minds they may wait until the Lord
> performs what they pray for, and, being thus relieved
> from all trouble and anxiety, they may cast on God the

burden of their cares. This ease and security ought not,
however, to abate their earnestness in prayer, for he who
is certain of a happy event ought not to abstain from
praying to God. For the certainty of faith by no means
generates indifference or sloth. The apostle meant that
everyone should be tranquil in these necessities when he
has deposited his sighs in the bosom of God.[18]

## The intercession of Christ

Christ, being our High Priest, is also our intercessor who represents us before God, in order that we may receive the salvation
which he purchased on the cross for us, and in order that our
prayers may be heard (Heb. 8:1; 7:24-25).

It is owing to Christ's eternal and unchangeable priesthood
that, according to 1 John 3:21-22, 'We have confidence
towards God. And whatever we ask we receive from him,
because we keep his commandments and do those things that
are pleasing in his sight.' Calvin sees the intercession of Christ
as the indispensable ground of our confidence concerning our
prayers:

> These two things are connected: confidence and prayer.
> As before he showed that an evil conscience is inconsis-
> tent with confidence, so now he declares that none can
> really pray to God but those who with a pure heart fear
> and worship him...
>
> He does not mean that a good conscience must be
> brought before God as though it obtained favour to our
> prayers... The faithful cannot come to God's tribunal in
> any other way than by relying on Christ the mediator.
> But as the love of God is ever connected with faith, the
> apostle, in order that he might the more severely reprove
> hypocrites, deprives them of that singular privilege with
> which God favours his own children: that is, that the

hypocrites should think that their prayers have an access
to God.[19]

The faithful do have access to God, however, at all times
and in all places. This is because by Christ's intercession we
have been reconciled to God. Having entered the heavenly
sanctuary after his ascension (Heb. 4:14), Calvin writes,

> Christ continually appears in the presence of the Father
> as our advocate and intercessor. He attracts the eyes of
> the Father to his righteousness, so as to avert them from
> our sins. He reconciles him to us, so as to procure for us,
> by his intercession, a way of access to his throne, which
> he replenishes with grace and mercy, but which otherwise
> would be pregnant with horror to miserable sinners.[20]

In one of his pastoral sermons, Calvin points to Christ as the
'mediator who has opened the way whereby we may come to
God' and offer our prayers with confidence in God's grace and
mercy. We are assured that our prayers are not offered in vain
because, says Calvin,

> Jesus Christ is called a mediator not only because he has
> made reconciliation by his death, but also because he
> appears now before the majesty of God, in order that
> through him we may be heard... Jesus Christ has re-
> deemed us by his death and passion, so that there is no
> hindrance why God should not accept us, and now he
> still makes intercession for us before God.[21]

Christ's continual intercession should be a comfort to those
who are tormented by pain or trouble. With this thought in
mind, Calvin said to his worshipping congregation,

> Since it has pleased God to give us such an advocate and
> mediator as his own Son, let us not be afraid to come

---

and present ourselves before him and call upon him for all our needs… When we pray to God, our prayers must be sanctified and consecrated by the blood of our Lord Jesus Christ… And we may rest assured that God will not reject the sacrifice with which he is very well content … and by which he has become reconciled to us and made one with us for ever.[22]

## The intercession of the Holy Spirit

We have many models of prayer in the Scriptures, including the incomparable Lord's Prayer (Matt. 6:9-13); yet we cannot by our own wisdom frame our prayers in a truly spiritual manner. Since 'We do not know what we should pray for as we ought', the Holy Spirit helps our weaknesses and 'makes intercession for us with groanings which cannot be uttered' (Rom. 8:26). We are not only 'taught by the Spirit how to pray and what to ask in our prayers' but also, states Calvin, 'He has annexed prayers to the anxious desires of the faithful; for God does not afflict them with miseries so that they may inwardly feed on hidden grief, but that they may unburden themselves by prayer, and thus exercise their faith.'[23]

We are truly indebted to the Holy Spirit for his sensitive understanding of our anxiety and our grief and for the Spirit's communicating our deepest desires to our heavenly Father. Calvin says:

Though … it does not appear that our prayers are heard by God, yet Paul concludes that the presence of the celestial favour does already shine forth in the mere desire for prayer, for no one can of himself give birth to devout and godly aspirations. The unbelieving do indeed blab out their prayers, but they only trifle with God, for there is in them nothing sincere or serious or rightly formed. Therefore the manner of praying properly must be suggested by the Spirit; and Paul calls *unutterable* those groanings into which we break forth by the impulse of the Spirit, for this reason: they far exceed the capability of our own minds. And the Spirit is said to *intercede,* not because he really humbles himself to pray or groan, but because he stirs up in our hearts those desires which we ought to entertain. He also affects our hearts in such a way that those desires by their fervency penetrate into heaven itself. And Paul has spoken in this way so that we might more significantly ascribe everything to the grace of the Spirit. We are indeed bidden to knock; but no one can of himself premeditate even one syllable, except that God by the secret impulse of his Spirit knocks at *our* door, and thus opens for himself our hearts.[24]

God, who searches our hearts, knows the mind of the Spirit (Rom. 8:27), and therefore we are assured that our prayers do not dissipate into thin air. Calvin says,

This is a remarkable reason for strengthening our confidence, namely, that we are heard by God when we pray through his Spirit, for he thoroughly knows our desires, even as he knows the thoughts of his own Spirit... As Paul had previously testified — that God aids us when he draws us as it were into his own bosom — so now he adds another consolation: that our prayers, of which he is the director, shall by no means be disappointed.[25]

God's favour and blessing sometimes are withheld for a time from those who are devoted to his service. This seems to have been the psalmist's experience as he had to contend with adversaries. 'Consider my affliction and deliver me, for I do not forget your law,' he prayed (Ps. 119:153). Calvin, who faced almost daily conflict with opponents of the Reformation movement, saw his own painful experiences in the light of the psalmist's, and assures us that we too have access through faith to the all-sufficient grace of God: 'The psalmist teaches by his

own example that those who are devoted to the service and
fear of God must not be discouraged though they are not
rewarded for it in this world. Their condition on earth is one of
warfare, and therefore they should not be dismayed by adversity, but rather rest satisfied with the consolation that *the gate of
prayer is always open* to them.'[26]

## When God seems not to hear our prayers

It is natural for us to become impatient, and even discouraged,
if God's help is delayed — especially when we have prayed
earnestly and faithfully. But instead of abandoning hope, we
should remember that God is faithful too. He may be simply
trying our patience or calling us to the discipline of prayer.
Calvin comments:

> When God does not promptly afford assistance to his
> servants, it seems to the eye of sense that he does not
> observe their needs. David, for this reason, asks God to
> look upon him and to help him... God knew, of course,
> David's need, but the Holy Spirit purposely accommo-
> dates to our understanding the models of prayer recorded
> in Scripture. If David had not been persuaded that God
> had his eyes upon him, it would have availed him noth-
> ing to cry to God — this persuasion was the effect of
> faith. In the meantime, until God actually puts forth his
> hand to give relief, carnal reason suggests to us that he
> shuts his eyes and does not notice us. God, however,
> because he does in fact observe our need, hears us and,
> having compassion upon us, is moved and induced to
> help us.[27]

We can, therefore, pray with confidence for ourselves
in the manner in which David does for himself, but only
when we fight under the standard of God and are obedi-

ent to his orders, so that our enemies cannot obtain the victory over us without wickedly triumphing over God himself.[28]

'My God, my God why have you forsaken me?' is a cry not unknown by those whose suffering is unbearable (Ps. 22:1). But such a complaint issues from faith — otherwise God's name would not be invoked. Calvin comments,

> When the psalmist speaks of being forsaken and cast off by God, it seems to be the complaint of a man in despair; for can a man have a single spark of faith remaining in him when he believes that there is no longer any help available to him from God? And yet, in twice calling God his own God and depositing his groanings into God's bosom, he makes a very distinct confession of his faith. With this inward conflict the godly must necessarily be exercised whenever God withdraws from them the tokens of his favour, so that, in whatever direction they turn their eyes, they see nothing but the darkness of night. I say that the people of God, when wrestling with themselves, on the one hand reveal the weakness of the flesh, and on the other give evidence of their faith.[29]

Third World countries in Asia, Africa, and Latin America are populated by the poorest people on earth. Scenes of squalor and disease, wretched shanties and emaciated children that occasionally fill our TV screens raise the question of God's goodness and common grace. Has God forgotten to be gracious to the needy of our world? The answer must be that we ourselves have forgotten to be gracious to them by relieving their wants, so far as is possible. Prayer alone, without sharing, will do little to relieve their poverty and misery. Is it possible that God's answer to our entreaties in behalf of the poor awaits our generous assistance? We are assured in any case that 'God will not forsake the poor for ever, though they may indeed seem to be forsaken for a time.'[30]

There are needy people in every country, of course — in Brazil and Britain, in Romania and Russia, in Argentina and America. For anyone who feels the pinch of poverty and thinks that God has forgotten to be gracious, Calvin has a word of counsel:

> Let us remember that God has promised his assistance to us, not in the way of preventing our afflictions, but of at length helping us after we have been long subdued under the cross. David in Psalm 9:18 speaks expressly of hope or expectation, thereby to encourage us to prayer. The reason why God seems to take no notice of our afflictions is because he would have us to awaken him by means of our prayers; for when he hears our requests (as if he began only then to be mindful of us), he stretches forth his powerful hand to help us. David again repeats that this is not done immediately, in order that we may persevere in hoping well, even though our expectations may not be instantly gratified.[31]

Persistence in prayer is a mark of one who is faithful. Our Lord encourages us to continue to ask and to expect to receive, in due time, an answer to our entreaties. Jesus' parable of the persistent widow who pestered a hard-hearted judge to grant her justice teaches us 'that men always ought to pray and not lose heart' (Luke 18:1-5). After many entreaties the unjust judge gave in, saying, 'Though I do not fear God or regard man, yet because this widow troubles me I will avenge her, lest by her continual coming she weary me' (vv. 4-5).

The Judge in the court of heaven, by contrast, is 'abundant in mercy to all who call upon [him]' (Ps. 86:5). If one truly believes that the gate of prayer is open to all, he or she will not hesitate to bring troubles of all sorts to God whose grace is super-abundant. Calvin's comment on this verse may seem elementary, but when trouble comes, one needs to be reminded that God will not turn a deaf ear:

> It would avail the afflicted nothing to have recourse to God and to lift up their desires and prayers to heaven, if they were not persuaded that he faithfully rewards all who call upon him... God is bountiful and inclined to compassion; his mercy is so great as to render it impossible for him to reject any who implore his aid... The psalmist says *all,* meaning that everyone, without exception, from the greatest to the least, may be encouraged confidently to take himself [or herself] to the goodness and mercy of God.[32]
>
> It is evident that the psalmist was oppressed with no ordinary degree of grief, and also agitated with extreme anxiety... From this example we are taught that those who, having once engaged in prayer, allow themselves immediately to give up that exercise if God does not at once grant them their desire, betray the coldness and inconstancy of their hearts... By repeating the same requests, the saints, little by little, discharge their cares into the bosom of God, and this importunity is a sacrifice of a sweet savour before him. When the psalmist says, 'God will hear me when I cry in the day of my trouble', he makes a particular application to himself of the truth which he had just stated: that God is gracious and merciful to all who call upon him.[33]

Our prayers for relief from suffering may be answered, not according to our petitions, but in some other way that seems best to God. Paul's three prayers for relief from his 'thorn in the flesh' are a case in point (2 Cor. 12:7-10). Calvin writes:

> It may seem ... that Paul had not ... prayed in faith, if we believe all the promises of God. Some may say, 'We read everywhere in Scripture that we shall obtain whatever we

ask in faith; Paul prays and does not obtain.' I answer
that as there are different ways of asking, so there are
different ways of obtaining. We ask in simple terms for
those things for which we have an express promise — for
example, the perfecting of God's kingdom and the hallowing of his name (Matt. 6:9); the remission of our sins
and everything that is advantageous to us. But when we
think that the kingdom of God *can,* no, *must* be advanced in this or that particular manner, and that this
thing, or that, is necessary for the hallowing of his name,
we are often mistaken in our opinion. Likewise, we often
fall into a serious mistake as to what ends promote our
own welfare. Therefore we ask those former things confidently and without any reservation — but it does not
belong to us to prescribe the means... Now Paul was not
so ignorant as not to know this. Thus, as to the *object* of
his prayer, there can be no doubt that he was heard, although he met with a refusal as to the specific *form.* By
this example we are admonished not to give way to despondency, as if our prayers had been lost labour when
God does not gratify or comply with our wishes, but to be
satisfied with his grace; that is, in respect of our not being
forsaken by him.[34]

To sum up the matter of 'unanswered prayer', we turn to
Calvin's *Institutes*:

If, with minds framed to obedience, we allow ourselves to
be governed by the laws of divine providence, we will
easily learn to persevere in prayer. Suspending our own
desires, we will wait patiently for the Lord, assured, however little it appears, that God is always present with us
and will in his own time show how very far he was from
turning a deaf ear to our prayers — though to the human
eye they may seem to be disregarded. This will be a very
present consolation, preventing us from fainting or giving

way to despondency if at any time God does not grant an immediate response to our prayers. There are those who often, in invoking God, are so borne away by their own fervour, that unless he yields on their first importunity and gives present help, they immediately imagine that he is angry and offended with them; and abandoning all hope of success, they quit praying. On the contrary, deferring our hope with well-tempered equanimity, let us insist on that perseverance which is strongly recommended to us in Scripture. We may often see in the psalms how David and other believers, after they are almost weary of praying and seem to have been beating the air by addressing a God who would not hear their petitions, yet did not stop praying — because the authority of the divine Word is not maintained unless it is fully believed, in spite of the appearance of any circumstances to the contrary.[35]

## Faith is indispensable

Throughout Scripture faith is the foundation of prayer. Certainly the psalmist's prayer in Psalm 143 was undergirded by faith: 'I spread out my hands to you.' His open hands stretched forth in expectation of divine help were a symbol of faith in God's readiness to help him in his time of need. Calvin comments:

Prayer, indeed, springs from faith. As practical proofs of the favour and mercy of God confirm this faith, they are means evidently fitted for dissipating languor. The psalmist uses a striking figure to set forth the ardour of his desire: His soul longs for God like a thirsty land. In times of extreme heat we see that the earth is cracked and opens, as it were, its mouth to heaven for moisture. David likewise drew near to God with passionate desire, as if the very sap of life failed him. In verse 7 he gives another

proof of his extraordinary faith. Feeling himself weak and
ready to sink into the very grave, he does not vacillate
between this and the other hope of relief, but fixes his
sole dependence upon God. And heavy as the struggle
was that he underwent with his own felt weakness, the
fainting of spirit of which he speaks was a better stimulant
to prayer than any stoical obstinacy he might have shown
in suppressing fear, grief, or anxiety. We must not overlook this: In order to induce himself to depend exclusively
upon God, he dismisses all other hopes from his mind
and makes a chariot for himself ... in which he ascends
upwards to God.[36]

Calvin frequently encourages his readers (and his congregation) to pray with the same faith as the psalmists exercised and
to experience answers to our prayers, as they did. One example
is in Psalm 34:6 — 'This poor man cried out, and the LORD
heard him, and saved him out of all his troubles.' Calvin says,

David here introduces all the godly, speaking of himself,
the more emphatically to express how much weight there
is in his example to encourage them. This poor man, they
say, cried; therefore the Lord invites all the poor to cry to
him. They contemplate in David what belongs to the
common benefit of all the godly; for God is willing and
ready at this day to hear all the afflicted who direct their
sighs, wishes, and cries to him *with the same faith as God
was at that time to hear David.*[37]

Another poor man — the composer of Psalm 88 — cries
out, 'Your wrath lies heavy upon me, and you have afflicted me
with all your waves' (v. 7). Calvin makes good use of the
maritime metaphor, encouraging the faithful, however desperate their plight may be, to cast the anchor of faith in the safe
haven of heaven: 'The psalmist declares that he sustained the
whole burden of God's wrath: he was afflicted with all God's

"waves". Yet, so dreadful a flood did not prevent him from lifting up his heart and prayers to God. So we may learn from his example *to cast the anchor of our faith and prayers directly into heaven in all the perils of shipwreck to which we may be exposed.*'[38]

When we pray in a time of trouble, God does not regard our goodness or kindness or generous treatment of others; he looks, rather, upon his Son, our intercessor, in whom we trust. Trust or confidence in God, Calvin states, 'is the mother of all true religion'. He continues, 'Therefore, although we may have the testimony of an approving conscience, and although God may be the best witness of our innocence [as in the case of Job], it is necessary for us to commit our hopes and anxieties to him.'[39]

Our trust and confidence must rest, ultimately, in Christ, our reconciler and intercessor. Even the psalms do not limit access to God to the people of Israel. David envisions the way to God being open to all people everywhere. It is as if David anticipates the future coming of the kingdom of Christ: 'O you who hear prayer, to you all flesh will come. Iniquities prevail against me; as for our transgressions, you will provide atonement for them' (Ps. 65:2-3). Again, we turn to Calvin for his comment:

> None could venture into God's presence without the persuasion of his being open to entreaty; but when he anticipates our fears and comes forward declaring that prayer is never offered to him in vain, the door is thrown open wide for the admission of all... Before we can approach God acceptably in prayer, it is necessary that his promises should be made known to us, without which we can have no access to him. This is evident from the words of the apostle Paul in Ephesians 3:12, where he tells us that all who would come to God must first be endued with such a faith in Christ as may animate them with confidence... Invaluable is the privilege, which we enjoy by the gospel, of free access to God. When the psalmist uses the expression 'all flesh', he intimates that the privilege

which was peculiar to the Jews would be extended to all
nations. It is a prediction of Christ's future kingdom.[40]

## How then should we pray?

### *Persevere in prayer*

Following the example of the apostles, we are to 'Pray without
ceasing' (1 Thess. 5:17). Calvin knew the difficulties of following
this rule of thumb:

> We know how difficult it is to rise above all doubts and
> boldly to *persevere in a free and unrestrained course of
> prayer*. Here, then, the faithful call to remembrance the
> proofs of God's mercy and working, by which he certi-
> fied, through a continued series of ages, that he was the
> King and Protector of the people whom he had chosen.
> By this example we are taught that, as it is not enough to
> pray with the lips unless we pray also in faith, we ought
> always to remember the benefits by which God has given
> a confirmation of his fatherly love towards us, and should
> regard them as so many testimonies of his electing love.[41]

David utters a prayer of faith in a time of great distress
(Ps. 6). 'I am weary with my groaning', he laments. David's
sorrow, Calvin says, was truly severe and bitter, not because of
bodily distress due to injury or sickness, but because he regarded God as 'greatly displeased with him' and 'He saw, as it
were, hell open to receive him; and the mental distress which
this produces exceeds all other sorrows.' Calvin perceives that
'Nothing prevents us at this day from experiencing in ourselves
what David describes', namely 'the terrors of his conscience'.
Although he was burdened with grief and 'almost wholly wasted

away with protracted sorrow ... *yet all the while he never ceased from praying to God*.[42]

When God's answer to our prayers seems not to be forthcoming and our patience is being tried, the need for perseverance in prayer is very pressing. God sometimes holds us in suspense, 'Yet he listens and is favourable to our prayers, so that our hope founded on his Word is never disappointed.' When faithful praying saints like Hannah were afflicted, desolate, and half-dead, they could 'become dispirited and rush on to despair if they were not comforted with the thought that God looks on them with favour, and that there will be an end to their present troubles. But however secure their hopes may stand, they do not cease to pray, since prayer unaccompanied by perseverance leads to no result.'[43]

Perseverance in prayer is a mark of David's life of devotion. Pressed to the limit of endurance, his heart severely pained within him, and overwhelmed with horror, he moans noisily (Ps. 55:4-5). Calvin says:

> Though there was no apparent method of escape and he stood on the brink of immediate destruction, he declares his resolution to continue in prayer and expresses his assurance that it would be successful. In Psalm 55:17 he engages more particularly to show perseverance in prayer: 'Evening and morning and at noon I will pray and cry aloud, and he shall hear my voice.' He says that he would cry aloud to denote passionate supplication on account of the grief and anxiety to which he was subjected. He intimates that no extremity of present trouble would prevent him from directing his complaint to God and cherishing a confident hope of deliverance.[44]

Living a transformed life includes, according to Paul, 'rejoicing in hope, [being] patient in tribulation [and] continuing steadfastly in prayer' (Romans 12:2, 12). 'Joy derived from hope and patience in adversities', Calvin insists, are possible only if we persevere in prayer.

> But as both these things (joy and patience) are far above our strength, we must be diligent in prayer, continually calling upon God, that he may not allow our hearts to faint and be pressed down, or to be broken by adverse events. Paul not only stimulates us to prayer but expressly requires perseverance in it; for we have a continual warfare, and new conflicts arise daily. Even the strongest are not able to sustain the battle unless they frequently gather new rigour. That we may not then be wearied, the best remedy is diligence in prayer.[45]

## Pray with a humble spirit

> It is to be observed that it is chiefly when men are sorely oppressed by adversity that they are made to feel their nothingness in the sight of God. David, for example, acknowledged that 'Every man at his best state is but vapour.' Prosperity so intoxicates them that, forgetful of their condition and sunken in insensibility, they dream of an immortal state on earth. It is very profitable for us to know our own frailty, but we must be careful not to fall into such a state of sorrow on account of our weakness that we begin to murmur and fret. David speaks truly and wisely in declaring that man, even when he seems to have risen to the highest state of greatness, is only like a bubble which rises on the water and is blown about by the wind. But he is at fault when he takes occasion from this to complain about God. *Let us, therefore, so feel the misery of our present condition that, however cast down and afflicted, we may, as humble suppliants, lift up our eyes to God and implore his mercy.* This we find David does a little later, after having corrected himself; for he does not continue to indulge in rash and inconsiderate

lamentations, but, lifting up his soul in the exercise of faith, he attains heavenly consolation.[46]

Psalm 131 is a lovely cameo of humble trust in God. Whether it arose from a troubled heart we cannot say, but because it is a prayer of faith and hope we can view it as an example of the way in which we must approach God in our own prayers. Calvin, however, thinks that it expresses David's humble spirit as he undertook his headship over God's people. 'He is desirous to show that he had not been influenced, in anything which he had attempted, by ambition or pride, but had submitted himself with a quiet and humble spirit to the divine disposal.'[47]

The psalm is a beautifully touching portrait of a quiet and humble spirit that prays with trust and hope:

LORD, my heart is not haughty,
Nor my eyes lofty.
Neither do I concern myself with great matters,
Nor with things too profound for me.
Surely I have calmed and quieted my soul,
Like a weaned child with his mother;
Like a weaned child is my soul within me.
O Israel, hope in the LORD
From this time forth and for ever.

Calvin continues, 'It teaches us a very useful lesson, and one by which we should be ruled in life — to be contented with the lot which God has marked out for us, to consider what he calls us to, and not to aim at fashioning our own lot; to be moderate in our desires, to avoid entering upon rash undertakings, and to confine ourselves cheerfully within our own sphere, instead of attempting great things.'[48]

If we are ruled in life by a humble and quiet spirit, our daily prayers and our cries for help in times of trouble will be framed in that same spirit.

## Pray in accordance with God's will

We cannot know God's secret will for our lives, except as God has revealed it to us in Christ and in Scripture. This is why 'We do not know what we should pray for as we ought' (Rom. 8:26). The enlightenment of the Holy Spirit and the insight which the Spirit gives — sometimes called 'common sense' — may serve as guides for prayer that is attuned to the will of God. But if we expect to pray for things agreeable to his will, God's Word must be our primary guide. Calvin makes this point crystal clear in his comment on Psalm 91:15:

> That affection and desire which is produced by faith prompts us to call upon God's name. I have touched upon this truth formerly — that prayer is properly grounded upon the Word of God. We are not at liberty in this matter to follow the suggestions of our own mind and will, but must seek God only in so far as he has in the first place invited us to approach him. The context of Psalm 91:15, too, may teach us that faith is not idle or inoperative, and that one test by which we ought to try those who look for divine deliverances is whether they have recourse to God in a right manner.[49]

Our confidence in God as we utter our petitions before him is this: 'If we ask anything *according to his will,* he hears us' (1 John 5:14, emphasis added). Calvin comments:

> By this expression he meant to remind us what is the right way or rule of praying, even when we submit our own wishes to God. For though God has promised to do whatever his people may ask, yet he does not allow them unbridled liberty to ask whatever may come to their minds. At the same time, he has prescribed to them a law according to which they are to pray. Doubtless nothing is better for us than this restriction; for if every one of us

were allowed to ask what we pleased, and if God were to
indulge us in our wishes, it would be to provide very
badly for us. For we do not know what may be expedient; no, we boil over with corrupt and hurtful desires. But
God supplies a twofold remedy, lest we should pray otherwise than according to what his own will has pre-
scribed: he teaches us by his Word what he would have
us ask, and he also sets over us his Spirit as our guide
and ruler, to restrain our feelings, so as not to allow them
to wander beyond due bounds. For what or how to pray
we do not know, says Paul, but the Spirit helps our weakness and stimulates in us unutterable groans. We ought
also to ask the mouth of the Lord to direct and guide our
prayers; for God in his promises has fixed for us, as it has
been said, the right way of praying.[50]

Since it is the Holy Spirit who helps us with our prayers, it is
important that we pray for his guidance, not only in our prayers
but in our life as a whole. 'Teach me to do your will' is a most
important petition to that end. In his comments on Psalm 143,
Calvin says,

The psalmist now rises to something higher [deliverance
from enemies]: praying not merely for deliverance from
outward troubles, but what is of still greater importance — the guidance of God's Spirit, that he might not
turn aside to the right hand or to the left, but be kept in
the path of rectitude. This is a request which should never
be forgotten when temptations assail us with great severity, as it is particularly difficult to submit to God without
resorting to unwarrantable methods of relief. As anxiety,
fear, disease, weariness, or pain often tempt persons to
take particular steps, David's example should bid us to
pray for divine restraint, that we might not be hurried
through impulses of feeling into unjustifiable courses. We
must mark carefully his way of expressing himself, for

what he asks is not simply to be taught what the will of
God is, but to be taught and brought to the observance
and doing of it.[51]

One of David's prayers that may well serve as a model for us
is found in Psalm 25:1-7. In verses 4 and 5 he petitions God
that he might be led in right and godly pathways in accordance
with the Word of God:

Show me your ways, O LORD;
Teach me your paths.
Lead me in your truth and teach me,
For you are the God of my salvation;
On you I wait all the day.

Calvin writes:

There is in this prayer an allusion to those sudden and
irregular emotions which arise in our minds when we are
tossed by adversity and by which we are precipitated into
the devious and deceitful paths of error, *till they are in
due time subdued or allayed by the Word of God.* Thus
the meaning is, 'Whatever may happen, do not permit
me, O Lord, to fall from your ways, or to be carried away
by a wilful disobedience to your authority, or any other
sinful desire; but rather let your truth preserve me in a
state of quiet repose and peace, by humble submission to
it...' As often, then, as any temptation may assail us, we
ought always to pray that God would make the light of
his truth to shine upon us, lest by having recourse to sinful devices we should go astray and wander into devious
and forbidden paths.[52]

## Pray in hope

If we pray with sincere and confident trust in God's unfailing goodness, we will be rewarded with hope that 'does not disappoint' (Rom. 5:5; Ps. 25:20).

> There is nothing better suited to impart a holy ardour to our prayers than when we are able to testify with sincerity of heart what we confide in God. And, therefore, it behoves us to ask with so much more care that God would increase our hope when it is small, awaken it when it is dormant, confirm it when it is wavering, strengthen it when it is weak; and that he would even raise it up when it is overthrown.[53]

## Pray with thanksgiving

Prayer is necessary for Christians, according to the *Heidelberg Catechism*, 'because prayer is the most important part of the thankfulness which God requires of us. Moreover, God will give his grace and the Holy Spirit only to those who constantly and with heartfelt longing ask him for these gifts and thank him for them'.[54]

Our prayers, then — even those we offer in the direst circumstances — should begin and end in thanksgiving to God for his all-sufficient grace. Calvin recognizes the close association of petition and thanksgiving:

> Though prayer is properly restricted to wishes and petitions, yet there is so great an affinity between petition and thanksgiving that they may be justly comprehended under the same name... The Scripture, not without reason, enjoins us in the continual use of both. We have elsewhere said that our need is so great; and experience itself proclaims that we are molested and oppressed on every

side with such numerous and great perplexities that we all
have sufficient cause for unceasing sighs and groans and
ardent supplications to God. For though some Christians
enjoy freedom from adversity, yet the guilt of their sins
and the innumerable assaults of temptation ought to
stimulate even the most eminent saints to pray for relief.
Of the sacrifice of praise and thanksgiving there can be
no interruption without guilt, since God does not cease to
lavish on us his various benefits according to our respective cases, in order to constrain us, inactive and sluggish
as we are, to the exercise of gratitude. Finally, we are
almost overwhelmed with such great and copious out-
pourings of his generosity. We are surrounded, wherever
we turn our eyes, by such numerous and amazing mira-
cles of his hand that we never lack matter for praise and
thanksgiving.[55]

Paul exhorts the Philippians, regarding prayer, to render
thanks to God for his bountiful grace whenever they pray: 'Be
anxious for nothing, but in everything by prayer and supplication, with thanksgiving, let your requests be made known to
God' (Phil. 4:6). 'In everything' means 'in every circumstance'.
In sickness or in health, in poverty or prosperity, in loneliness or
bereavement, we should thank God for his saving grace, his
mercy, and his unfailing love in Christ our Saviour. Calvin
knows that not all believers are grateful, and some grumble in
their prayers:

As many often pray to God amiss, full of complaints or
murmurings, as though they had just ground for accusing
God, while others cannot tolerate delay if he does not
immediately gratify their desires, Paul on this account
joins thanksgiving with prayers. It is as though he had
said that we ought to request from the Lord those things
that we need in such a way that we, nevertheless, place
our affections in subjection to his good pleasure and give

thanks while presenting petitions. And unquestionably,
gratitude will have this effect upon us — that the will of
God will be the grand sum of our desires.[56]

Calvin takes his application of Philippians 4:6 further,
making the point that offering thankful prayer to God can help
to alleviate suffering:

> In that passage ... Paul presents as a source of joy a calm
> and composed mind, one that is not unduly disturbed by
> injuries or adversities. Lest we be borne down by grief,
> sorrow, anxiety, and fear, he bids us to rest in the provi-
> dence of God. And as intrusive doubts frequently cause
> us to wonder whether God cares for us, Paul also pre-
> scribes the remedy — that by prayer we disburden our
> anxieties as it were into God's bosom, as David com-
> mands us to do in Psalm 37:5 and Psalm 55:22; and Pe-
> ter also, after his example (1 Peter 5:7). As, however, we
> are unduly hasty in presenting our desires, Paul imposes
> a check upon them — that, while we desire what we are
> in need of, we at the same time do not cease to give
> thanks... Further, Paul would have us hold God's bene-
> fits in such esteem that the recognition of them and medi-
> tation upon them will overcome all sorrow. And unques-
> tionably, if we consider what Christ has conferred upon
> us, there will be no bitterness of grief that is so intense
> that it cannot be alleviated and give way to spiritual joy;
> for if this joy does not reign in us, the kingdom of God is
> at the same time banished from us, or we from it. Very
> ungrateful to God is that man who does not set so high a
> value on the righteousness of Christ and the hope of
> eternal life as not to rejoice in the midst of sorrow... God
> has such a disposition towards us in Christ that even in
> our afflictions we have large occasion for thanksgiving, for
> what is more suitable for pacifying us than when we learn

that God embraces us in Christ so tenderly that he turns to our advantage and welfare everything that befalls us?[57]

## One of John Calvin's prayers

Grant, Almighty God, that as thou dost not only invite us continually by the voice of thy gospel to seek thee, but also dost offer to us thy Son as our mediator, through whom an access to thee is open, that we may find thee a propitious Father — O grant that, relying on thy kind invitation, we may throughout life exercise our lives in prayer; and as so many evils disturb us on all sides and so many wants distress and oppress us, may we be led more earnestly to call upon thee, and in the meantime never be wearied of this exercise of prayer, until having been heard by thee throughout life, we may at length be gathered to thy eternal kingdom where we shall enjoy the salvation which thou hast promised us, and of which thou dost daily testify to us by the gospel, and be forever united to thy only begotten Son, of whom we are now members; that we may be partakers of all the blessings which he has obtained for us by his death. Amen.

*Suffering — understanding
the love of God*

Selections from the writings of John Calvin

---

## Chapter 6

## Waiting for God

---

'To wait calmly and silently
for God's favour ... is the
undoubted evidence of faith.'

# 6.
# Waiting for God

*How poor are they that have not patience! What wound did
ever heal but by degrees?*

William Shakespeare[1]

Nelson Mandela, the militant leader of the antiapartheid
movement in South Africa, epitomized the struggle of the black
citizens during his imprisonment, from 1964 to 1990. Mandela
also symbolized the test of patience that kept the movement
alive until in 1994, after his release from prison and his election
as president of South Africa, a new constitution was adopted
guaranteeing free speech, free political action, and recompense
for land seized by the apartheid regime.

One can only guess how many times during his long imprison-
onment Nelson Mandela must have cried out bitterly, 'How
long, O Lord?' Yet he never gave in to the temptation to stop
fighting for the cause of freedom for black South Africans.
Despite the maximum security and harsh conditions of Robben
Island prison, where he spent eighteen years, Mandela was able
to keep in touch with other leaders of the antiapartheid movement. Later, when he was moved to a maximum-security prison
near Cape Town, he became an international symbol of
resistance to discrimination on grounds of race. His autobiogra-
phy, most of which he wrote secretly in prison and which was
smuggled out and eventually completed and published, he
called *Long walk to freedom*. The title itself is a reminder that

his life was marked particularly by patience and perseverance, two human virtues which are invariably linked.

Patience and perseverance, longsuffering and endurance — these virtues also marked the lives of the great men and women of the Bible: Abraham and Sarah, Isaac and Jacob, Moses and Elijah, David and Job, Hannah, Naomi and Ruth, Peter and Paul, and many others. Their patience was a God-given virtue, though it was not consistently exercised. Tried by adversity and afflictions, they became impatient, frustrated, and angry — until their faith in God's promises prevailed and their patience was rewarded. It is this faith-foundation of patience that we must look at in more detail.

## Patience springs from faith

Paul, writing to the Christians of Thessalonica, praises them because, he says, 'Your faith grows exceedingly', and he added, 'We ourselves boast of you among the churches of God for your patience and faith in all your persecutions and tribulations that you endure' (2 Thess. 1:3-4). Calvin recognizes, from his own experience as well as from Scripture, that faith and patience are exceptional virtues in those who suffer:

> Paul did not boast of the faith of the Thessalonians from a spirit of ambition... Nor does he say that he boasts in their faith and love, but in their *patience* and *faith.* Hence it follows that patience is *the fruit and evidence of faith.* What Paul is saying is this: 'We glory in the patience which springs from faith, and we bear witness that it eminently shines forth in you...' Undoubtedly, there is nothing that sustains us in tribulations as faith does — which is sufficiently manifest from this, that we altogether sink down as soon as the promises of God leave us. Hence, the more proficiency anyone makes in faith, the more he

will be endued with patience for enduring all things with fortitude. On the other hand, softness and impatience under adversity betoken unbelief on our part. Especially when persecutions are to be endured for the gospel, the influence of faith in that case reveals itself.[2]

Many there are who can identify with David, whose faith and patience sustained him in trial. In Psalm 40:1-2 he tells in graphic terms of his plight and his deliverance from it: 'I waited patiently for the Lord; and he inclined to me, and heard my cry. He also brought me up out of a horrible pit, out of the miry clay, and set my feet upon a rock, and established my steps.' Calvin writes:

> David here comprehends a multitude of dangers from which he had escaped. He had certainly been more than once exposed to the greatest danger, even of death, so that, with good reason, he might be said to have been swallowed up in the gulf of death and sunk in the 'miry clay'. It nevertheless appears that his faith had continued firm, for he did not cease to trust in God, although the long continuance of the calamity had nearly exhausted his patience. He tells us not merely that he had waited, but by the repetition of the same expression [which in Hebrew is, 'in waiting I waited'] he shows that he had been a long time in anxious suspense. In proportion then as his trial was prolonged, the evidence and proof of his faith in enduring the delay with calmness and equanimity of mind was so much the more apparent. The meaning is, in short, that although God delayed his help, yet David's heart did not faint or grow weary from delay; but that after he had given, as it were, sufficient proof of his *patience,* he was at length heard.
>
> In his example there is set before us this very useful truth, that although God may not immediately appear for our help but rather by design may keep us in suspense

and perplexity, yet we must not lose courage, inasmuch as faith is not thoroughly tested except by long endurance. The result, too, of which he speaks in terms of praise [v. 3] ought to inspire us with increased fortitude. God may come to our aid more slowly than we desire, but when he seems to take no notice of our condition, or, if we may so speak, when he seems to be inactive or to be asleep, this is totally different from deceit: for if we are enabled by the invincible strength and power of faith to endure, the fitting season of our deliverance will at length arrive.[3]

When we are suffering any adversity, whether prolonged illness, loss of income, unsuccessful job hunting, continuing conflict in personal relations, or something else, our troubles may seem to drag on and on without any prospect of relief. In such circumstances, God may be quietly saying, 'Just hold on a little longer; in my own time help will come. Be patient and trust me.' David had implicit trust in God and, confident that God keeps his promises to us and answers our prayers, he anticipated God's soul-satisfying goodness even before there was evidence of it. This is the import of Calvin's comment on Psalm 63:5 — 'My soul will feast and be satisfied, and I will sing glad songs of praise to you.'[4] Calvin continues:

If we would evidence a strong faith, we must anticipate the divine favour before it has been actually manifested and when there is no appearance of its forthcoming. From the instance here set before us, we must learn to be on our guard against despondency, especially in circumstances when we may see the wicked wallowing and rioting in the abundance of the things of this world while we ourselves are left to pine under the want of them. David, in the present pressure to which he was exposed, might have given way to despair, but he knew that God was able to fill the hungry soul and that he could want for

nothing so long as God possessed an interest in his favour. It is God's will to try our patience in this life by afflictions of various kinds. Let us bear the wrongs which
may be done to us with meekness, till the time comes
when all our desires shall be abundantly satisfied.[5]

Another psalmist whose distress seemed unbearable, despite
his devotion to God's law, complained to God that his persecutors made his life miserable; but his complaint, recorded in
Psalm 119:81-82, was not without hope: 'My soul faints for
your salvation, but I hope in your word. My eyes fail from
searching your word, saying, "When will you comfort me?"'[6]
Calvin says,

> The psalmist intimates that, although worn out with con-
> tinual grief and perceiving no issue to his calamities, trou-
> ble and weariness had not produced such a discouraging
> effect upon his mind as to prevent him from always re-
> posing with confidence in God… He affirms that *he trusts
> in God, and this is the foundation of all.* But intending to
> express the invincible constancy of his trust, he tells us
> that he patiently endured all the distresses under which
> others succumb. We see some embracing with great ea-
> gerness the promises of God, but their ardour within a
> short time vanishes, or at least is quenched by adversity.
> It was far otherwise with David.[7]

When we are suffering, we feel alone, abandoned and cut
off from the love of others around us. Facing adversity, we may
become bitter and faithless, believing that God has let us
down — again. In our worst moments we would find it hard to
take seriously the rather puzzling exhortation of James, the
'bondservant of God': 'My brethren, count it all joy when you
fall into various trials, knowing that the testing of your faith
produces patience. But let patience have its perfect work, that
you may be perfect and complete, lacking nothing' (James 1:1-

3). How could anything bitter be regarded as sweet? Calvin has some answers that might surprise you:

> James called adversities 'trials' or 'temptations' because they serve to test our faith... It might be objected, 'How can we judge as sweet something which we sense is bitter?' James then shows by the effect of trials that *we ought to rejoice in afflictions because they produce fruit that ought to be highly valued, even patience.* If God provides for our salvation, he affords us an occasion of rejoicing... We certainly dread diseases and want and exile and prison and reproach and death because we regard them as evils; but when we understand that they are turned, through God's kindness, into helps and aids to our salvation, it is ingratitude to murmur and complain and not to submit willingly to being paternally dealt with in this way.
>
> Paul says in Romans 5:3 that we are to glory in tribulations; and James says here that we are to rejoice. 'We glory' [NIV, 'rejoice'], says Paul, 'in tribulations, knowing that tribulation produces patience...' Probation or trial is said by James to produce patience; for were God not to test us, but leave us free from trouble, there would be no patience, which is nothing else than fortitude of mind in bearing evils. But Paul means that as we conquer evils by enduring trials, we experience how much God's help avails in necessities; for then the truth of God is as it were manifested in us. Hence it is that we dare to entertain more hope as to the future; for we believe more fully the truth of God known by experience. Consequently, Paul teaches that hope is produced by such a trial, that is, by such an experience of divine grace — not that hope only then begins, but that it increases and is confirmed. But both Paul and James mean that tribulation is the means by which patience is produced.[8]

Calvin acknowledges that our minds 'are not so formed by nature that affliction of itself produces patience'. But because of God's providential ordering of human affairs, 'The faithful learn patience from troubles.'[9]

If patience is to have 'its perfect work', as James says, it requires perseverance. 'Real patience', in other words, 'is that which endures to the end', Calvin says. He continues,

> 'Work' here means the effort not only to overcome one contest, but to persevere through life... I explain 'Let patience have it perfect work' to mean *constancy*. For there are many, as we have said, who at first show a heroic greatness and shortly afterwards grow weary and faint. He therefore bids those who would be perfect and complete [i.e., mature] to persevere to the end.[10]

## Satan takes advantage of our impatience

John Milton in *Paradise lost* gives sage advice in regard to enduring suffering:

> Arm th' obdur'd breast
> With stubborn patience as with triple steel.[11]

The only way to arm oneself with triple-steel patience is to have triple-strong faith. But, unfortunately, faith is likely to weaken in times of adversity, and we give way to all sorts of negative emotions. If we were honest, we would have to admit, as David did, that in those desperate moments of suffering, soul and body 'wastes away with grief' (Ps. 31:9). Calvin takes the Hebrew word *kaas* (grief) to mean *anger*. David was angry as well as vexed by his troubled life. Calvin in his comment is not exactly sympathetic towards David.

By giving way to anger, David shows that he was not at all times of such iron-like firmness, or so free from sinful passion, as that his grief did not now and then break forth into an excess of impetuosity and keenness.[12]

From this we infer that the saints have often a severe and arduous conflict with their own passions; and that although their patience has not always been free from peevishness, yet by carefully wrestling against it, they have at least attained this much — that no accumulation of troubles has overwhelmed them.[13]

Emotions often run the gamut from sorrow to self-pity to anger. The experience of David is rather typical. He tried to suppress his sorrow, but it only became more inflamed as he kept it to himself: 'I was mute with silence. I held my peace even from good; and my sorrow was stirred up. My heart was hot within me; while I was musing, the fire burned... (Ps. 39:2-3). Calvin comments:

From this we may learn a very profitable lesson — that the more strenuously one sets himself to obey God, employing all his endeavours to attain the exercise of patience, the more vigorously he is assailed by temptation. Satan, while he is not so troublesome to the indifferent and careless and seldom looks near them, displays all his forces in hostile array against that patient individual. If, therefore, at any time we feel ardent emotions struggling and raising a commotion in our breasts, we should remember this conflict of David, so that our courage may not fail us, or at least that our infirmity may not drive us headlong into despair... Whenever, therefore, the flesh shall put forth its efforts and shall kindle a flame in our hearts, let us know that we are exercised with the same kind of temptation which occasioned so much pain and trouble to David... In the course of his prayer he acknowledges that the severity of the affliction with which

he was visited had at length overcome him and that he
had allowed foolish and ill-advised words to pass from his
lips. In his own person he sets before us a mirror of human infirmity, so that, being warned of the danger to
which we are exposed, we may learn in good time to
seek protection under the shadow of God's wings.[14]

In January 2001, Taliban Supreme Leader, Mullah
Mohammad Omar, issued a decree making it a capital offence
for an Afghan to convert from Islam to Christianity, or for
anyone to propagate the Christian faith. Afghanistan is one
country among several with a 'hidden' church. An estimated
1,000 Afghan Christians meet secretly in homes to worship and
encourage each other. They live among 25 million Afghans
who dwell in abject poverty and endure appalling suffering and
sadness. Because of prevailing antichristian restrictions and total
lack of religious freedom, most Afghans may never hear the
message of the gospel.

The organization Free Church for China reported from
Beijing on 21 July 2002, that five adults and twenty-five children were arrested in south-eastern China for engaging in
religious activities. One of the adults, Sister Chen Mai, was
sentenced without a trial to fifteen days in jail for teaching
catechism in the village of Dongan in the Lianjiang district of
Fujian province. The other four adults received a warning from
Chinese authorities and were released the day after their arrest,
as were the children who received the catechesis.

Persecuted Christians in such countries undoubtedly find
comfort and encouragement from passages like Hebrews 10:32-
39, which urges steadfastness, patience, and perseverance:
'Recall the former days in which, after you were illuminated,
you endured a great struggle with sufferings: partly while you
were made a spectacle by reproaches and tribulations, and
partly while you became companions of those who were so
treated... knowing that you have a better and enduring possession for yourselves in heaven. Therefore do not cast away your

confidence, which has great reward. For you have need of endurance, so that after you have done the will of God, you may receive the promise...'

Behind the church's struggle in this world are satanic powers (Eph. 6:12), and there will always be the temptation to yield to the pressures of Satan's assaults. Calvin knows this, and he perceives that the writer of Hebrews is urging those Christians who are tempted to fall back in the face of persecution to stay in the race to the end, sustained by patience:

> The writer of Hebrews says that patience is necessary, not only because we have to endure to the end, but because Satan has innumerable schemes by which he harasses us; unless we possess extraordinary patience we shall a thousand times be broken down before we come to the half of our course. The inheritance of eternal life is indeed certain to us, but as life is like a race we ought to go on towards the goal. In our way are many hindrances and difficulties which not only delay us but which would also stop our course altogether, unless we have great firmness of mind to pass through them. Satan craftily suggests every kind of trouble in order to discourage us. So Christians will never advance two paces without fainting, unless they are sustained by patience.[15]

Whatever our circumstances, whether we are ridiculed because of our faith or just tired of the struggle, we are in need of endurance if we expect to arrive at the finish line as a winner in life's race. And endurance requires exercises of patience, faith, prayer, and continuance in the way of righteousness. This may sound like a mere platitude, but it is a truth exemplified by the apostles themselves and deeply imbedded in their inspired writings. Peter, for example, urges the congregations, composed mainly of Gentile converts to the Christian faith, not to be surprised at the 'fiery ordeal' which has come upon them. They can rejoice even in their trials, because by participating in the

sufferings of Christ they will demonstrate the genuineness of
their faith. Peter goes so far as to say, 'But even if you suffer for
righteousness' sake, you are blessed' (1 Peter 3:14). Calvin
explains:

> The meaning is that the faithful will do more towards ob-
> taining a quiet life by kindness than by violence and hasty
> revenge. When they neglect nothing to secure peace,
> were they to suffer, they are still blessed because they
> suffer for the sake of righteousness. This, indeed, differs
> much from the judgement of our flesh; but Christ has not
> without reason declared, nor has Peter without reason
> repeated the sentence from Christ's mouth; for God will
> at length come as a deliverer and then will appear openly
> what now seems incredible — that *the miseries of the
> godly have been blessed when endured with patience.*[16]

## Patience is not just 'putting up with things'

Suffering in silence is not necessarily being patient. You can
suffer without hope; but true patience can be sustained only if
you hope that things will get better. When you have a painful
toothache, you do not simply 'put up with it'; you seek help and
expect, after proper treatment, to experience relief. 'It is only in
the Lord's school that we can ever learn to maintain composure
of mind and a posture of patient expectation and trust under
the pressure of distress', writes Calvin. 'The psalmist in
Psalm 94:12-13 declares that the wisdom which would bear us
onward to the end with an inward peace and courage under
long-continued trouble is not natural to any of us, but must
come from God. Accordingly, he exclaims that those are truly
blessed whom God has habituated through his Word to the
endurance of the cross and prevented from sinking under

adversity by the secret supports and consolations of his own Spirit.'[17]

Silent acceptance of suffering is often mistaken for patience. This point is made rather tersely by François, Duke of Rouche-foucauld: 'We often in our misfortunes take that for constancy and patience which is only dejection of mind; we suffer without daring to hold up our heads, just as cowards let themselves be knocked on the head because they have not courage to strike back.'[18]

For a Christian, vengeance is not an option, of course; the better part of wisdom is submitting to God in the face of misfortune and suffering. This at least is Calvin's view of the matter:

The Word of God provides us with abundant ground of comfort; it ensures that no one who rightly avails himself of it need ever to count himself unhappy, or yield himself to hopelessness and despondency. One mark by which God distinguishes the true from the false disciple is that of being ready and prepared to bear the cross and of waiting quietly for the divine deliverance without giving way to fretfulness and impatience. True patience does not consist in presenting an obstinate resistance to evils, or in that unyielding stubbornness which passed as a virtue with the Stoics, but in a cheerful submission to God, based upon confidence in his grace.

Even supposing that a man should bear trials without a tear or a sigh, yet if he champs at the bit in sullen hopelessness ... this is obstinacy rather than patience, and there is concealed opposition to God in this contempt of calamities under colour of fortitude. The only consideration which will subdue our minds to a tractable submission is that God, in subjecting us to adversity, has in view our being ultimately brought into the enjoyment of a rest. Wherever there reigns this persuasion of a rest prepared for the people of God and refreshment provided under the heat and turmoil of their troubles, so that they might not perish with the world around them — this will prove enough and more than enough to alleviate any present bitterness of affliction.[19]

Those who experience constant pain and who know that they will die 'any day now', and those whose homes have been blown to bits by a hurricane or destroyed by the torrential rain and flooding that tropical storms produce would probably find Calvin's instruction difficult and, perhaps, even depressing. Calvin seems to present an ideal that only the most saintly Christians could live up to:

Pious minds ought to manifest tranquillity and endurance; these must be extended to all the accidents to which this present life is liable. He alone, therefore, has properly denied himself who has resigned himself entirely to the Lord, placing the whole course of his life entirely at his disposal. Happen what may, he whose mind is thus composed will neither deem himself wretched nor murmur against God because of his lot. The necessity of this attitude becomes clear if you consider the many accidents to which we are liable. Various diseases are always attacking us: at one time pestilence rages; at another we are involved in all the calamities of war. Frost and hail, destroying the promise of the year, cause unfruitfulness, which reduces us to extreme poverty; wife, parents, children, and other relatives are carried off by death; our house is destroyed by fire. These are the events which make men curse their life, detest the day of their birth, execrate the light of heaven, even censure God, and, as they are eloquent in blasphemy, charge him with cruelty and injustice.

The believer must in these circumstances contemplate the mercy and truly paternal indulgence of God. Accordingly, should he see his house by the removal of kindred reduced to solitude, even then he will not cease to bless the Lord; his thought will be, 'Still the grace of the Lord, which dwells within my house, will not leave it desolate'. If his crops are blasted, mildewed, cut off by frost, or struck down by hail, and he sees famine before him, he will not become despondent or murmur against God, but maintain confidence in him... If he is afflicted with disease, the sharpness of pain will not so overcome him as to make him break out with impatience and expostulate with God; but recognizing justice and leniency in the rod used for chastisement, he will patiently endure. In short, whatever happens, knowing that it is ordered by the Lord, he will receive it with a placid and grateful mind and will not disobediently resist the government of him at whose disposal he has placed himself and all that he has.[20]

When tragedy strikes and a family is deeply grieved, a friend may say something like, 'This must be part of God's plan for you'. While a statement like that may be well-intentioned, it may carry the implication that God is really rather cruel. And yet, Calvin does not hesitate to remind us that when bereavement, disease, and other forms of suffering affect us, 'We must think that none of them happens except by the will and providence of God.'[21] He continues:

If we are faithful disciples of Christ, we will endeavour to permeate our minds with such reverence and obedience to God as may tame and bring under control all emotions that are contrary to God's appointment. In this way, whatever may be the kind of cross to which we are subjected, we shall in the greatest straits firmly maintain our patience.[22]

We should not, however, think that when we are sorrowful or suffering loss we are being patient if only we keep a stiff upper lip. 'To bear the cross patiently', Calvin tells us, 'is not to have your feelings altogether blunted and to be absolutely insensible to pain.' This was the ideal of the ancient Stoics, whose hero was one who, divested of humanity, was like a stone, not affected by anything — grief or joy, prosperity or adversity. Such tolerance of pain and suffering is only 'a shadow of patience'.[23]

A truly patient sufferer, to the contrary, hurts and is not too proud to admit it; but, feeling pain and shedding tears, he or she takes it to the Lord in prayer. Calvin says,

> Adversity will have its bitterness and sting us. When afflicted with disease, we shall groan and be disquieted and long for health. Pressed with poverty, we shall feel the stings of anxiety and sadness, feel the pain of ignominy, contempt, and injury, and pay the tears due to nature at the death of our friends. But our conclusion will always be: the Lord so willed it, therefore let us follow his will. No, amid the pungency of grief, among the groans and tears, this thought will necessarily suggest itself and incline us cheerfully to endure the things with which we are so afflicted.[24]

## The enabling power of God's grace

We cannot bear patiently the hardship of poverty or the trauma of serious injury without strong and stable faith. But sometimes we find it hard to pray and to affirm the goodness of God. In such times of weakness we need the prayers of a friend or a pastor for consolation and strength. On the other hand, we ourselves may act as intercessors for friends who need someone to pray for *them* in a time of distress. Paul, for example, prays for his fellow believers, that they may be 'strengthened with all might, according to his glorious power, *for all patience and*

*longsuffering with joy* (Col. 1:11; emphasis added). Calvin
writes:

> In describing the content of his prayer, Paul puts them in
> mind of their own weakness, for he says that they will not
> be strong otherwise than by the Lord's help; with the
> view of magnifying this exercise of grace, he adds, 'ac-
> cording to his glorious power'. So far from anyone's be-
> ing able to stand through dependence on his own
> strength, the power of God shows itself illustriously in
> helping our infirmity. Lastly, he also shows that the
> strength of believers ought to display itself in 'all patience
> and longsuffering'. For they are constantly, while in this
> world, exercised with the cross, and a thousand tempta-
> tions daily present themselves so as to weigh them down,
> and they see nothing of what God has promised. They
> must, therefore, arm themselves with an admirable pa-
> tience, so that what Isaiah says may be accomplished: 'In
> quietness and confidence shall be your strength'
> (Isa. 30:15).[25]

The faithful, by remaining patient when tested by adversity,
'show their strength by resisting and overcoming their grief'.
They also exhibit 'joy and cheerfulness when, wounded by
sadness and sorrow, they rest in the spiritual consolation of
God'.[26] The consolation in which we rest is mediated by the
Word of God. 'Blessed is the man whom you instruct, O LORD,
and teach out of your law, that you may give him rest from the
days of adversity' (Ps. 94:12-13). Calvin's comment on this
verse is instructive as well as helpful:

> The man is blessed who has learned to be composed and
> tranquil under trials. The rest intended would then be that
> of an inward kind, enjoyed by the believer even during
> the storms of adversity... The truly happy man is he who
> has so far profited by the Word of God as to sustain the

assault of evils from without, with peace and composure.[27]

Paul picks up the psalmist's thought in his letter to the Romans: 'For whatever things were written before were written for our learning, that we through the patience and comfort of the Scriptures might have hope' (Rom. 15:4). Paul, Calvin says, 'does not include the whole of that benefit which is to be derived from God's Word; but he points out the main end — the Scriptures are especially serviceable for this purpose — to raise up those who are prepared by patience and strengthened by consolations to the hope of eternal life'. Only when God mitigates our adversities with consolation are we prepared to bear them with patience. Submitting to God and tasting of 'his goodness and paternal love renders all things sweet to us: this nourishes and sustains hope in us, so that it does not fail'.[27]

We cannot have the consolation of God's Word and Spirit unless our patient waiting is a time of prayerful trust in God's mercy. 'Wait on the LORD; be of good courage, and he shall strengthen your heart; wait, I say, on the LORD' (Ps. 27:14). Calvin comments:

We are encouraged to wait on God when, withdrawing his grace from us, he permits us to languish under afflictions. David stirs himself up to collect strength, as if he had said, 'If fearfulness steals upon you, if temptation shakes your faith, if the feelings of the flesh rise in tumult, do not faint, but rather endeavour to rise above them by an invincible resolution of mind.' From this we may learn that the children of God overcome not by sullenness but by patience, when they commit their souls quietly to God. As David did not feel himself equal to great and difficult efforts, he borrows strength from God by prayer. He knew that God would be at hand to strengthen his heart, and plainly shows that when the saints strive vigorously they fight in the strength of another, and not their own.

David knew that new conflicts would daily arise and that
the troubles of the saints are often protracted for a long
period; therefore he repeats what he had said about relying upon God: 'Wait only on the Lord.'[28]

The British television comedy series, 'Waiting for God', while
intentionally humorous, is often too sad to be funny. The setting
is that of a stylish residence for elderly people who have little to
do, while they wait for the inevitable, but to play croquet, chat
about the good old days, and think up pranks to play on the all-
too-serious but not-too-swift supervisor. The only religious
element in the series is an occasional funeral of one of Bay-
view's inmates whose time has run out.

Such a dismal outlook on life is all too typical of elderly
people who are merely putting in time playing 'Bingo', waiting
for death to knock on their doors. But many of them, on the
other hand, are devout Christians who continue to live produc-
tive lives, and who wait for God in a truly biblical sense: 'I wait
for the LORD, my soul waits, and in his word do I hope. My soul
waits for the LORD more than those who watch for the morning — yes, more than those who watch for the morning'
(Ps. 130:5-6).

Patiently and prayerfully waiting for God is the rule of life,
not only for the elderly but for the youth and their middle-age
parents as well; yet, as Calvin remarks, 'There is hardly one in
ten who, when removed from the inspection of his fellow men,
in his own heart waits for God with a quiet mind. The psalmist
intimates that what supported his patience was the confidence
by which he reposed in the divine promises.'[29]

## The prophets as an example of suffering and patience

'Indeed we count them blessed who endure' (James 5:10).
James does not mention any of the prophets by name when he

points to the prophets as an example of suffering and patience. Probably there were too many who suffered reproach and bodily harm to name them individually.

We can think of several offhand. Take Elijah, who ran for his life to escape from the murderous intent of Jezebel and went into hiding in the wilderness (1 Kings 19:1-4). Take Zechariah, the son of Jehoiada, as another example of suffering. Zechariah, a prophet during the reign of Joash of Judah, was stoned by the people because of his unpopular preaching (2 Chron. 24:20-22). And there was Jeremiah, the 'weeping prophet'. His repeated warnings of imminent invasion by the Chaldeans were met with scorn, and the king's ministers wanted to kill him but were afraid of the king's retaliation. They charged him with desertion to the enemy; then struck him and imprisoned him in a dungeon. The Judean king Zedekiah later released him from the dungeon, but, refusing to listen to the prophet's message ('You will be delivered into the hand of the king of Babylon'), he ordered that Jeremiah be committed to the court of the prison and given daily only a piece of bread (Jer. 37:6-21).

Jeremiah was not as patient as he might have been, however. In a deeply despondent frame of mind, he complained bitterly and cursed the day of his birth, crying in desperation, 'Why did I come forth from the womb to see labour and sorrow? (Jer. 20:14, 18). Calvin would not advise us to view Jeremiah as an example of patience (though he was a true servant of God, through whom God spoke to the people of Judah). Calvin is unsparing in his criticism of the weeping prophet:

> After having cursed his birth day ... Jeremiah now expostulates with God. It thus appears how great his madness was, for thus we must speak... There is then no doubt that he raged furiously against God, for his expostulation is that of a man wholly desperate. He asks why he was not slain from the womb, as though he did not regard it

as a kindness that he came alive into light. But this life, though exposed to many sorrows, ought nevertheless to be counted as an evidence of God's inestimable favour. As the prophet, then, not only despised this goodness of God but contended with God himself, because he had been created a man and brought into light — how great was his ingratitude!

What just cause can we have to contend with God? Jeremiah was created to sorrow and trouble; this is the condition of all; why then should God be blamed? His days were spent in reproach, but there was nothing new in his case, for many who have received an honourable testimony from God have suffered many wrongs and reproaches. Why then did he not look to them as examples, so that he might bear with patience and resignation what had happened to other holy men?[30]

We might be loath to take Jeremiah as an example of patience, but in other respects he was exemplary. Calvin, in his unique pastoral way, charges us to eschew the prophet's unreasonable impatience but to emulate his faithfulness as a servant of God:

Let us learn to check our feelings, so that they may not break out thus unreasonably. Let us at the same time know that God's servants, though they may excel in firmness, are nevertheless not wholly divested of their corruptions. And should it happen at any time to us to feel such emotions within us, let not such a temptation discourage us, but as far as we can and as God gives us grace, let us strive to resist it, until the firmness of our faith at length gains the ascendancy, as we see was the case with Jeremiah. For when overwhelmed with such a confusion of mind as to lie down as it were dead in hell itself, yet he was restored to such soundness of mind that he afterwards courageously executed his own office and also gloried in the help of God.[31]

We have, besides the ancient prophets, many other 'holy men' to whom we can look for inspiration and guidance. Take Abraham for example, and Moses, Samuel, Gideon, Daniel, John the Baptist. Each of them suffered in some way, and all were patient, though not perfectly so. 'Indeed', writes James, 'we count them blessed who endure' (James 5:11). 'You have heard of the perseverance of Job', he continues.

'The patience of Job' is proverbial. He is reputed to have been the most patient of all men. He suffered the loss of his family and of his property, and was stricken with 'painful boils from the sole of his foot to the crown of his head' (Job 2:7). Yet, if you read the story of Job, you discover that he is patient only for two chapters. After that, like Jeremiah, 'He cursed the day of his birth' (Job 3:1). He challenged God to explain himself, as if to say, 'What have I done to deserve this?' Yet, for all his complaints, Job suffered submissively and patiently, waiting for God to make it up to him — which God eventually did.

From Calvin we learn why Job is properly held before us as an example, and why he deserved to be commended by James. Job, he says, is 'an example remarkable above all others'.

No one, as far as we can learn from histories, has ever been overwhelmed with troubles so hard and so various as Job; and yet he emerged from so deep a gulf. Whoever, then, will imitate his patience will no doubt find God's hand, which at length delivered him, to be the same. We see for what end Job's history has been written. If God did not permit his servant Job to sink, because he patiently endured his afflictions, then God will disappoint the patience of no one.[32]

'James has done well for us', writes Calvin; 'for he has laid before our eyes a pattern, that we may learn to look at it whenever we are tempted to impatience or to despair; and he takes this principle for granted: the prophets were blessed in their afflictions, for they courageously sustained them. Since that is so, James concludes that the same judgement ought to be formed of us when we are afflicted.'[33]

## Peace and joy the rewards of patience

Life is not all sweetness and light, even when it is lived faithfully and when adversities are borne cheerfully and patiently. Fear, temptation, and distress continue to buffet the most devout of God's children, but, confiding in God's grace and remembering past experiences of God's care, the bitter becomes sweet and dark days become bright with the light of God's presence. David experienced this transformation, and when agitated with fear of death or pangs of conscience, he remembered God's goodness, saying to himself, 'Return to your rest, O my soul, for the LORD has dealt bountifully with you' (Ps. 116:7). Calvin gives a realistic but consoling comment on this verse:

It may be asked whether the experience of the grace of God alone can allay the fear and trepidation of our minds, since David declares that, having experienced relief through divine aid, he would for the future be at rest. If the faithful regain their peace of mind only when God manifests himself as their deliverer, what room is there for the exercise of faith, and what power will God's promises possess? Assuredly, to wait calmly and silently for God's favour … is the undoubted evidence of faith. And strong faith quiets the conscience and composes the spirit, so that, according to Paul, 'the peace of God, which surpasses all understanding' reigns supremely there

(Phil. 4:7). And so the godly remain unmoved, though the whole world is about to go to ruin... Confiding in the promises, they throw themselves upon God's providence; and still they are sorely distressed by disquieting fears and sadly buffeted by the storms of temptation ... but from the manifestation of God's grace they are supplied with grounds of joy and gladness.[34]

# Suffering — understanding the love of God

Selections from the writings of John Calvin

---

## Chapter 7

## Continuing by grace

---

'When we draw near to our finishing-line and can
look back and see that while we were running ...
though we stumbled many times ... our God rescued
us and lifted us up before we came to grief.'

# 7.
# Continuing by grace

*When our faith is tested by suffering 'as gold is tried in a fur-*
*nace' and we depend with confidence on God and rely entirely*
*on his help, we will be granted 'the most excellent gift of pa-*
*tience' and through faith 'We may victoriously persevere to the*
*end.'*

John Calvin[1]

John Calvin himself was a sterling example of perseverance.
Threatened and defamed by opponents of the Reformation —
whom he referred to as 'enemies' — Calvin continued on his
course, preaching with zeal and defending the truth of the
gospel by whatever means were at his disposal. At the same
time he endured sorrowful personal experiences: the loss of his
son, and soon afterwards the illness and death of his wife. His
poor health also made his life painful and difficult, and as he
neared the end of his life he was often confined to his bed. But
despite his wretched physical condition he managed to continue
his preaching, lecturing, and dictating letters and expositions of
the Scriptures.

Throughout the years of his ministry, especially at Geneva,
he faced unpopularity, vicious rumours, and bitter criticism of
his teaching and of the rules of civility and morality which he
sought to impose on the citizens of Geneva. In his most sombre
days he preached a sermon in which he said, 'If it were up to
me, I would want God to remove me from this world, and that I

should not have to live here three days in such disorder as there is here.'[2] But Calvin was a survivor; he did not succumb to the pressures of conflict with the foes of the Reform movement, but continued with extraordinary vigour to defend the truth and to espouse the cause to which God had called him.

During those darker days, Calvin and his fellow Reformer Pierre Viret encouraged each other. In the thick of the fight against a mob of villains called Libertines, when Calvin was considering leaving Geneva, Viret recalled him to his duty and reminded him of the sufferings of Christ, of Moses, and of Paul. 'Tears and prayers are our weapons', Viret wrote in a letter to him. 'As for the idea of leaving your post, that would be nothing else than kindness to the wolves and leaving the sheep to the fate the wolves deserve... Courage! Go on as you are doing until the day when you will be glorified with that servant whom you now follow and who said, "I have fought the good fight, I have run the race, I have kept the faith."'

Calvin in fact preached a sermon on that text, 2 Timothy 4:7, in the Church of St Pierre in Geneva. The sermon has a pastoral tone and speaks also to present-day readers about perseverance in the face of personal tragedy or misery:

> We must realize that when God calls us, it is to the end that we should be dedicated to him, not to be active in the service and to make an offering to him for one day only, but to continue to do so all the days of our life. Though we may languish, though we may seem to be perishing in our miseries, let us, nevertheless, stick at it. And when the time of our death approaches, we must know that it is the time for us to be more courageous in exercising ourselves, as mariners do when they draw near to the shore. Though they were weary before, yet they rejoice at the mere sight of the haven, for they think, 'Come now, within two or three hours we shall be able to rest and eat our fill.'

When we see these poor men, who are completely exhausted and utterly wasted and broken, take heart only because they have seen the haven, what must we do when we draw near to our finishing-line and can look back and see that while we were running God always held us fast by the hand, and that though we stumbled many times — yes, and sometimes even fell — our God rescued us and lifted us up before we came to grief? Must we not strive earnestly to come to God and to draw all the closer to him? This, then, is what we need to learn from this phrase: 'I have finished the race.'[3]

Calvin knew that perseverance in the race of life is not just 'hanging in there' until, by dint of strenuous effort, we arrive at the finish line. He lived long before John Newton (1725–1807), but he would have heartily endorsed Newton's 'Amazing Grace':

'Tis grace has brought me safe thus far,
And grace will lead me home.

Yes, we must 'keep the faith in a good conscience', but it is God who helps us through to the end. Calvin writes:

Let us therefore note well that we must have this upright-ness and good conscience, walking in the fear of God and holding fast the promises of his goodness and grace, or else we shall never be determined to keep right on to the end of the race. Let us, then, hold fast a good con-science, so that we may keep our faith; and though we may be held back to some extent by our own feebleness, though we may be dismayed at the fierce assaults and the alarms to which we must be exposed, even though we may be hindered from going forward, nevertheless we shall surely achieve it, because God will not forsake us.[4]

Hebrews 12:1-2 calls us to 'Run with endurance the race that is set before us.' In order to persevere to the finish line, we must always 'look to Jesus', who 'endured the cross', choosing suffering 'instead of joy, which includes every kind of enjoyment'.

'Patience' is closely related to 'perseverance', and both imply endurance. Without patience there is no endurance, and, without endurance, no perseverance. Calvin encourages us to look to Jesus and trust him for patience and perseverance in the race that is set before us:

> The author of Hebrews commends to us the patience of Christ on two accounts: he endured the bitterest death and he despised the shame. He then mentions the glorious end of his death, so that the faithful might know that all evils which *they* may endure will end in their salvation and glory, provided they follow Christ.[5]

That servant whom Calvin followed (as his friend Pierre Viret put it) was the apostle Paul, who suffered many perils and afflictions, including a 'thorn in the flesh'. The answer to Paul's prayer (asking that the thorn be removed) was renewed spiritual strength and consolation, both gifts of divine grace. Calvin, from his own experience, knew what that meant:

> God answers us when he strengthens us inwardly by his Spirit and sustains us by his consolation, so that we do not give up hope and patience. He bids Paul to be satisfied with his grace, and in the meantime not to refuse chastisement. Hence we must *bear up under evil of ever-so-long continuance,* because we are admirably well dealt with when we have the grace of God as our support. The term *grace* does not mean here, as it does elsewhere, the favour of God in general, but the aid of the Holy Spirit, which comes to us from the unmerited favour of God; and it ought to be sufficient for the pious, inasmuch as it

is a sure and invincible support against their ever giving
way.[6]

Calvin and his fellow Reformers faced vigorous opposition
from the Sorbonne, a college within the University of Paris. Its
faculty of theology was regarded by Roman Catholics as an
authority on questions concerning the Christian faith. The
Sorbonists, as Calvin called them, contended that 'The faithful
are in doubt with respect to their final perseverance.' Calvin
countered their 'fabrication', as he called it, in his exposition of
Psalm 16:8: 'I have set the LORD always before me; because he
is at my right hand I shall not be moved.' He writes:

David, in very plain terms, extends his reliance on the
grace of God to the time to come. And certainly it would
be a very miserable condition to be in, to tremble in uncertainty every moment, having no assurance of *the continuance of the grace of God towards us.*[7]

Calvin is constantly encouraging us to 'recline on God
alone', to be aware of our own weakness, and to 'transfer [our]
confidence to God', trusting in his help, so as to 'continue
invincible to the end, standing by his grace'.[8]

Reliance on the grace of God and the strength of the Holy
Spirit guarantees our perseverance. At a time when we are
ready to say with David, 'My spirit is overwhelmed within me;
my heart within me is distressed' (Ps. 143:4), we should 'recall
the former kindness which God may have shown us'.[9] This
exercise of trust helped David to get a fresh grip on his emotions, to overcome his fears and to persevere through his trials.
Calvin would have us to do the same:

David acknowledges the feebleness of his spirit ... and,
overwhelmed with grief ... he owed his support entirely
to faith and *the grace of the Spirit.* We are taught by his
example not to throw up the conflict in despair, however

much we may be weakened and even exhausted by afflictions, for God will enable us to surmount them, if we
only rise to him with our hearts amid all our anxieties...
David ... gathered confidence from the past mercies of
God. The very best method for obtaining relief when we
are about to faint under the burden of adversities is to call
to mind the former loving kindness of the Lord.[10]

David's heart was devoted to God with steadfast perseverance... He had good reason to persevere, without
fainting, in following close behind God (Ps. 63:8), when
he considered that he had been preserved in safety, up to
this time, by the divine hand. But I would understand the
words, 'My soul follows close behind you', as having a
more extensive application, and consider that David here
speaks of the *grace of perseverance* which would be bestowed upon him by the Holy Spirit. To say that he
would cleave to God with an unwavering purpose, whatever dangers he faced, might have sounded like vain
boasting, had he not added that he would do this in so
far as he was sustained by the hand of God.[11]

## Perseverance and endurance are gifts of grace

A marvellous example of these gifts of grace is Robert Moffat
(1795–1883), the Scottish pioneer missionary to South Africa.
Moffat ministered to the natives of 'the Dark Continent' for over
fifty years. When I think of Robert Moffat, I am reminded of
Paul, that great missionary to the nations, who endured cruel
indignities and brutality at the hands of his opponents. Amid the
'many dangers, toils, and snares' through which he went, Paul
wrote this testimony to the grace which sustained him: 'We are
hard pressed on every side, yet not crushed; we are perplexed,
but not in despair; persecuted, but not forsaken; struck down,
but not destroyed' (2 Cor. 4:8-9).

Life for the Moffats was primitive and dangerous. He went on long arduous journeys into the interior, preaching and establishing mission stations wherever the native villagers welcomed him. There were few railroads and hardly any passable roads — he travelled across meadows and scorching desert sand, and his journeys were dangerous and sometimes life-threatening. Unable to avoid swamps, rivers, and forests, he managed somehow to cross them. The sun was fiery hot by day and the nights were shivering cold. Ferocious animals sometimes came too close for comfort. Lions, hyenas, jackals, crocodiles, snakes, and unfriendly monkeys were lurking everywhere. And warlike tribes of savage Bushmen made his cross-country treks dangerous and frightening. A Mr James Chapman, who spent fifteen years in South Africa hunting and trading, observed missionary life and labour at close range. He bore this honourable testimony concerning the endurance of those early missionaries:

> The lot of a missionary in Africa is a hard one; his life is one of trial and self denial. Deprived, often for months together, of the common necessaries of life, cut off from society, from friends and relations, with the prospect of never seeing them more... I have seen a great deal of missionary life, and have every reason to sympathize with them. Their labours are difficult, their trials many, their earthly reward a bare subsistence...[12]

Robert Moffat, faithful to his missionary call, was able to surmount the obstacles that stood in his way, and through faith, prayer, and determination he persevered in his missionary tasks. Over time, he became proficient in African customs and languages, and he developed leadership skills that enabled him to train and civilize thousands of natives. His long missionary ministry makes him one of God's most honourable servants, and his life and labours exhibit the grace of God by which endurance of the most distressing adversities made him a blessing to God's elect children in the primitive outback regions of South Africa.

Calvin lived in a more 'civilized' country, but he endured many painful conflicts, among them defamatory rumours and malicious designs on his life. But he received strength from God enabling him to climb to the summit of faith and to persevere through all his trials. Calvin's comments on Habakkuk 3:19 seem to apply also to him: 'The LORD God is my strength; he will make my feet like deer's feet, and he will make me walk on the high hills.'

> Habakkuk sought no strength but in God alone... The prophet, by calling God his strength, sets him apart from all other supports; for he wishes to encourage the faithful to persevere in their hope, however grievously God might afflict them. His meaning, then, is that even when evils impetuously rage against us, and when we vacillate and are ready to fall any moment, God ought then to be our strength; for the aid which he has promised for our support is all-sufficient.[13]

We may forget that the instruction given by the apostles to the early Christians, as well as the warnings and prayers and benedictions, are God's Word to us as well as to them. The benediction which Paul pronounced upon the Christians of Thessalonica should be consoling to any of us who are struggling to stay the course without faltering or giving up: 'Now may our Lord Jesus Christ himself, and our God and Father, who has loved us and given us everlasting consolation and good hope by grace, comfort your hearts and establish you in every good word and work' (2 Thess. 16-17). Writes Calvin,

> The term *hope* has this object in view — that they [the Thessalonians] may confidently expect a never-failing continuance of grace. But what does Paul ask in this prayer? He asks that God may sustain their hearts by his

consolation, for this is his office: to keep them from giving way through anxiety or distrust; and further, *that he may give them perseverance,* both in the pious and holy course of life and in sound doctrine.[14]

## God's grace prevails even over death

David, Calvin's model of perseverance, states that he is weary with his crying (Ps. 69:3). Calvin writes:

> When seeking and calling upon God, when his affairs were in such a confused and desperate condition, David exhibited an instance of rare and wonderful patience... By the word *weary* he does not mean that he gave up with prayer, as if he had cast from him all love to and delight in that exercise upon finding that it proved unavailing as a means of deliverance. We perceive, then, that although his bodily senses failed him, the vigour of his faith was by no means extinguished.
>
> When we reflect that David has spoken, as it were, out of the mouth of Christ and out of the mouths of all true saints who are the members of Christ, we ought not to think that any strange thing happens to us, if at any time we are so overwhelmed with death as to be unable to discern the slightest hope of life. Rather, let us learn early on, while God spares us, to meditate on this truth and desire the aid which it is fitted to impart under calamity — that even in the most profound depths of adversity faith may hold us up. What is more, that faith may elevate us to God, since, as Paul testifies in Romans 8:39, there is no height or depth which can separate us from the infinite love of him who swallows up all the depths — even hell itself.[15]

With the love of God supporting us, how can we *not* endure all things and persevere in faith and hope to the very end of life? The same God who sustained David in his trials also maintains his true church throughout all the ages. As the church awaits her consummation 'mid toil and tribulation and tumult of her war', God continues to bless her and show his sovereign grace to her members, so that they may persevere in all their trials.

'For this is our God, our God forever and ever; he will be our guide even unto death' (Ps. 48:14). Calvin comments:

> When the faithful here declare that God will continue unchangeably steadfast to his purpose in maintaining the church, their object is to encourage and strengthen themselves to persevere in a continued course of faith... *He will be our guide even unto death*. In making this statement, the people of God assure themselves that he will be their guide and keeper forever. They are not to be understood as meaning that they will be safe under the government and conduct of God in this life only, and that he will abandon them in the midst of death; but they express ... that God will take care of all who rely on him, even to the end.[16]
>
> As God has from the beginning carefully preserved and maintained his church, even as a father brings up children from their infancy, so he will continue to act in the same manner.[17]

The church in every age must contend against 'rulers of the darkness of this age [and] against spiritual hosts of wickedness in the heavenly places' (Eph. 6:12). In her militant struggle with satanic evil, some 'Christian soldiers' will become fainthearted and seek refuge in some safe retreat. But we must remind ourselves that we are called to persevere in the defence of the truth. Calvin reminded his congregation at St Pierre of this divine calling, and his pastoral concern should be assuring to anyone who has doubts about 'the perseverance of the saints'. Following is an excerpt from his sermon on 2 Timothy 2:1-3, entitled 'Strength for the battle':

> Since Jesus Christ is our captain and we are under him, we need not fear in the slightest. Even if our enemies are imbued with a murdering spirit and are full of madness, malice, and betrayal, let them do the worst they can — we will still go on boldly. And why is this? Because we shall be safe in the hands of the one who has promised that he will not lose even the smallest part of that which the Father has given him, but will keep it so well and so securely that he will give the Father a good account of it at the last day.[18]

## 'Endurance': Shackleton's voyage to the Antarctic

In 1914 Sir Ernest Shackleton and a crew of twenty-seven set sail on an expedition to the Antarctic continent. Their adventure turned out to be one of the greatest tests of endurance in the history of exploration. Within eighty-five miles of the continent their ship *Endurance* became trapped in sea ice and was slowly crushed and destroyed by ice pressure; the crew was forced to abandon ship. Under Shackleton's encouraging leadership, the crew struggled to stay alive in one of the most inhospitable regions of the world. After camping on the ice for five months, Shackleton made two open boat sailings, one of which — a treacherous 800-mile ocean crossing to South Georgia Island — is now considered one of the most daring voyages in nautical history. After crossing the densely wooded mountains of South Georgia, Shackleton arrived at a remote whaling station, organized a rescue team, and saved all the men he had left behind.

Such endurance is almost superhuman, but by the grace of God and human fortitude, the crew of the abandoned ship *Endurance* returned to England after an ordeal that lasted twenty months — and not one man was lost!

One suspects that Calvin would have been fascinated by the legendary expedition of Ernest Shackleton and the courageous crew of the *Endurance*. The Reformer in his preaching and written works often illustrated a point using examples of maritime experiences, as well as athletic events such as foot races. In his comments on Isaiah 40:31 he combines these figures, running and sailing:

'Those who wait on the Lord ... shall run and not be weary.' It is as if the prophet had said that the Lord will assist them, so that they shall pursue their course without molestation. It is a figurative expression by which he suggests that believers will always be ready to perform their duty with cheerfulness. But it will be said, 'There are so many troubles which we must endure in this life; how then does he say that we shall be free from weariness?' I reply: Believers are indeed distressed and wearied, but they are at length delivered from their distresses and feel that they have been restored by the power of God; for it happens to them according to the saying of Paul, 'While we are troubled on every side, we are not overwhelmed...' Let us therefore learn to flee to the Lord, who, after we have encountered many storms, will at length conduct us to the harbour. He who has opened up a path and has commanded us to advance in that course in which he has placed us does not intend to assist us only for a single day and to forsake us in the middle of our course, but will conduct us to the goal.[19]

**Fortitudine vincimus** — 'by endurance we conquer' — by God's continuing grace

*Suffering — understanding
the love of God*

Selections from the writings of John Calvin

---

## Chapter 8

## Standing in the shadow

---

'Although God's people may be subject,
like others, to the miseries of human life,
yet his shadow is always at their side to
shield them from any harm.'

# 8.

# Standing in the shadow

*He shall cover you with his feathers, and under his wings you shall take refuge.*

Psalm 91:4

During Calvin's time in Geneva, a sect of 'spiritual libertines', described by Calvin as 'the most pernicious and execrable sect there ever was in the world', took deadly aim at Calvin and his followers. The libertines were radical antinomians, believing themselves to be completely liberated from the constraints of all law, moral and civil. They advocated leading a dissolute life, and they themselves gave 'free rein to complete carnal license'.

A large number of French Christians had settled in Geneva seeking refuge from religious persecution and were supporters of the Reformation. On 15 June 1555, Calvin wrote a letter to his fellow Reformer Henry Bullinger describing the libertines' intention to wipe out the community of French refugees:

One cry was everywhere heard: 'The Frenchmen must be massacred: the city has been betrayed by them.' But the Lord in a wonderful manner, watching over his wretched exiles, threw them into so deep a sleep that during these horrid outcries they were tranquilly reposing in their beds. This strengthened their hearts so that they were not dismayed by the threats or fears of danger. What is certain is that none of them stirred out of the house. And by this singular interference of God, the rage of the ungodly was defeated because no one presented himself to the conflict.[1]

Calvin closed his letter with this appeal to his friend Bullinger: 'May the Lord grant that the remembrance of so great a deliverance may continually stir us up to gratitude and bind us to our duty.'[2]

The libertines' diabolical plot and God's 'singular interference' remind us of God's promise of protection in Psalm 91:5 — 'You shall not be afraid of the terror by night.' Calvin comments:

The psalmist continues to insist upon the truth ... that if we place our trust with implicit reliance upon the protection of God, we will be secure from every temptation and assault of Satan. It is important to remember that those whom God has taken under his care are in a state of absolute safety. Even those who have reached the most advanced experience find nothing more difficult than to rely upon the divine deliverance; especially when, overtaken by some of the many forms in which danger and death await us in this world, doubts will insinuate themselves into our hearts, giving rise to fear and disquietude. There was reason, therefore, why the psalmist should enter upon a specification of different evils, encouraging the Lord's people to look for more than one mode of deliverance and to bear up under various and accumulated calamities. Mention is made of the fear of the night because people are naturally apprehensive in the dark, or because the night exposes us to dangers of different kinds, and our fears are apt at such a season to magnify any sound or disturbance... But we must assure ourselves that there is no kind of calamity which the shield of the Almighty cannot ward off and repel.[3]

## Are we always secure under God's care?

One of the most important concerns in the Western world is national security. A massive attack by radical Islamic operatives is a dreaded prospect in many countries of the world today. The organization called Al Qaeda has openly publicized its intention to destroy everything related to Western Christians and other non-Islamic peoples — their military bases, means of transportation, water supplies, gasoline refineries, and government buildings. These 'will soon be the target of our future operations', their report stated, 'with the help of God [Allah] in our cause for the [military] jihad that we shall continue in the upcoming period. We pray to Allah for the triumph of his religion, the rise of his word above any other, and the defeat of his enemies.'

Can we rely on our God to protect us against such attacks? That depends. Although strong military defence is necessary, the Bible presents no call to arms; it summons us instead to prayer for national security and demands that we relinquish all national pride in armoured tanks and attack helicopters, and that we begin to rely more confidently on the invincible power of God.[4]

Should we then not fear the threats of terrorist tactics? Should we not rather 'fear the Lord'? Psalm 112 details the blessed state of 'the man who fears the LORD':

He will not be afraid of evil tidings;
His heart is steadfast, trusting in the LORD.
His heart is established;
He will not be afraid,
Until he sees his desire upon his enemies (vv. 7-8)

Calvin thinks that the children of God, if they rely upon God for security, can rise above their fear and anxiety when 'heightened security alerts' are posted:

> The righteous, unlike unbelievers, who tremble at even the slightest rumour, calmly and peacefully confide in God's paternal care amid all the evil tidings which may reach them.
>
> The children of God however may also manifest symptoms of fear at the prospect of impending danger. If they completely disregarded calamities, such indifference would be the result, not of confidence in God, but of insensibility. But should they not be able to lay aside all fear and anxiety, acknowledge God as the guardian of their life, and pursue their usual activities, entrusting themselves to his preserving care and cheerfully resigning themselves to his disposal? This is that magnanimity of the righteous, under the influence of which the psalmist declares that they can disregard those rumours of evil which strike them with alarm... A sense of calamities, while it alarms and disconcerts the faithful, does not make them fainthearted, because it does not shake their faith, by which they are rendered bold and steadfast. In a word, they are not insensible to their trials, but the confidence which they place in God enables them to rise above all the cares of the present life.[5]

David counselled his people, 'Do not fret because of evildoers', because he was confident that 'Evildoers shall be cut off' (Ps. 37:1, 9). The upright among God's people, on the other hand, have an inheritance that will never be taken away from them (v. 18). The one condition is that they 'Trust in the LORD and do good' (v. 3). Is it always true, then, that good people will not have bad things happen to them? Calvin never states that the upright are exempt from trials and troubles. He does however affirm God's goodness, his love in Christ towards those who put their trust in him, and he certifies that 'Everything *in the end* shall be well with the righteous, because they are under the protection of God.'[6] Then follows the condition on which they shall be blessed:

> But as there is nothing better or more desirable than to enjoy the fostering and protecting care of God, the psalmist exhorts them to put their trust in God and at the same time to follow after goodness and truth. It is not without good reason that he begins with the doctrine of faith, or trust in God; for there is nothing more difficult for men than to preserve their minds in a state of peace and tranquillity, undisturbed by any disquieting fears while they are in the world, which is subject to so many changes.[7]

The 'protecting care of God' does not guarantee complete freedom from suffering while we are in the world, and Calvin knows this. During the reign of Edward VI, the Duke of Somerset established the Reformation in England. Eventually, he was overthrown by the nobility and imprisoned in the Tower of London. Calvin corresponded with him, assuring him that God is able to protect those who suffer for the sake of the gospel. His letter, written in October 1548, offered the Duke an encouraging word: Since 'In the present day God has the defence of the truth as much at heart as ever, never doubt that he will come to your aid, and that not once only, but in all the trials he may send you.' Calvin's encouraging word may have given the Duke temporary peace and tranquillity, but shortly afterwards he was hanged, a victim of hatred towards the Reformers.[8]

Despite the bad things that happen to good people, Psalm 121 offers an ironclad guarantee that God will protect from all harm those who lift up their eyes and know that their help comes from the Lord: 'He will not let your foot slip' (NIV). But sometimes it does. Fred Nahas comes out of a barber shop, catches his foot on the threshold, and falls on the concrete pavement, fracturing his pelvis and shoulder bones. As he sits in a wheelchair in his hospital room he suffers intense pain. Would Fred find Psalm 121 comforting? 'The LORD will keep you from all harm — he will watch over your life; the LORD will watch over your coming and going both now and forevermore' (vv. 7-8, NIV).

Would Fred say, 'If God is my keeper, why did he let me stumble over that threshold?' Being a devout believer, he would say, 'In spite of this accident, I still say, "God is my keeper."' Calvin, too, strongly affirms the protective care of God in all circumstances:

> The psalmist not only attributes power to God, but also teaches that he so cares about us that he will preserve us in all respects in perfect safety... In this passage (Psalm 121:3-8), God is exhibited to the faithful as their guardian, so that they may rest with assured confidence on his providence.
>
> The psalmist declares that the purpose for which God is our keeper is that he may hold us up. The Hebrew word *mot*, which is here used, signifies both *sliding* or *falling* and *trembling* or *staggering*. Now, although it often happens that the faithful stagger and are even ready to fall altogether, yet because God sustains them by his power they are said to stand upright. And since amid the many dangers which every moment threaten us, it is difficult for us to get rid of all anxiety and fear, the psalmist at the same time testifies that God keeps watch unceasingly over our safety.[9]

It is not only difficult for us to eliminate anxiety and fear when we face danger, but it also is difficult for us to acknowledge God's protective care:

> How few there are to be found who yield to God the honour of being a keeper, in order that they may be assured of their safety and led to call upon him in the midst

of their perils! On the contrary, even when we seem to
have largely experienced what this protection of God
implies, we still tremble at the noise of a leaf falling from a
tree, as if God had quite forgotten us.[10]

So, which is it? Either God protects us from all kinds of
trouble, or he does not. Calvin seems to want it both ways. The
psalmist, he says, 'declares in general that the faithful shall be
safe from all adversities, defended as they are by divine power'.
In the same context he acknowledges that the faithful often do
suffer, like everyone else:

> Although God's people may be subject, like others, to the
> miseries of human life, yet his shadow is always at their
> side to shield them from any harm. The psalmist does
> not, however, promise the faithful a condition of such
> felicity and comfort as implies an exemption from all
> trouble; he only, for the purpose of assuaging their sor-
> rows, sets before them this consolation — that being in-
> terested in the divine layout, they shall be secure from all
> deadly harm... God will keep his own people from all
> evils, so as to maintain their life in safety.[11]

## In the shadow of God's wings

'Shadow' is a metaphor signifying God's presence. And since
God is everywhere present, he can, and does, protect and
deliver from trouble his faithful ones who look to him for help.
Take the strange case of St Felix.

Catholic tradition has a legend (who knows but that there
may be some truth to it?) about Felix of Nola, a town near
Naples, Italy. Felix was ordained as a priest in the year 250.
Soon afterwards persecution broke out, and Bishop Maximus
was forced to flee for his life. The persecutors then seized Felix,

and he was cruelly whipped, bound with chains, and thrown into prison. One night an angel appeared to him and commanded him to go to help Maximus. His chains fell off, the door opened, and the saint was able to bring relief to the bishop, who was then suffering from cold and hunger. The persecutors went after Felix, who had taken refuge in a dry well. Soon after he entered his hiding-place, a spider wove her web over the opening of the hole into which he had just crept. His pursuers, seeing the spider's web, assumed that the priest could not be hiding there, and sought their prey elsewhere. Felix is said to have remarked, after emerging from the dry well in which he had lain hidden for six months, 'Where God is, a spider's web is a wall; where God is not, a wall is but a spider's web.'[12]

Paul and Silas's release from prison in Philippi is an authentic example of God's miraculous protection and deliverance from further persecution. 'Suddenly there was a great earthquake, so that the foundations of the prison were shaken; and immediately all the doors were opened and everyone's chains were loosed' (Acts 16:26). Concerning this divine intervention Calvin states, 'It is not to be doubted that the Lord did then show a token of his power, which should be profitable for all ages, so that the faithful may fully assure themselves that he will be with them as often as they are about to enter combats and dangers for the defence of the gospel.'[13]

When Saul was pursuing David, David went into hiding in the desert. Saul sought him day after day, but God protected David: 'God did not deliver him into his hand' (1 Sam. 23:14). In Psalm 63 David acknowledged that 'he owed to God his preservation' while in those desert strongholds.' 'He was resolved', observes Calvin, 'to rejoice and triumph *under the shadow of God's wings,* feeling the same peace and satisfaction in reliance upon God's protection as he could have done had no danger existed.'[14] Applying to all believers David's reliance on God for safety, Calvin writes, 'The experience of the divine goodness should dispose us to prayer as well as praise.'[15]

Those who are safe under God's protection are designated 'sheltered ones'. Those who hate God, says the psalmist, 'have taken crafty counsel against [God's] people, and consulted together against [his] sheltered ones' (Ps. 83:3). Although the psalmist goes on the pray for the destruction of the enemies of Israel, Calvin sees in this verse a pastoral opportunity; he wishes to encourage the church to see herself safe under God's sheltering care:

> To keep us from thinking that we are abandoned to the snares and traps of our enemies, the psalmist here suitably sets before us a consideration calculated to afford the highest consolation and hope: he calls us God's hidden, or sheltered, ones... The purpose of this designation is simply to teach that we are *hidden under the shadow of God's wings,* for although to outward appearance we lie open and are exposed to the will of the wicked and the proud, we are preserved by the hidden power of God.
>
> It is, however, at the same time to be observed that none are hidden or sheltered under the keeping and protection of God, but those who go with fear and trembling to him, renouncing all dependence on their own strength... We will best ensure our own safety by taking shelter under the shadow of the Almighty and, conscious of our own weakness, committing our salvation to him, placing it, so to speak, into his bosom.[16]

In those times of uncertainty, fear, or affliction which all of us experience, it is helpful to remember that 'Your life is hidden with Christ in God' (Col. 3:3). The psalmist was no less confident in God's protective love; he looks to God and prays, 'You are my hiding place and my shield; I hope in your word' (Ps. 119:114). Calvin writes:

> The meaning is that the psalmist, persuaded that the only way in which he could be safe was by lying hidden under

the wings of God, confided in God's promises and therefore feared nothing. And assuredly, it is of primary importance that the faithful should hold it as a settled principle:
that amid the many dangers to which they are exposed,
the preservation of their life is entirely owing to the protection of God — in order that they may be eager to flee
to him, and, leaning on his Word, may confidently wait
for the deliverance which he has promised... We must
remember ... that when we have learned from the Word
of God that we have in him a safe hiding place, this truth
is to be cherished and confirmed in our hearts, as we are
made conscious of our absolute need of divine protection.[17]

We cannot read many of the Psalms without being made
conscious of God's protection. Psalm 27 is another expression
of confidence in God's keeping us safe, as though we had
found asylum in a house of worship:

One thing I have desired of the LORD,
That will I seek:
That I may dwell in the house of the LORD,
All the days of my life,
To behold the beauty of the LORD,
And to inquire in his temple.
For in the time of trouble
He shall hide me in his pavilion;
In the secret place of his tabernacle
He shall hide me;
He shall set my feet upon a rock (vv. 4-5).

The tabernacle was a symbol of God's presence, which affords divine protection to all those who are faithful in prayer. Says Calvin,

> Everyone who seeks God sincerely and with a pure heart shall be safely concealed under the wings of his protection. It is in the temple that God, so to speak, spreads forth his wings to gather true believers under his protection. Since David had no greater desire than to flee under these wings for refuge, there would be a shelter ready for him, under the divine protection, in times of adversity.[18]

It is vitally important that we do not think of God as a last resort, a guardian whom we contact in prayer and worship only in emergencies. David longs to 'dwell in the house of the Lord all the days of [his] life' (Ps. 27:4), and he encourages us to do the same if we expect God to keep us safe, preserve our faith, and protect us from 'the arrow that flies by day'. *Living* in the presence of God must be our habit: 'He who dwells in the secret place of the Most High shall abide under the shadow of the Almighty. He shall cover you with his feathers, and under his wings you shall take refuge' (Ps. 91:1, 4, 5). Calvin explains:

> This figure, which is employed in other parts of Scripture, is one which beautifully expresses the singularly tender care with which God watches over our safety. When we consider the majesty of God, there is nothing which would suggest a likeness such as is here drawn between him and the hen or other birds, which spread their wings over their young ones to cherish and protect them. But in accommodation to our limitation, he does not hesitate to descend, as it were, from the heavenly glory which belongs to him and to encourage us to approach him under such a humble illustration. Since he condescends in such a gracious manner to our weakness, surely there is noth-

ing to prevent us from coming to him with the greatest freedom so that we might enjoy safety and security.[19]

Having such access to God, through our Lord Jesus Christ (Rom. 5:1-2), we can come to God and receive assurance that, even when we are going through a time of suffering, we are under God's care and protection because we are his children. We may pray with confidence, as David prayed: 'Keep me as the apple of your eye; hide me under the shadow of your wings' (Ps. 17:8).

> The two phrases which David joins together — the 'apple of the eye' and the little birds which the mother keeps 'under her wings' — are introduced for illustrating the same subject. God, to express great care which he has of his own people, compares himself to a hen and other fowls that spread out their wings to cherish and cover their young, and declares them to be no less dear to him than the apple of the eye (the most sensitive part of the body) is to man.[20]

On several occasions David was 'on the run', driven from place to place by his adversaries, particularly Saul and Absalom. Psalm 61 reflects such a flight to a place of safety, which David recalls after returning from his banishment. Of special interest is David's testimony regarding God's protection and safe keeping: 'You have been a shelter for me, a strong tower from the enemy. I will abide in your tabernacle forever; *I will trust under the shadow of your wings*' (vv. 3-4, emphasis added). Calvin comments:

> Once re-established within his own palace, David's heart was set more upon the worship of God than all the wealth, splendour, and pleasures of royalty. We have his testimony in other parts of his writings that in the worst calamities which he endured he experienced nothing

which could be compared to the bitterness of being shut out from the ordinances of religion; and now he counts it a higher pleasure to lie as a suppliant before the altar than to sit upon the throne as king... He did not ... attach a superstitious importance to the mere externals of religion, adding that *he found safety under the shadow of God's wings.*[21]

## Do angels protect us?

The subject of angels has recently been quite popular; the result has been several misconceptions regarding these special messengers sent by God. A great deal of popular mythology surrounds the nature of angels. They do not have physical bodies or human faces, or wings, as depicted in medieval art such as that of Raphael and Michelangelo.

Angels, as Scripture portrays them, are spiritual beings who serve at God's command and will to deliver his messages, protect his people, and punish his enemies. Hebrews 1:14 identifies angels as 'ministering spirits sent forth to minister for those who will inherit salvation'; and Hebrews 12:22 informs us that the angels are 'an innumerable company'.

Does each person, then, have a special 'guardian angel' assigned to him or her for guidance, help, and protection? Who knows for certain? The Bible does not say that each of God's children has a guardian angel. What it does say is that God 'shall give his *angels* charge over you, to keep you in all your ways', so that 'no evil shall befall you, nor shall any plague come near your dwelling' (Ps. 91:10-11). On this point Calvin has several enlightening things to say:

> Whether each of the faithful has a particular angel assigned to him for his defence I cannot venture certainly to affirm. When Daniel introduces the angel of the Persians

and the angel of the Greeks (Dan. 10:13, 20; 12:1), he clearly signifies that certain angels are appointed to preside over kingdoms and provinces. Christ also, when he says that the angels of children always behold the face of the Father (Matt. 18:10), suggests that there are certain angels who are charged with the children's safety. But I know not whether this justifies the conclusion that every one of them has his or her particular guardian angel. Of this, indeed, we may be certain, that not one angel only has the care of every one of us, but that they all with one consent watch for our salvation. For it is said of all the angels together that they rejoice more over one sinner who has turned to repentance than over ninety-and-nine just persons who have preserved their righteousness (Luke 15:7). Of more than one angel it is said that they carried the soul of Lazarus into the bosom of Abraham (Luke 16:22).[22]

Calvin, in his comments on Psalm 91, addresses the matter of God's concern for his people and encourages us to trust God in all our adversities:

In this psalm we are taught that God watches over the safety of his people and never fails them in the hour of danger. They are exhorted to advance through all perils, secure in the confidence of his protection. The truth inculcated by Psalm 91 is of great use, for though many talk much of God's providence and profess to believe that he exercises special guardianship over his own children, few are found actually willing to entrust their safety to him.[23]

When all attempts to encourage us have been tried and God finds that we still linger and hesitate to approach him or cast ourselves upon his sole and exclusive protection, he next makes mention of the angels and proffers them as guardians of our safety. As an additional illustration of his indulgent mercy and compassion for our weakness, he represents those whom he has ready for our defence as being a numerous host; he does not assign one solitary angel to each saint, but commissions all the armies of heaven to keep watch over every individual believer. It is the individual believer whom the psalmist addresses, as we read in Psalm 34:7 — that 'Angels encamp round about those who fear him.'[24]

How encouraging it is to know that 'The angel of the LORD encamps all around those who fear him, and delivers them'! (Ps. 34:7). Calvin comments:

David here speaks in general of God's fatherly favour towards all the godly; and as their lives are exposed to innumerable dangers, he at the same time teaches us that God is able to deliver them. The faithful especially, who are as sheep in the midst of wolves, surrounded as it were with death in every form, are constantly harassed with the dread of some approaching danger. David therefore affirms that the servants of God are protected and defended by angels... Although the faithful are exposed to many dangers, yet they may rest assured that God will be the faithful guardian of their life. But in order to confirm them more in this hope, he adds ... that those whom God would preserve in safety he defends by the power and ministry of angels. The power of God alone would indeed be sufficient of itself to perform this; but in deference to our limited capacity to understand, he graciously pledges to employ angels as his ministers.

It serves not a little for the confirmation of our faith to know that God has innumerable legions of angels who are always ready for his service as often as he is pleased to aid us. Moreover, the angels also ... are ever intent upon the preservation of our life, because they know that this duty is entrusted to them. God is indeed our fortress and place of defence; but, accommodating our present imperfect state, he displays the presence of his power to aid us through the instrumentality of angels. Furthermore, what the psalmist here says of one angel in the singular number ought to be applied to all the other angels, for they are distinguished by the general designation: 'ministering spirits sent forth to minister for those who will inherit salvation' (Heb. 1:14). Whenever he knows it to be for his people's benefit, the Lord appoints many angels to take care of each of them (2 Kings 6:15; Ps. 91:11; Luke 16:22).

The sum of it is this: However great may be the number of our adversities and the dangers surrounding us, the angels of God, armed with invincible power, constantly watch over us and arrange themselves on every side to aid and to deliver us from evil.[25]

A striking example in the New Testament of the ministry of the angel of the Lord is recorded in Acts 12:3-11, the account of Peter's release from prison. Peter was put in prison for his bold preaching of salvation through Christ. But God intervened. 'Peter was sleeping, bound with two chains between two soldiers, and the guards before the door were keeping the prison. Now behold, an angel of the Lord stood by him, and a light shone in the prison; and he struck Peter on the side and raised him up, saying, "Arise quickly!" And his chains fell off his hands.' Then the angel said to him, '"Put on your garment and follow me." So he went out and followed him, and did not know that what was done by the angel was real, but thought that he was seeing a vision.' Later, 'When Peter had come to himself, he said, "Now I know for certain that the Lord has sent his angel, and has delivered me from the hand of Herod and from all the expectation of the Jewish people."'

Calvin is straightforward in his acceptance of the miracle; he does not explain Peter's escape as some modern interpreters have done: that Peter knew some friendly guards who set him free. Peter's release is God's doing.

> Assuredly, Peter might have gathered by the strange light that God was present... When the angel struck Peter's side, it demonstrated what care God has for his faithful servants: he watches over them when they are asleep and raises them when they are drowsy.
>
> It is said that immediately after the angel had said the word, the chains were loosed. We gather from this that there is enough power in the command of God alone to remove all kinds of obstructions, when things seem to be barred on all sides... Luke's setting down both the words of the angel and also the course of the matter serves as stronger witness that it was actual history, so that it may in every respect appear that Peter was delivered by God.
>
> He says that the angel was sent from God, according to the common understanding of the godly, who hold that the angels are appointed to be ministers, to care for and to take charge of their safety; unless he had been thus persuaded, he would not have spoken of the angel. And yet he does not commend the angel as the author of grace, but ascribes all the praise to God alone. The angels help us to this end — that they may not derive for themselves even the least particle of God's glory.[26]

## God's protection when the church is under fire

Christians in many countries around the world are being tested by severe and unrelenting persecution. The church in China, India, Indonesia, Pakistan, Afghanistan, Sudan, and other nations is facing increasingly tense situations as governments have outlawed minority religions, especially Christianity. Christians in Sudan, for example, were denied their freedom to worship and witness when the Arab Government of Sudan (GoS) decided to 'Islamize' the nation. The black African Christians have struggled to reclaim their freedom, but the government's offensive is 'violent, merciless, and driven by the Islamic notion of jihad. It includes brutal, institutionalized slavery on a massive scale, constant bombing, massacres, and scorched-earth raids led by the GoS and other Islamic jihad forces... By razing entire regions, the government also inflicts mass starvation on the southern Sudanese, killing tens of thousands at a time. It is the inveterate practice of the GoS to block humanitarian aid to southern regions or else permit its delivery to coincide with their massacres and slave raids, with the intention of also taking the delivered food and medical supplies.'[27]

We Christians in the Western world, who are relatively safe from such brutality, must pray for the persecuted church, as well as support humanitarian aid efforts in behalf of suffering Christians. John Calvin in his day pledged his intercession in behalf of the suffering church in France. In November 1859 he wrote a letter from Geneva to the 'brethren' of France, stating his hope and prayer, that 'Since our merciful Father has once confided you to the keeping of our Lord Jesus Christ, he would cause you to feel how safe you are under so good a protector, to the end that you may cast all your cares upon him; and that he would be pleased to have compassion on you and all those who are in affliction, delivering you from the hands of the ungodly.'[28]

Christ built his church upon a solid rock and promised that 'the gates of Hades shall not prevail against it' (Matt. 16:18). Does this promise mean that the church will never come under fire, that it will be safe from all attacks and protected from persecution? We know the answer — the church in many countries is being constantly attacked.

Christ's promise does mean, however, that the church will
never be destroyed by the assaults of Satan. Calvin writes:

> Against all the power of Satan the firmness of the church
> will prove to be invincible, because the truth of God on
> which the faith of the church rests will ever remain un-
> shaken... It is a promise which eminently deserves our
> observation, that all who are united to Christ and ac-
> knowledge him to be Christ and Mediator will remain to
> the end safe from all danger. What is said of the body of
> the church belongs to each of its members, since they are
> one in Christ. Yet this passage also instructs us that, so
> long as the church shall continue to be a pilgrim on earth,
> she will never enjoy rest but will be exposed to many at-
> tacks. When it is declared that Satan will not conquer the
> church, this implies that he will be her constant enemy.
>    While, therefore, we rely on the promise of Christ and
> feel free to boast against Satan, and already triumph by
> faith over all his forces, let us learn, on the other hand,
> that this promise is, as it were, the sound of a trumpet
> calling us to be always ready and prepared for battle.[29]

The prophet who ministered to the people of God during the
years of their exile told them that God would always protect
Jerusalem, once it was restored. He declared, 'No weapon
formed against you shall prosper' (Isa. 54:17). Calvin makes it
clear that the prophet was speaking of the church of Christ as
well as the church in Isaiah's time:

> The prophet implies ... that wicked men, even though
> they exert themselves to the utmost, will gain nothing. He
> uses the phrase 'every weapon', meaning by it that
> wicked men will have the means of attempting many and
> various methods for destroying the church, but that their
> efforts will be vain and fruitless, for the Lord will restrain
> them. Heaven permits them ... in order to try the pa-

tience of believers, but when God thinks it proper, he strips them of their strength and armour.[30]

Martin Luther's stirring hymn, 'A mighty fortress is our God', has a consoling message, one would think, for the Christians in Sudan and Pakistan. Its assurance that 'God is a bulwark never failing' echoes the opening words of Psalm 46: 'God is our refuge and our strength, a very present help in trouble.' But those believers who are enslaved or imprisoned or are suffering starvation because they are Christians may sing Luther's hymn, or Psalm 46, with reservations, because in their troubles God seems *not* to be a very present help. And to think, 'The church will survive the violence of evil men, even if I don't', may not be very consoling. Calvin of course looked beyond the troubles which the church of his day had to endure. His understanding of the psalmist's assurance in Psalm 46:1-2 of God's presence would be that, while the faithful are not shielded from trouble, the church will survive the attacks of Communist atheists in China, radical Islamic jihad forces in Sudan, and post-modern liberals in America and Europe.

Calvin remarks that in the exodus from Egypt, 'Proof had been given to all succeeding ages of the love which God has for his church.'[31] God, he says, is 'sufficiently able to protect his own people, and he gives them sufficient ground to expect it'.[32] He continues:

> It is obvious that the psalmist's purpose in Psalm 46:1 is to extol the power of God and his goodness towards his people and to show how ready God is to grant them assistance, so that they may not gaze around them on every side seeking human help, but rest satisfied with God's protection alone. The psalmist therefore says expressly that God acts in such a manner towards them, in order to let the church know that he exercises a special care in preserving and defending her.

The faithful, therefore, have no reason to be afraid, since God is always ready to deliver them and is also armed with invincible power... The true and proper proof of our hope consists in this, that when things are so confused that the heavens seem to fall with great violence, the earth to remove out of its place, and the mountains to be torn up from their very foundations, we nevertheless continue to preserve and maintain calmness and tranquillity of heart. It is an easy matter to manifest the appearance of great confidence, so long as we are not placed in imminent danger; but if, in the midst of a general crash of the whole world, our minds continue undisturbed and untroubled, this tranquillity is an obvious proof that we attribute to the power of God the honour which belongs to him.[33]

## In life or in death, God is our protector

We ought to assure ourselves, writes Calvin, that 'We are not forsaken by God either in life or in death, for those whom God brings safely by his power to the end of their course he at last receives to himself at their death.'[34]

Seeing, therefore, that God condescends to undertake the care of our lives and to support them, although they are often exposed to various kinds of death, let us learn always to flee to this refuge... Let this be our shield against all dangerous attacks, our haven amid all the tossing and tempests: although our safety may be beyond all human hope, God is the faithful guardian of it... This confidence will make everyone ... resolutely and fearlessly struggle onward to the end of his course.[35]

In Psalm 35:1-3, God is portrayed both as an advocate in a law court and as a warrior who with sword and shield protects and defends his people:

> Plead my cause, O LORD, with those who strive with me;
> Fight against those who fight against me.
> Take hold of shield and buckler,
> And stand up for my help.
> And draw out the spear,
> And stop those who pursue me.
> Say to my soul,
> 'I am your salvation.'

> Since our understanding is limited, when troubles and dangers arise, when terrors assail us on every side, when even death presents itself to our view, it is difficult to realize the secret and invisible power of God, which is able to deliver us from all anxiety and fear. In order that our faith, therefore, may ascend little by little to the heavenly power of God, he is here introduced as one who is armed after the manner of men, with sword and shield.[36]

Those Christians who are sentenced to death for their faith and loyalty to Christ cannot but anticipate death's sting with terrible anxiety. They know that believers are supposed to be armed with the shield of faith (Eph. 6:16), but they are none the less fearful as they face the terrors of death. Calvin understands this, but he is nevertheless reasonably optimistic when he says that 'To withstand these assaults, faith arms and fortifies itself with the word of God.' Faith is our shield, he reminds us, and when the darts strike it, faith 'either wards them off entirely, or at least breaks their force and prevents them from reaching the vitals'.

> Thus, when faith is shaken, it is just as when, by the violent blow of a javelin, a soldier standing firm is forced to

step back and yield a little; and again, when faith is wounded, it is as if the shield were pierced but not perforated by the blow. The pious will always rise and be able to say with David, 'Yea, though I walk through the valley of the shadow of death, I will fear no evil; for you are with me' (Ps.23:4).

Doubtless it is a terrifying thing to walk in the darkness of death, and it is impossible for believers, however great their strength may be, not to shudder at it; but since ... God is present and providing for their safety, the feeling of security overcomes that fear. As Augustine says, whatever the engines are which the devil erects against us, since he cannot gain entrance to the heart where faith dwells, he is cast out.[37]

Calvin may have been speaking from experience as well as from the teaching of Scripture. He did do battle with adversaries, and he was protected by the shield of faith. He was so detested and maligned that he might have been killed by his enemies, had he not been under the protection of God. On the other hand he was keenly aware that God protects the faithful *in* death, but not necessarily *from* death. And he knows that many believers are gripped with 'despairing fears' when death approaches. Calvin, however, takes his stand beside the psalmist: death will mean the destruction of the body, 'But God will redeem my soul from the power of the grave, for he shall receive me' (Ps. 49:15).

The psalmist's meaning is that God would redeem his soul from death by undertaking the guardianship of it when he came to die. The despairing fears which so many entertain when descending to the grave spring from the fact that they have not commended their spirit to the preserving care of God. They do not consider it in the light of a precious deposit which will be *safe in his protecting hands*. Let our faith be established in the great truth that our soul, though it appears to vanish upon its separation from the body, is in reality only gathered to the bosom of God, to be kept there until the day of the resurrection.[38]


## We are under the protection of Christ

It is humbling to realize that we are helpless to defend ourselves against the schemes of the devil, unless we have Christ as our guardian. And to have Christ as our guardian we must humbly acknowledge our helplessness apart from him, for 'with righteousness [God] shall judge the poor' — that is, the poor in spirit (Isa. 11:6; Matt. 5:3). 'The persons to whom the grace of Christ strictly belongs', says Calvin, 'are those who, humbled by a conviction of their poverty, have laid aside those proud and lofty dispositions which commonly swell the minds of men, till they have learned to be meek through the subduing influence of the Word of God.'[39]

> The prophet therefore declares that God will be the protector and guardian, not of all men, but of those who know that they are poor and destitute of everything good. This was also declared by Christ to John's disciples, when he said that 'The gospel is preached to the poor' (Matt. 11:5). Who are they that are capable of receiving this teaching? Not all men without exception, but those who, having laid aside the glory of the flesh, come under that heavenly protection.
>
> That spiritual poverty which the prophet recommends to all the members of Christ is to have no lofty views, but to be truly humbled by a conviction of our poverty and nakedness, so as to depend on Christ alone. When we have been brought to this state of mind, the faithful king and guardian will undertake to secure our salvation and

will defend us to the last against all our enemies. We also learn whom Christ invites to come to him: all you who labour and are burdened (Matt. 11:28).[40]

*This invitation stands by the parting of the ways where worldly and earthly sufferings have set down their crosses, and calls out: Come hither, all ye poor and wretched ones, ye who in poverty must slave in order to assure yourselves, not of a carefree, but of a toilsome, future; ah, bitter contradiction, to have to slave for assuring oneself of that under which one groans, of that which one flees!*

Søren Kierkegaard

*Suffering — understanding the love of God*

Selections from the writings of John Calvin

---

## Chapter 9

## Joy in the morning

---

`It is in fact Christ, present in the midst of the congregation, who brings "joy in the morning" to the worshipping church and renders its worship acceptable to our heavenly Father.`

# 9.
# Joy in the morning

*Our vows are heard betimes! And heaven takes care*
*To grant, before we can conclude the prayer:*
*Preventing angels met it half the way,*
*And sent us back to praise, who came to pray.*

John Dryden[1]

An outbreak of Hepatitis A in November 2003 was linked to a restaurant in Pennsylvania and traced to raw green onions from Mexico. At least 660 people contracted the disease; many of them required serious medical treatment, and four persons died. Rich Miller was one of the survivors who spent many weeks in a hospital. On his return to his home, he wrote a testimony to God's gracious care and healing mercy. His letter, published in his church's newsletter, is reproduced here for the encouragement of those readers who may have a family member suffering a similar ordeal.

Most of you are aware that recently I had an emergency liver transplant due to the Hepatitis A virus I contracted at a local eatery. After being sick for about a week, I became much worse and on Thursday, 6 November, Linda called the paramedics, who took me to The Medical Center and they transferred me by ambulance to UPMC Presbyterian Hospital.

That evening I was put in the liver transplant intensive care unit and was immediately diagnosed with total liver failure due to fulminating Hepatitis A. This type of hepatitis is referred to as fulminating because it totally takes over and destroys the liver. Because fulminating Hepatitis A can be fatal within hours, I was moved to the top of the transplant list. On Friday night, 7 November, an organ donor was found in Philadelphia and an organ recovery team was dispatched via helicopter to obtain my life-saving organ. Surgery was scheduled for 5 a.m. on Saturday, 8 November, and by late afternoon Linda was told that my liver was functioning. After ten days of being unconscious, I finally awoke. I had no idea I had received a liver transplant, because the last thing I remembered was being at home, sick in bed.

This was a traumatic time for Linda, our entire family, and me. However, I want to tell you about a brief moment that I remember most vividly. While unconscious, I had terrible nightmares. (I had no knowledge of how severe my condition was or that I had received a liver transplant.) At some point during these nightmares, I consciously prayed to Jesus to save me from what I believed was certain death. I then became calm for what seemed to be a few minutes, and then I became fully aware of what I had just prayed for, and I said to God, 'Why am I asking you to save my life? Isn't my goal to be with you?' Then I said to him, 'Whatever your will is...' Finally, I had a feeling of peace, knowing that all was well in his hands.

So, what's my point? Faith! Faith in the fact that, no matter what happens, the Lord is going to take care of me, one of his own. I believe the only reason he didn't take me was that it wasn't his time. I don't believe in happenstance, luck of the draw, or a whole bunch of other clichés as to why I made it through this ordeal. The Lord has his plans for each one of us. I believe he has something for me to do for his glory before I join him. Maybe it's writing this letter — who knows? Only God knows.

The next time you go through one of those deep valleys in your life, think about the peak at the end of it. For as surely as the Lord will carry you through the darkest time of your life, he will pull you up to the brightest, most wonderful times, and he will *always* be with you.[2]

Rich Miller

## Darkness, then light; sorrow, then joy

'Weeping may endure for a night, but joy comes in the morning' (Ps. 30:5). Calvin comments:

> The psalmist does not simply mean that affliction would be only for one night, but if the darkness of adversity should fall upon the people of God, as it were, in the evening, or at the setting of the sun, light would soon arise upon them to comfort their sorrow-stricken spirits. David's instruction amounts to this: If we were not too headstrong, we would acknowledge that the Lord, even when he appears to overwhelm us for a time with the darkness of affliction, always — in his own time — ministers matter for joy, just as the morning arises after the night.[3]

Paul exhorts the Christians of Philippi (and his readers, including us) to 'Rejoice in the Lord always' (Phil. 4:4). Even in the darkness of adversity we are to rejoice in the Lord. Rejoicing does not mean wearing a smile always, or singing, upon awaking, 'O what a beautiful morning!' Joy is a quiet gladness of heart as one contemplates the goodness of God's saving grace in Jesus Christ. It is joy that comes from faith (Phil. 1:25) and it is given by the Holy Spirit (Rom. 14:17).

Calvin observes,

> The apostle Paul might have had special occasion of sorrow. For if the Philippians are appalled by persecutions, or imprisonment, or exile, or death, here is the apostle who, setting himself forward ... amid imprisonments, in the very heat of persecution and even amid an apprehension of death is not merely joyful himself, but even stirs up others to joy. The sum, then, is this: Come what may, believers, because they have the Lord on their side, have ample and sufficient grounds for joy.
>
> Let this be your strength and stability — to rejoice in the Lord, not merely for a moment, but also that your joy in him may be perpetuated... The Christian's joy unquestionably differs from the joy of the world in this respect: We know from experience that the joy of the world is deceptive, frail, and fading... Only a settled joy in God is a joy that is never taken away from us.[4]

When the psalmist praises God for the joy of forgiveness, he rejoices that he can count on God for future help, and he prays, 'You shall preserve me from trouble; you shall surround me with songs of deliverance' (Ps. 32:7). True joy in God is bound to break forth in songs of praise. Calvin writes:

> By the word *surround*, he means manifold and various kinds of deliverance, as if he had said that he should be under obligation to God in innumerable ways and that he should, on every side, have abundant matter for praising God. We may observe in the meantime how he offers his service of gratitude to God, according to his usual method — putting *songs of deliverance* instead of *help*.[5]

When God delivers us from deep trouble, we ought to remember David's testimony to God's marvellous grace. God, he exclaimed, brought him up out of a horrible, muddy pit. David responded by singing praise to God: 'He has put a new song in my mouth' (Ps. 40:2-3). When God's mercy lifts me out of any difficulty, it is not enough that 'In my *heart* there rings a melody'; the song of joy should also ring out from my mouth as well. Calvin comments:

> In whatever way God is pleased to help us, he asks nothing else from us in return but that we should be thankful for it and remember it. As often, therefore, as he bestows benefits upon us, so often does he open our mouths to praise his name. Since God, by acting liberally towards us, encourages us to sing his praises, David with good reason reckons that, having been so wonderfully delivered, the matter of a new song had been furnished to him. He uses the word *new* in the sense of exquisite and not ordinary — even as the manner of his deliverance was remarkable and worthy of everlasting remembrance. It is true that there is no benefit from God so small that it ought not to call forth our highest praises; but the more mightily he stretches forth his hand to help us, the more it becomes us to stir up ourselves to fervent zeal in this holy exercise, so that our songs may correspond to the greatness of the favour which has been conferred upon us.[6]

Like David, we should tune our hearts to praise God even before God grants deliverance from our troubles. This is, of course, a matter of faith and hope. David says that he has 'sorrow in his heart daily' (Ps. 13:2). 'But I have trusted in your mercy; my heart shall rejoice in your salvation. I will sing to the LORD, because he has dealt bountifully with me' (Ps. 13:5-6).

Calvin, in his comments on these verses, again gives pastoral counsel to all who may be praying and hoping for God's deliverance from adversity:

The psalmist does not yet feel how much he has profited by praying; but, depending upon the hope of deliverance which the faithful promise of God enabled him to entertain, he makes use of this hope as a shield to repel those temptations that might greatly distress him with their terror. Therefore, although he is severely afflicted, and many different cares urge him to despair, he resolves to continue firm in his reliance upon the grace of God and in the hope of salvation. With the very same confidence all the godly ought to be furnished and sustained, so that they may duly persevere in prayer. From this, also, we gather ... that it is by faith that we apprehend the grace of God, which is hidden from and unknown to the understanding of the flesh... David here wishes to testify that he continued firm in the hope of deliverance promised to him, and would continue to do so even to the end, however heavy the burden of temptations which might press upon him.

David, it is true, had not yet obtained what he earnestly desired, but being fully convinced that God was already at hand to grant him deliverance, he pledges himself to give thanks to God for it. And surely it becomes us to engage in prayer in such a frame of mind as at the same time to be ready to sing the praises of God... We may not be wholly free from sorrow, but it is nevertheless necessary that this cheerfulness of faith rise above it and put into our mouth a song, on account of the joy which is reserved for us in the future, although we do not yet experience it — just as we see David here preparing himself, before he perceives the outcome of his troubles, to celebrate in songs the grace of God.[7]

In contrast, the desperate outcry of the prophet Jeremiah seems to be devoid of faith and hope: 'Cursed be the day in which I was born! Let the day not be blessed in which my mother bore me.'[8]

The weeping prophet had to know in his heart of hearts that his outburst was entirely inappropriate for one who had been called to proclaim God's Word of judgement and grace. Indeed, as Søren Kierkegaard has said, 'It takes moral courage to grieve; it requires religious courage to rejoice.' Calvin, on the other hand, cuts Jeremiah some slack, allowing that the prophet's burden of sorrow was indeed unbearable, given the abuse and ridicule and resistance to his ministry which he had experienced. But Jeremiah's expression of grief is part of God's Word to us, and Calvin sees it as an occasion for counselling us to look beyond our dark distress to brighter days, when God will be pleased to cheer and comfort us.

> We are here reminded how much vigilance we ought to exercise over ourselves. In most instances when we become weary of life and desire death and hate the world, even though we have the light and blessings of God, it is because we are influenced by disdain that reigns within us, or by reproaches that we cannot bear with resignation, or by poverty too grievous for us, or by troubles that press upon us too heavily. It is not that we are influenced by a zeal for God. Since we see the prophet, who had no regard to himself nor private reason to gain or lose, become exasperated and so vehement — no, seized with so violent a feeling — we surely ought to exercise more care to restrain our feelings. Though many things daily happen to us that may produce weariness or overwhelm us with so much disdain as to render all things hateful to us, we ought to contend against such feelings. If we cannot repress and subdue them by our first effort, we at least, according to the example of the prophet Jeremiah, ought to learn to correct them by degrees, until God cheers and comforts us, *so that we may rejoice and sing a song of thanksgiving.*[9]

## Celebrate God's mercy with joy and thanksgiving

Whenever God's people (the church in the time of the Old Testament) experienced a remarkable deliverance from some calamity, they went to the place of worship to offer sacrifices — burnt offerings — of rams and goats. Such offerings were expressions of thanksgiving, and they were accompanied by vows of continued trust in God's mercy (Ps. 66:13-15). Today, the sacrifices of the Law having been abolished, the distressed church offers the sacrifice of praise, in keeping with the call to worship given in the context of the church's suffering: 'Therefore by him [Jesus] let us continually offer the sacrifice of praise to God, that is, the fruit of our lips, giving thanks to his name' (Heb. 13:15). Calvin writes:

> We are taught that when God at any time helps us in our adversity, we do an injustice to his name if we forget to celebrate our deliverances with solemn acknowledgements. More is spoken of in this passage (Ps. 66:13-15) than thanksgiving. The psalmist speaks of vows having been contracted by him in his affliction, and these evidenced the constancy of his faith. The exhortation of the apostle James is worthy of our special notice — 'Is any among you suffering? Let him pray. Is anyone cheerful? Let him sing psalms' (James 5:13).
>
> How many there are who lavish their hypocritical praises upon God in their career of their good fortune. When they are subjected to difficult situations, the fervour of their love is dampened, or gives place to the violence of fretfulness and impatience. The best evidence of our true piety is when we sigh to God under the pressure of our afflictions and show by our prayers a holy perseverance in faith and patience; while afterwards we come forward with the expression of our gratitude.[10]

The psalmist's pledge, in Psalm 17:7, to praise the Lord for his faithfulness and to sing to the name of 'the Lord Most High' is, for the individual believer and for the church, a distinct call to offer the sacrifice of praise. Calvin comments, 'The design of God in the deliverances which God grants his servants is that they may render to him in return the *sacrifices of praise*.' David, in ascribing to God praise for his deliverance from Saul's murderous intention, 'confirms in one word … that he is indebted for his life to the grace of God, who had not permitted Saul to take it from him'.[11]

Joy and thanksgiving expressed in prayer and praise according to the Word of God are the heart of the church's worship. Our heavenly Father, Calvin says, consoles us by the assurance that in the very cross with which he afflicts us he provides for our salvation. In the world we will have tribulations, but 'Why', Calvin asks, 'should we not receive them with calm and grateful minds?'

> The effect of these thoughts is that to whatever extent our minds are contracted by the bitterness which we naturally feel under the cross, to the same extent they will be expanded with spiritual joy. From this arises thanksgiving, which cannot exist unless joy is felt. But if the praise of the Lord and thanksgiving can emanate only from cheerful and gladdened breasts, and there is nothing which ought to interrupt these feelings in us, it is clear that it is necessary to temper the bitterness of the cross with spiritual joy.[12]

## God's Word is the ground of our joy

As we need the Holy Spirit's help to pray (Rom. 8:26), so we need his Word to teach us how we should praise God; and surely the psalms provide ample material for acceptable praise of God's works of creation, providence, and redemption. Psalm 57:17, which follows a plea for defence against persecution, sets the tone for the church's praise: 'I will praise the LORD according to his righteousness, and will sing praise to the name of the LORD Most High.'

In times of trouble we can find consolation in many of the psalms, and we can learn from them how to praise God properly. David, when tormented by his enemies, had ample reasons to praise God. God's promises were as good as gold, and his Word trustworthy. 'In God (I will praise his Word), in God I have put my trust; I will not fear. What can flesh do to me?' (Ps. 56:4). Calvin comments:

> He was now in possession of a triumphant confidence and rejoiced in the certainty of hope. The ground of his joy is said to be *the divine Word*, and this implies that, however much he might seem to have been forsaken and abandoned by God, he satisfied himself by reflecting on the truthfulness of God's promises. He would glory in God in spite of his seeming abandonment, and although there should be no outward appearance of help … he would rest contented with the simple security of God's Word. It was no small attainment for David — that he could thus proceed to praise the Lord in the midst of dangers and with no other ground of support but the Word of God.[13]

When the people of Israel were delivered from exile and returned to Zion, their sorrow was turned to joy. During their long period of exile 'by the rivers of Babylon', they wept when they remembered Zion. Asked by their captors to sing 'one of the songs of Zion', they replied, 'How shall we sing the LORD'S song in a foreign land?' But when the Lord brought them back from captivity, they said, 'Then our mouth was filled with laughter and our tongue with singing'. Calvin says:

The psalmist would have the people rejoice on account of their return, so as not to bury in forgetfulness the grace of God. He therefore describes no ordinary rejoicing, but such rejoicing that fills their minds as to constrain them to break forth into extravagance of gesture and of voice. At the same time he intimates that there was good ground for this joy, in which it was fitting for the children of God to indulge, on account of their return to their own land.

With a similar joy it becomes us at the present day to exult when God gathers together his church, and it is undoubted evidence that we are hard-hearted if her miserable dispersion does not produce in our minds grief and lamentation... God's power and operation were so conspicuous in that deliverance from exile that they burst forth into the open acknowledgement that God had done great things for his people... When he adds that they were glad, there is an implied antithesis between this fresh joy and the long-continued sorrow with which they were afflicted in their captivity.[14]


## The call to praise God is 'for all the saints'

David exclaims, 'I will bless the LORD at all times' (Ps. 34:1). He also calls upon others to join him in praising God: 'O magnify the LORD with me, and let us exalt his name together' (v. 3).

Calvin understands this to be a call to united service of praise, addressed to the whole church:

The psalmist shows still another fruit which would be the result of his giving thanks to God, namely, that he shall induce others by his example to the same exercise of devotion. More than that, he calls upon all the godly to unite with him in this exercise, inviting and exhorting them heartily and with one accord to extol the Lord. Let us therefore learn from the many instances in which God may have given help to any of his people to abound in hope; and when each recites the personal benefits which he or she has received, let all be moved with united hearts and in a public manner to give praise to God. We give thanks publicly to God, not only that others may be witnesses of our gratitude, but also that they may follow our example.[15]

The prophet Jeremiah, immediately after his release from imprisonment (on account of his rebukes to the nation), prayed that God might vindicate his sorrows (Jer. 20:7-12). It was in this prayer that the prophet cursed the day in which he was born (v. 14). Ironically, in the verse which precedes this outburst of cynicism he calls upon others to praise God for his mercy: 'Sing to the LORD! Praise the LORD! For he has delivered the life of the poor [i.e., the defenceless] from the hand of evildoers' (Jer. 20:13). Calvin writes:

Here the prophet breaks out into an open expression of joy, and not only gives thanks himself to God that he had been freed from the intrigue and violence of the wicked, but he also summons others and encourages them to sing praises — as though he had said that his deliverance was such a favour that not only he should be thankful to God for it, but that all should join to celebrate it... As, then, he had really found that God was victorious and that his safety had been defended by God's invincible power against all the ungodly, he in full confidence expressed his thanks and wished all God's servants to join with him.[16]

## Praising God when we are sorrowful, ill, or depressed

There are times when the burden of grief, or the lingering pain of an injury, or the darkness of despair make thanksgiving and praise most difficult, even for people of great faith. I have ministered in hospital rooms to some of God's children who were wallowing in self pity and brooding over their personal misery, unable to lift up their hearts to praise God in their dreary solitude. It often helps to remind such patients of Paul's exhortation in 1 Thessalonians 5:16-18: 'Rejoice always, pray without ceasing, in everything give thanks; for this is the will of God in Christ Jesus for you.'

Rejoicing, Calvin says, refers to 'moderation of spirit, when the mind keeps itself in calmness under adversity and does not give indulgence to grief'. Constant praying, he insists, is 'the way of rejoicing perpetually, for by this means we ask from God alleviation in connection with all our distresses'.[17]

'Give thanks in all circumstances' (v. 18, NIV). Calvin may seem to be rather unrealistic when he urges suffering saints to pray and give thanks, an exercise, he says, that produces 'as a source of joy a calm and composed mind that is not unduly disturbed by injuries or adversities'. But we can experience joy in adverse circumstances ... 'by holding God's benefits in such esteem that the recognition of them and meditation upon them shall overcome all sorrow'. Calvin continues:

> And unquestionably, if we consider what Christ has conferred upon us, there will be no bitterness of grief so intense that it may not be alleviated and give way to spiritual joy... Very ungrateful is that one who does not set so high a value on the righteousness of Christ and the hope of eternal life as to rejoice in the midst of sorrow. But because our minds are so easily dispirited that they give way to impatience, we must observe the remedy that Paul offers: On being cast down and laid low we are raised up again by prayers, because we lay upon God what burdens us... And our prayers must always mingle thanksgiving with our desires.[18]

God has such a disposition towards us in Christ that even in our afflictions we have a large occasion of thanksgiving. For what is more suitable for pacifying us

than when we learn that God embraces us in Christ so
tenderly that he turns to our advantage and welfare everything that befalls us? Let us therefore bear in mind that
this is a special remedy for correcting our impatience —
to turn away our eyes from looking at present evils that
torment us and to direct our views to a consideration of a
different nature: how God stands affected towards us in
Christ.[19]

In hospital rooms where I have given pastoral care, encouraging and praying for patients who are recovering from surgery
or dealing with cancer, I often have noticed a Bible at the
bedside, and not a few have testified that they found that
reading the psalms lifted their spirits and gave them joy and
hope. One such meditation might be on Psalm 140:13: 'Surely
the righteous shall give thanks to your name; the upright shall
dwell in your presence.' Calvin writes:

Though the godly may be silenced for a time, and though
the force of trouble may not raise the praises of God,
David expresses his conviction that what was taken away
would be speedily restored, and that they would celebrate
the loving kindness of the Lord with joy and cheerful
readiness. As this is not easily believed in circumstances
of trial, David assures the godly that help is on the way.
We must endeavour, though with a struggle, to rise to a
confident persuasion that however low they may be
brought, the Lord's people will be restored to prosperity
and will soon sing his praises.[20]

## Praise is a lifelong exercise

'You have turned for me my mourning into dancing; you have
put off my sackcloth and clothed me with gladness, to the end

that my glory may sing praise to you and not be silent. O LORD
my God, *I will give thanks to you forever.*' David's testimony
and pledge in Psalm 30:11-12 remind us that we should not
limit our praise of God only to those times when we have been
extricated from some difficulty. Calvin comments,

> David concludes the psalm as he had begun it, with
> thanksgiving. He affirms that it was by the help and bless-
> ing of God that he had escaped safely; and then he adds
> that the final object of his escape was that he might em-
> ploy the rest of his life in celebrating the praises of God.
>    'I will celebrate your praise forever' is David's pledge
> in view of God's gracious help. His meaning therefore is:
> O Lord, I know that you have preserved me for this pur-
> pose: that your praises may resound from my tongue. I
> will faithfully discharge this service to you and perform
> my part even unto death... My tongue shall not be mute,
> nor deprive God of his due praise; it shall, on the con-
> trary, devote itself to the celebration of his glory.[21]

I have known a few devout Christians who include in their
everyday conversation the pious cliché, 'Praise the Lord', and I
have wondered how sincere their 'praise' was. David, on the
other hand, declares with evident sincerity that his praise of
God will never cease: 'I will bless the LORD at all times; his
praise shall continually be in my mouth' (Ps. 34:1). Shouldn't
continual praise of God be the rule for *all* believers? Hear what
Calvin has to say:

> David here extols the greatness of God, promising to
> keep in remembrance during his whole life the goodness
> which God had bestowed upon him. God assists his peo-
> ple daily, that they may continually employ themselves in
> praising him. Yet, it is certain that the blessing which is
> said to be worthy of everlasting remembrance is distin-
> guished ... from other benefits which are ordinary and

common. This, therefore, is a rule which should be observed by the saints: They should often call into remembrance whatever good has been bestowed upon them by God. If at any time he should display his power more illustriously in preserving them from some extraordinary danger, it is fitting that they should so much the more earnestly testify to their gratitude.

Now if by one benefit alone God lays us under obligation to him all our life, so that we may never lawfully cease from setting forth his praises, how much more when he heaps upon us innumerable benefits? In order to distinguish the praise which he had said before would be continually in his mouth from the empty sound of the tongue (in which many hypocrites boast), David adds ... that it would proceed from the heart.[22]

David 'intersperses throughout Psalm 35 testimonies of his thankfulness; he concludes the psalm by saying that after he has been delivered he will *celebrate the praises of God all his life.*'[23] Other psalmists also recognized God's abundant grace and goodness towards them and were firmly committed to lifelong praise of God. In Psalm 104:33, that commitment is expressed with joyful acknowledgement of God's mighty works of creation and providence: 'I will sing to the LORD as long as I live: I will sing praise to my God while I have my being.'

Here, by his own example, the psalmist points out to others their duty, declaring that throughout the whole course of his life he will proclaim the praises of God without ever growing weary of that exercise. The only boundary which he fixes to the celebration of God's praises is death — not that the saints, when they pass from this world into another state of existence, desist from this religious duty, but because the end for which we are created is that the divine name may be celebrated by us on earth.[24]

## Christ is our mediator and leader

Central in the church's worship is the presence of Christ, and, contrary to recent trends that make the Sunday morning service a musical performance, authentic worship is a celebration of God's works, especially his redemptive work through Jesus Christ. It is in fact Christ, present in the midst of the congregation, who brings 'joy in the morning' to the worshipping church and renders its worship acceptable to our heavenly Father. At the centre of the Israelites' worship, sacrifices of rams, bulls, and goats were offered (Ps. 66:13-16). Christian worship, when true to the regulative principles of God's Word, is a joyful celebration of Christ's atoning sacrifice. Calvin in his writings has a great deal to say about Christ as our mediator, through whom our prayers and praises ascend to God as an acceptable sacrifice (Heb. 2:12; 13:15):

> However we might propose to ourselves to praise the name of God, we could only profane it with our impure lips, had not Christ once offered himself up as a sacrifice to sanctify both us and our services (Heb. 10:7). It is through him, as we learn from the writer of Hebrews that our praises are accepted. The psalmist (Ps. 66:13-16), by way of commendation of his burnt offering, speaks of its incense or sweet savour; for although in themselves vile and loathsome, the rams and other victims, so far as they were figures of Christ, sent up a sweet savour unto God. Now that the shadows of the Law have been abolished, attention is called to the true spiritual service... In calling, as he does, upon all who fear God, the psalmist teaches us that if we duly feel the goodness of God, we will be eager to publish it abroad, that others may have their faith and hope confirmed by what they hear of God's goodness, as well as *join with us in a united song of praise*.[25]

It is most remarkable that Christ, the Son of God, 'very God of very God', is not ashamed to call us his brothers and sisters, and in the midst of the worshipping church he proclaims the name of God and even leads our praises. Quoting Psalm 22:22, he says to the worshipping flock, 'I will declare your name to my brethren; in the midst of the assembly I will sing praise to you.' Calvin says:

> Hence it appears plainly that the proclamation of God's praises is always promoted by the teaching of the gospel; for as soon as God becomes known to us, his boundless praises sound in our hearts and in our ears. At the same time Christ encourages us by his own example publicly to celebrate them, so that they may be heard by as many as possible. For it would not be sufficient for each one of us to thank God individually for benefits received, unless we testify openly our gratitude, and thus mutually stimulate one another. And it is a truth which may serve as a most powerful stimulant, leading us most fervently to praise God, when we hear that *Christ leads our songs and is the chief composer of our hymns.*[26]

This chapter is not about sorrow and trouble, but about praising God for his saving grace in Jesus Christ. It is not about bad news; it is about the good news that Jesus heals, Jesus cares, Jesus saves. 'Tears may flow in the night, but joy comes in the morning' (Ps. 30:5, TEV). But there can be *songs* in the night, too. The apostle Paul and his missionary companion Silas were seized and beaten and thrown into prison because they magnified the name of Jesus Christ. But in that dark, damp dungeon where they lay wounded and restrained by shackles, they praised God and their praises resounded throughout the prison. They were bound with stocks, but the Word of God was not bound. All was dark and cheerless, 'But at midnight Paul and Silas were praying and singing hymns to God, and the prisoners were listening to them' (Acts 16:25). Calvin's observations may encourage us in a dark hour of distress:

> For even when they lay bound with fetters ... they lauded God. By this it appears that neither the reproach which they suffered, nor the stripes which made their flesh smart, nor the stink of the deep dungeon, nor the danger of death, which was close at hand, could hinder them from giving thanks to the Lord joyfully and with glad hearts.[27]

Those moments of devout praise were suddenly interrupted by an earthquake so violent that it shook the foundations of the prison. The earthquake was not a sign of God's *judgement,* but of his presence and power. Earthquakes invariably cause damage and ruin, but that earthquake brought deliverance and release. Miraculously, it opened the door of every cell and loosed the chains of every prisoner.

The prisoners were listening to prayers and songs in the night. The jailer was listening. And yes, others will listen to a Christian under trying circumstances in a midnight hour of sorrow. If others can hear you praying and praising God in your dark and desolate hour of trouble, they too, like the prison governor, will come running to ask, 'What must I do to be saved?' The answer is the same now as then: '*Believe on the Lord Jesus Christ, and you will be saved.*'

After their dark ordeal and the conversion of the jailer, Paul and Silas were vindicated and released from the magistrates' custody. Was Psalm 37 one of the 'hymns' which they sang that night? If so, the words of verse 6 would have encouraged their hearts with God's promise of vindication: 'He shall bring forth your righteousness as the light, and your justice as the noon-day.' Calvin's comment on this promise applies to the two singing prisoners and to any of God's servants who may be suffering for righteousness' sake:

God will not suffer our righteousness to be always hidden in darkness, but he will maintain it and bring it forth to the light... The psalmist alludes to the darkness of the night, which is soon dispelled by the dawning of the day — as if he had said, 'We may be often grievously oppressed, and God may not seem to approve of our innocence; yet this unpleasant change of circumstances should no more disturb our minds than the darkness of the night which covers the earth; for then the expectation of the light of day sustains our hope.'[28]

O Father, gracious was that word which clos'd
Thy sovran sentence, that man should find grace;
For which both heav'n and earth shall high extol
Thy praises, with th' innumerable sound
Of hymns and sacred songs, wherewith thy throne
Encompass'd shall resound thee ever blest.

John Milton, *Paradise lost*

*Suffering — understanding*
*the love of God*

Selections from the writings of John Calvin

---

## Chapter 10

## The fellowship of his sufferings

---

'In suffering for the cause of
God, we are walking step by
step after the Son of God and
have him for our guide.'

# 10.

# The fellowship of his sufferings

*But it is time to show in reality that when you have set yourself frankly to follow Jesus Christ, you have not done so without being resolved to hold fellowship with him at the cross, since he has done us that honour to be crucified in us, to glorify us with himself.*

John Calvin, to Monsieur de Falais, 1545[1]

During his years in Geneva, Calvin was the butt of endless jokes and the victim of vicious rumours about his personal life — all without foundation. He was vilified and humiliated by gangs of hoodlums who gathered in taverns to mock and belittle him. His strict enforcement of a moral code for the residents of Geneva made Calvin the target of abuse and even of threats against his life. The persecution that Calvin suffered is well documented in Bernard Cottret's biography of Calvin and numerous other works on the Reformer's life and ministry. As we shall see, Calvin viewed his own suffering as the price of following Christ in a world where license was valued more highly than truth. In his commentaries, sermons, and correspondence, he considers suffering for the sake of the gospel a privilege — even a blessing — since 'Persecutions are remnants of Christ's sufferings.'

The church since the days of the apostles has always been a 'suffering servant'. The church in the twenty-first century is no exception. Christians are the most persecuted religious group in the world today. In many countries they are suffering atrocities at the hands of dictatorial governments — many are arrested by police and fined or imprisoned; some are sold as slaves, others are tortured, brutalized, and executed — solely because of their faith. Hundreds of thousands, even some children, are being subjected to persecution and suffering, the cruelty of which we can scarcely begin to comprehend. The atrocities perpetrated against Christians spring chiefly from two ideologies that prevail throughout the world: godless Communism and radically militant Islam.

## Faith tested by persecution

In China and Vietnam, Communist governments are molesting non-registered house churches by disrupting worship and arresting their leaders. In the Middle East and certain parts of Africa and India, governments prohibit Christians from evangel-izing and forbid citizens from abandoning the state religion and converting to Christianity. Christians who share Bible truth with others are driven out of town, and some are beaten and brutal-ized.

From news reports gathered from online news services we learn of atrocities that are too brutal for words. Following are examples revealing the ruthless persecution of Christians by the enemies of Christ.

Muslims slaughtered an estimated 600 Christians during the week of 9 May 2004 in Kano, a city in northern Nigeria, accord-ing to the Christian Association of Nigeria. David Emmanuel, a factory worker, reported that he had seen two truckloads of corpses and counted at least thirty bodies lying in the street. Others testified that they had seen thirty-five mostly burned and mutilated bodies. The city morgue was filled to overflowing, according to eyewitnesses. Even a number of little children were killed. More than 30,000 residents, mostly Christian, were driven from their homes in Kano.

Barnabas Fund reports the killing of several hundred people 'when defiant mobs of Muslim youths armed with clubs and machetes and cutlasses rampaged at about 1 a.m.' 'Mobs went from house to house looking for Christian victims and in some cases trapped the occupants inside and torched the houses.'

In September 2003, 170 house-church Christians were arrested in central eastern Asia when a worship service was interrupted by the authorities. Most of them were fingerprinted, fined, and released, except for fourteen church leaders, who were detained.

A house church in Lisoning province was raided and forty Christians were tied up and arrested. They were released later the same day after being told that their 'illegal gathering' was prohibited.

Eighty Christians were arrested on 28 June 2003 when police raided a funeral in Hunan province.

On 5 January 2003, ten unidentified men burst into the home of Brother Hau Huiqi in Beijing, forced his family to lie down on the floor, and then beat them. Hau's eighty-year-old father suffered a broken leg in the attack. The intruders also confiscated the family's heaters, leaving them without heat in sub-zero temperatures.

These examples of present-day persecution may heighten our awareness of the suffering endured by hundreds of thousands of Christians — in Sudan, China, Vietnam, Pakistan, Saudi Arabia, North Korea, Myanmar, and other countries throughout the world.

Behind these attacks against Christians are the powers of spiritual darkness, which for the present seem to have he upper hand in persecuting of the church. Persecution of Christians is not simply the work of human opponents of Christianity; prompting it are 'the wicked spiritual forces in the heavenly world, the rulers, authorities, and cosmic powers of this dark age' (Eph. 6:12, TEV).

## We are destined to suffer for Christ

The apostles Barnabas and Paul encountered strong opposition when preaching the gospel in places like Iconium and Lystra in Asia Minor. Persuaded by unbelievers, a mob seized Paul, pelted him with stones, and dragged him out of their city, where they left him, 'supposing him to be dead' (Acts 14:19). But Paul, ever a survivor by God's grace, returned to the city and encouraged the Christians to continue in the faith, saying, 'We must through many tribulations enter the kingdom of God' (v. 22). Calvin understands *tribulations* to include, besides persecution, 'all the sorrows and miseries to which the life of the godly is subject'. He then continues:

> To these are added the reproaches and slanders of the wicked, for they consider followers of Christ the rubbish of the world, as it were... They use wicked mockery and scoffing, principally against God. Last of all, the lust of the wicked breaks out into open violence, so that believers must strive with many tribulations; their life will in due time be envied and unquiet amid so many enemies. But this is the best comfort, which is sufficient to confirm in their minds that this way (though it may be difficult and sharp) leads to the kingdom of heaven... Comfort is added, not to extol the dignity and merit of works, but only to encourage the godly, so that they do not faint under the burden of the cross... Let the faithful think that they must pass through continual miseries; that done, let them prepare themselves not for one kind of persecution only, but for various kinds.[2]

Our Lord warned his followers that they must expect persecution: wars, famine, pestilence, earthquakes; all these, he told them, are only the first pains of childbirth (Matt. 24:7-8). In addition to those challenges to their faith, 'Christ predicts for his disciples another kind of temptation which shall try their faith, namely, that besides the common afflictions that all people must suffer, they shall be hated and detested by the entire world.'[3]

> Here in Matthew 24:9, Christ is speaking of the afflictions which the disciples were to suffer for the gospel. What Paul says in Romans 8:29 is, of course, true. *Those whom God elects, he destines to bear a cross*, so that they may conform to the image of his Son. But there Paul means more than persecution at the hands of the enemies of the gospel. Here, on the other hand, Christ is speaking of the kind of cross which the faithful have to carry because of their witness to the gospel; for this makes it necessary for them to incur the hatred of the ungodly, to face their insults and provoke them to fury. He wants to warn his disciples that, as he had explained to them before, the teachings of the gospel, of which they were to become witnesses and heralds, would at no time please the world or receive its applause. So he prophesies that they will not be fighting with only a few enemies, but that everywhere they go nations shall rise against them.[4]

Nothing has changed. The gospel continues to be a scandal in our 'enlightened', politically correct society. Speaking of the modern anti-Christian bias, American columnist and commentator Ann Coulter writes, 'There is no surer proof of Christ's divinity than that he is still so hated some 2,000 years after his death.'[5]

Wherever in the world hatred of Christianity exists, there is bound to be repression of religious expression, vigorous opposition to Christian endeavours, and, in countries where Christians are a minority, persecution and bloodshed.

The innocent sufferer often struggles to understand God's ways. God, the psalmist says in Psalm 44, 'covered us with the shadow of death'. And with heart-searching disquietude he muses, 'If we had forgotten the name of our God, or stretched out our hands to a foreign god ... Yet for your sake we are killed all day long; we are accounted as sheep for the slaughter' (vv. 20, 22). Looking at the psalmist's complaint in the light of the gospel, Calvin cites 'the consolation which Christ offered', which, he says, 'appears very different from the words of the psalm' — 'Happy are those who are persecuted for righteousness' sake' (Matt. 5:10). Calvin also says,

> But I answer that although the best comfort for our sorrow is that the cause is connected with Christ, yet the faithful do not complain to God in vain, or wrongly, when they say that they are suffering unjustly for his sake. For in this way they want him to come forward with more vigour as their defender, since it is right that he himself should take care of his own glory when the impious insult and deal cruelly with his worshippers.[6]

Adoniram Judson, the first American missionary to Myanmar (formerly Burma), endured constant abuse, including imprisonment by tyrannical government authorities. One of his Burmese converts, Maung Shway-gnong, who suffered along with many other Christians for his faith, testified courageously, 'If I must die ... I shall die in a good cause. I know it is the cause of truth.'[7]

Suffering in the cause of truth is difficult to endure, but it is not without consolation. To the suffering church in the first century Peter writes, 'Beloved, do not think it strange concerning the fiery trial which is to try you, as though some strange thing happened to you; but rejoice to the extent that you partake of Christ's sufferings, that when his glory is revealed, you may also be glad with exceeding joy' (1 Peter 4:12-13). When Peter 'speaks of wrongs done to the faithful in the name of Christ', Calvin observes, they ought not to be dismayed, if by 'long meditation they have been prepared to bear the cross... In order to be in a prepared state of mind when the waves of persecution roll over us, we ought in advance to habituate ourselves to such an event by meditating continually on the cross.'[8]

The apostle Paul, writing to his younger associate Timothy, mentions the persecutions and afflictions which happened to him at Antioch, Iconium, and Lystra (described above), and he adds, 'Yes, and all who desire to live godly in Christ Jesus will suffer persecution' (2 Tim. 3:11-12). Calvin comments,

> Paul classes himself with the children of God, and at the same time he exhorts all the children of God to prepare for enduring persecutions. If this condition is laid down for all who wish to live a godly life in Christ, they who wish to be exempt from persecutions must necessarily renounce Christ. In vain shall we detach Christ from his cross, for it may be said to be natural that the world should hate Christ even in his members. Now, hatred is attended by cruelty, and hence arise persecutions. In short, let us know that we are Christians on this condition: that we shall be liable to many tribulations and various contests.[9]

## We are called to follow Christ

In July 1558, Calvin wrote a letter to Monsieur D'Andelot, who was imprisoned and had recanted his Protestant faith to spare himself from a death sentence. Calvin blames him for his weakness, telling him that the honour of God is more important than life itself, and that 'If we reflect properly on the shortness of life, it ought not to cost much to follow our Lord Jesus in his death and burial in order to be partakers of his glory.'[10]

'Jesus said to his disciples, "If anyone desires to come after me, let him deny himself, and take up his cross, and follow me. For whoever desires to save his life will lose it, but whoever loses his life for my sake will find it"' (Matt. 16:24-25). If we want to follow Christ, we must go with him to the cross. Calvin expands this idea, applying it to our whole life:

> Presenting himself to everyone as an example of self-denial and of patience, Jesus first shows that it was necessary for him to endure what Peter reckoned to be inconsistent with his character, and next invites every member of his body to imitate him. The words may be explained in this way: 'If any man would be my disciple, let him follow me by denying himself and taking up his cross, or, let him conform himself to my example.' The meaning is that none can be reckoned to be the disciples of Christ unless they are true imitators of him and are willing to pursue the same course... This self-denial implies that we ought to give up our natural inclinations and part with the affections of the flesh and thus give our consent to be reduced to nothing, provided that God lives and reigns in us... Jesus lays down this injunction to take up one's cross because, though there are common miseries to which people's lives are indiscriminately subjected, God is training his people in a particular manner, in order that they may be conformed to the image of his Son. We need not wonder that this rule is strictly addressed to them. It may be added that, although God lays on both good and bad men the burden of the cross, unless they willingly bend their shoulders to it, they are not said to bear the cross... Luke adds the word *daily,* which is very emphatic; Christ's meaning is that there will be no end to our warfare till we leave the world. Let it be the uninterrupted exercise of the godly, that when many afflictions have run their course, they may be prepared to endure fresh afflictions.[11]

Daily cross-bearing has been a way of life for many followers of Christ since the time of the apostles. Dietrich Bonhoeffer, a Lutheran pastor who led a resistance movement against the slaughter of innocents by the Nazis during the regime of Hitler, was thrown into prison, where he wrote *The Cost of Discipleship*. Most memorable are Bonhoeffer's challenges to our faith: 'When Christ calls a man, he bids him come and die' (and that means daily self-denial). 'The call of Christ sets a man in the middle of the daily arena against sin and the devil. Every day he must suffer anew for Jesus Christ's sake. The wounds and scars he receives in the fray are living tokens of his participation in the cross of our Lord.'

Calvin knew from his own experience, being in the middle of the arena where he had to contend almost daily with devils bent on destroying the Reform movement, that following Christ was not a safe and pleasant way of life. Expounding Hebrews 13:13 — 'Let us, then, go to him outside the camp, bearing the disgrace he bore' — Calvin writes,

> But as persecution is always harsh and bitter, let us consider how and by what means Christians may be able to fortify themselves with patience, so as unflinchingly to expose their lives for the truth of God... The writer of Hebrews says, 'Let us go forth from the city after the Lord Jesus, bearing his reproach.' In the first place he reminds us, although the swords are not drawn over us nor the fires kindled to burn us, that we cannot be truly united to the Son of God while we are rooted in this world. Therefore a Christian, even if not persecuted, must always have one foot lifted to march to battle; not only that, but he also must have his affections withdrawn from the world, though his body is living in it. Granted that this at first sight seems to us hard, still we must be satisfied with the words of Paul, 'We are called and appointed to suffer.' It is as if he had said, 'Such is our condition as Christians; this is the road by which we must go if we would follow Christ.'
>
> Meanwhile, to comfort us in our weakness and to mitigate the vexation and sorrow which persecution might

cause us, a good reward is held forth. In suffering for the cause of God, we are walking step by step after the Son of God and have him for our guide. Were it simply said that Christians must pass through all the insults of the world boldly, prepared to meet death at all times and in whatever way God may be pleased to appoint, we might apparently have some pretext for replying, 'It is a strange road to go when there is uncertainty as to where it leads.' But when we are commanded to follow the Lord Jesus, his guidance is too good and honourable to be refused.[12]

Christ is our example; we are called to follow in his steps, and this journey will lead us to the cross. So writes the apostle Peter, who himself, according to tradition (probably reliable), was put to death under the ruthless persecution by Nero.

In 1 Peter 2:21, the apostle reminds all the godly in common as to what the condition of Christianity is, as though he had said that we are called by the Lord for this end: patiently to bear wrongs. He says in another place that we are appointed to this. Lest, however, this should seem grievous to us, he consoles us with the example of Christ. Nothing seems more unworthy and therefore less tolerable than undeservedly to suffer; but when we turn our eyes to the Son of God, this bitterness is mitigated, for who would refuse to follow him going before us?[13]

## Following Christ means bearing the cross

Only one person in all history carried the actual cross on which Christ was crucified. That person was Simon of Cyrene, who had come to Jerusalem to celebrate the Passover (Mark 15:21). Simon was passing by as the Roman soldiers were leading Jesus away to be crucified, and they forced him to carry the cross. Many others since then in some mysterious way have

carried the cross of Christ in response to his summons: 'Whoever desires to come after me, let him deny himself, and take up
his cross, and follow me' (Mark 8:34). Believers are united with
Christ in his death in such a manner that they are said to have
died with Christ and that their old nature was crucified with him
(Rom. 6:5-6). The bond of union with Christ is so vital to
followers of Christ that Paul is able to say, 'I have been crucified
with Christ; it is no longer I who live, but Christ lives in me; and
the life that I now live in the flesh I live by faith in the Son of
God, who loved me and gave himself for me' (Gal. 2:20).

Cross-bearing is not a way of life for those whose worldly
interests are the 'chief end' for which they live. Martin Luther
(1483–1546) was an older contemporary of Calvin's. Although
Calvin was at odds with Luther regarding some points of
doctrine — the Lord's Supper, for example — he had much in
common with the German Reformer. Regarding cross-bearing,
Thesis 21 of Luther's *Heidelberg disputation* is a statement with
which Calvin would have concurred:

> This is clear: He who does not know Christ does not
> know God hidden in suffering. Therefore he prefers
> works to suffering, glory to the cross, strength to weak-
> ness, wisdom to folly... These are the people whom the
> apostle Paul calls 'enemies of the cross of Christ'
> (Phil. 3:18), for they hate the cross and suffering and love
> works and the glory of works. Thus they call the good of
> the cross *evil* and the evil of a deed *good*. God can be
> found only in suffering and the cross, as has already been
> said.

Calvin, I say, would have concurred with Luther's thesis, as
the following excerpt from Calvin's commentary on 1 Thessalonians 3:3 implies:

> As all would gladly exempt themselves from the necessity
> of bearing the cross, Paul teaches that there is no reason

why believers should feel dismayed on the occasion of persecutions — as though it were a thing that was new and unusual — considering that this is our condition that the Lord has assigned to us. This manner of expression — *we are appointed to it* — is as though Paul had said that we are Christians on this condition. He says, however, that they *know* it, because, to the extent that they had been forewarned, it enabled them to fight more bravely. In addition to this, incessant afflictions made Paul contemptible among rude and ignorant persons. On this account he states that nothing had befallen him but what he had long before, in the manner of a prophet, foretold.

Suffering after Christ's example is far from disgraceful, though it may seem bitter and painful. The sufferings of Christ, after all, are the means of forgiveness of sin and of eternal glory. Hebrews 2:9-10 affirms that Jesus 'tasted death' for everyone who trusts in him, 'For it was fitting for him, for whom are all things and by whom are all things, in bringing many to glory, to make the captain of our salvation perfect through sufferings.' There is, then, a certain consolation for suffering Christians, namely, that Christ suffered for us and that by our own suffering we are 'prepared for glory', as Calvin says:

> It is a singular consolation, calculated to mitigate the bitterness of the cross, when the faithful hear that by sorrows and tribulations they are sanctified for glory as Christ himself was. Hence they see a sufficient reason why they should lovingly kiss the cross rather than dread it. And when this is the case, then doubtless the reproach of the cross of Christ immediately disappears and its glory shines forth; for who can despise what is sacred — no, what God sanctifies? Who can deem that ignominious by which we are prepared for glory? And yet both of these things are said here of the death of Christ.[14]

'The Spirit himself bears witness with our spirit that we are children of God, and if children, then heirs — heirs of God and joint heirs with Christ, if indeed we suffer with him, that we may also be glorified together' (Rom. 8:16-17). Commenting on this statement, Calvin says that we share a glorious inheritance with Christ, 'provided ... we follow him in the same way in which he has gone before'. The inheritance 'has already been conferred on Christ, whose partners we have become; but since Christ came to it by the cross, we must come to it in the same manner'. This will mean suffering and sacrifice, as it did for Christ.

When one suffers 'reproaches' for the sake of the gospel, Calvin says in another context, in his commentary on 1 Peter 4:14, there is often more bitterness in them than in the loss of goods, or in the 'torments or agonies of the body'. When I think of Christ's demand that we must be 'poor in spirit' in order to have a place in the kingdom of heaven, I think of J. Hudson Taylor, the pioneer Christian missionary to China, who not only left mother and father and a promising future in England, but also suffered indignities and physical abuse for the sake of the gospel. On one of the missionaries' journeys, they were approaching Tungchow when persecution began. Taylor prayed, 'And now, Lord, behold their threatenings, and grant unto thy servants that with all boldness they may speak thy Word.'

Shortly afterwards the missionaries were confronted by a dozen or more soldiers of the Imperial Army, who took them into custody, threatening and brutalizing them almost to the point of exhaustion. After being so harshly mistreated, however, they were 'thankful at having been able to preach Jesus in spite of Satan's malice', and were later given permission by the city's magistrate to distribute their books freely.[15]

Fellowship with Christ may mean suffering abuse, ridicule, torture, and even death. The apostles, of course, are the prime examples of fellowship with Christ and participation in his sufferings. Peter and other apostles were put in prison because they were teaching in the name of the Lord Jesus and healing the sick, thus demonstrating the saving power of Christ. They were miraculously released from the prison by 'an angel of the Lord' and they afterwards resumed their teaching. Again the authorities took the matter in hand; after beating them and commanding them not to speak in the name of Jesus, they let them go. As they left the council chamber, they rejoiced that they were 'counted worthy to suffer shame for his name' (Acts 5:41). Calvin shows the significance of the apostles' painful experience for all who suffer persecution for the gospel:

> That which is counted most reproachful among men ex-cels in dignity and glory in the sight of God and his an-gels. We know that the kind of death which Christ suf-fered was most shameful, and yet he triumphed most nobly upon the cross. So, when we are made like him, we may worthily boast that it is a point of singular excel-lency that we suffer rebuke in the sight of the world. Thus Paul boasts of the marks of Christ (Gal. 6:17). For we must here respect the cause which associates us with Christ, who not only swallows up the shame of the world with his glory, but also turns reproaches, slanders, and mockery of the world into great honour.[16]

Paul endured not only slander and threats against his life, but also physical abuse — beatings, scourging, and stoning. Writing to the Galatians, he said, 'I bear on my body the marks of the Lord Jesus' (Gal. 6:17). Calvin asks, what were those marks?

> The marks of Jesus are imprisonment, chains, scourging, blows, stoning, and every kind of injurious treatment which he had incurred in bearing testimony to the gospel. Earthly warfare has its honours, in conferring which a general holds out to public view the bravery of a soldier. So Christ our leader has his own marks, of which he makes abundant use for conferring on some of his fol-

lowers a high distinction. These marks, however, differ from the other in one important respect: they partake of the nature of the cross, and in the sight of the world are disgraceful. This is suggested by the word translated *marks* (*stigmata*), for it literally denotes the marks with which barbarian slaves or fugitives or malefactors were usually branded. Paul, therefore, can hardly be said to use a figure of speech when he boasts of bearing those marks with which Christ is accustomed to honour his most distinguished soldiers, which in the eyes of the world were attended by shame and disgrace, but which before God and the angels surpass all the honours of the world.[17]

## We are called to renounce worldly goods

Jesus told his disciples that 'It is hard for a rich man to enter the kingdom of heaven' and 'It is easier for a camel to go through the eye of a needle than for a rich man to enter the kingdom of God' (Matt. 19:23-24). Jesus himself, as far as we know, had few possessions, and he counselled his followers to renounce the love of worldly goods.

Speaking for the disciples, Peter said to Jesus, 'Look, we have left everything and followed you; what then will we get?' (Matt. 19:27). Calvin seems not to have a great deal of sympathy with the disciples, though he does think that Peter's question had some merit:

Since they led a life of privation and wandering, and suffered insults and various vexations without hope of a better future, Peter asks rightly whether it was for nothing that they had left behind everything they had and devoted themselves to Christ. It was absurd that when they had been despoiled of everything by the Lord, they should not receive back more than they had lost.

But then, what were all those things they had left behind? Being poor and low-class folk, they did not even
have a house to leave behind; and so their boasting was
nothing less than ridiculous. Our own experience shows
that people commonly overestimate the things they do in
the service of God. There are people who are hardly
more than beggars ... but they go around arrogantly
complaining that they have made great sacrifices for the
sake of the gospel. There was some excuse for the disciples, however; although they did not possess splendid
fortunes, they lived by the labour of their hands and were
no less happy in their homes than people of great riches.
And we know that humble people who are used to a
quiet and decent life find it harder to be torn away from
their wives and children than those who are driven by
ambition, or thrown this way and that by the winds of
prosperous fortune. Of course, unless there was some
reward waiting for the disciples, they would have been
foolish to change their way of life. Still, although one
might excuse them on that ground, they were wrong to
demand a taste of triumph before their warfare was finished.[18]

Calvin himself lived a very frugal life, but it can hardly be
said that he literally left *all* and followed Christ, though he did
renounce the *love* of worldly goods, and he counselled others to
do the same. Monsieur de Falais, one of Calvin's contemporaries, was persecuted for his allegiance to the Reformers and was
reduced to poverty, his property having been sequestered by
the authorities. Calvin wrote a letter to him in which he said,
'We know not what it is to part with everything for the love of
him, until he has brought us to the test.' Calvin's view was that
whenever one has renounced his love of worldly goods he has
as much as 'sold all', but the real proof of this spiritual poverty is
'patiently to endure the loss of worldly goods, and without any

regret, when it pleases our heavenly Father that we should be despoiled of them'.[19]

## We are privileged to share in Christ's sufferings

'It is a real comfort to us that when we endure many miseries, which are called adversities and calamities, we partake of the sufferings of Christ... While we are "participating in his death", we are also being prepared for sharing his glorious resurrection.'[20]

Mrs. Zhang Hongmei, a Chinese house-church Christian, was arrested by police in Dongmiaodong village in Scandong province on 29 October 2003. That afternoon, police summoned Zhang's family and asked them to pay a bribe of 3,000 RMB (£217 or $400 USD) to secure her release. As this sum is more than a year's wages for many peasant families, they were unable to pay the money. When Zang's family went to the police station in the evening and pleaded with police officers, they saw her bound with heavy chains, injured and unable to speak with them. Next day they were again summoned to the police station, where they were told that Zhang had died at noon. An autopsy revealed wounds to her face, hands, and legs, and serious internal bleeding.[21]

In what sense did Zhang Hongmei share in Christ's sufferings when she endured such brutality and death at the hands of ruthless infidels? The answer of course is that she suffered and died for the sake of Christ. She died as Christ had died — for righteousness' sake. To use Paul's phrase, she was 'conformed to his death' and thus she participated in his sufferings.

When Christians are persecuted for their 'fellowship in the gospel', they are not sharing in the redemptive work of Christ, except in the sense that, in common with all believers, they enjoy the benefits of his redemptive work. The death of Christ, by which we are redeemed, is an all-sufficient sacrifice for the reconciliation of sinners to God. It need not be — indeed it

cannot be — augmented by any amount of suffering for his
sake. Calvin explains precisely how Christ's cross and ours are
related. After reminding us that 'Those whom the Lord has
chosen and honoured with his saving grace can expect to live
"a hard, laborious, troubled life ... full of many and various
kinds of evils"', Calvin goes on to say:

> All the children of God are destined to be *conformed to
> Christ.* Hence it affords us great consolation in hard and
> difficult circumstances, which men deem evil and ad-
> verse, to think that *we are holding fellowship with the
> sufferings of Christ* — that as he passed to celestial glory
> through a labyrinth of many woes, so we too are con-
> ducted to that place through various tribulations... Paul
> speaks in this way of his desire to follow Christ: 'that I
> may know him, and the power of his resurrection, and
> *the fellowship of his sufferings, being conformed to his
> death'* (Phil. 3:10). How powerfully it should soften the
> bitterness of the cross to think that, the more we are af-
> flicted with adversity, the surer we are made of our fel-
> lowship with Christ. By communion with him our suffer-
> ings are not only blessed to us, but tend greatly to the
> furtherance of our salvation.[22]

Is it then a *privilege* to suffer in conformity with Christ's
sufferings? Paul must think so, for when he boasts of the
Thessalonians' faith and patience 'in all your persecutions that
you endure', he insists that their suffering for Christ is evidence
of God's righteous judgement — 'that you may be counted
worthy of the kingdom of God, for which you also suffer'
(2 Thess. 4-5). Does suffering for Christ's sake make one *worthy*
of entrance into God's kingdom? Calvin explains:

> The worthiness spoken of is not that of merit, but as God
> the Father would have those whom he has chosen for his
> children to be conformed to Christ the firstborn, and as it

behoved Christ first to suffer and then to enter into his glory, so we also, through much tribulation, enter the kingdom of heaven. Therefore, while we suffer tribulation for the name of Christ, we in a manner receive the marks with which God usually stamps the sheep of his flock (Gal. 6:17). Thus we are accounted worthy of the kingdom of God, because we bear in our body the marks of our Lord and Master, these being the insignia of the children of God. It is in this sense that we are to understand these passages: 'always carrying about in the body the dying of the Lord Jesus, that the life of Jesus also may be manifested in our body' (2 Cor. 4:10) and 'that I may know him and the power of his resurrection, and the fellowship of his sufferings, being conformed to his death' (Phil. 3:10).[23]

The essence of our sharing in the sufferings of Christ, then, is *conformity to Christ* in our union with him, our self-denial and sacrifices for the kingdom. None of these, as Calvin has made clear, make us worthy — except by God's grace.

Christians who live in countries where Communist ideologies prevail or where militant Islamic operatives torment them need our prayers and support; but primarily they need the comfort of the Scriptures, that they might have hope, as Paul says in Romans 15:4. When one bears the cross and 'When there is need of comfort,' writes Calvin, 'it is admirably afforded in these words: "We are troubled on every side, yet not distressed; we are perplexed, but not in despair; persecuted, but not forsaken; cast down, but not destroyed, always bearing about in the body the dying of the Lord Jesus, that the life also of Jesus might be manifested in our body. If we be dead with him, we shall also live with him; if we suffer, we shall also reign with him."'[24]

Calvin takes up this theme in his commentary on Philippians 3:10, which is quoted above. The ground of comfort for Paul — and for Calvin — was their fellowship with Christ, not only in his sufferings, but especially in his resurrection. Calvin writes:

> Christ is rightly known when we feel how powerful his death and resurrection are, and how effective they are in us. All things pertaining to our salvation are there furnished to us: expiation and destruction of sin, freedom from condemnation, satisfaction of God's justice for the forgiveness of sin, victory over death, the attainment of righteousness, and the hope of a blessed immortality.
>
> Let everyone, therefore, who has become through faith a partaker of Christ's benefits acknowledge the condition that is presented to him — that the whole life be conformed to his death.
>
> There is a twofold participation and fellowship in the death of Christ. The one is inward — what is called the 'mortification of the flesh' or the 'crucifixion of the old man' (i.e., the sinful human nature apart from grace)... The other is outward — what is called 'the mortification of the outward man'. It is the endurance of the cross, which Paul discusses in the eighth chapter of Romans, and here also, if I am not mistaken. For after introducing along with this the power of his resurrection, Christ crucified is set before us, that we may follow him through tribulations and distresses; and so the resurrection of the dead is expressly mentioned, that we may know that we must die before we live.
>
> This, however, is a choice consolation: in all our miseries we are partakers of Christ's cross, if we are his members — so that through afflictions the way is opened up for us to everlasting blessedness, as we read elsewhere: 'If we die with him, we shall also live with him; if we suffer with him, we shall also reign with him' (2 Tim. 2:11).
>
> We must all therefore be prepared for this — that our whole life will represent nothing else than the image of

death, until it produces death itself, since the life of Christ is nothing less than a prelude to death. We enjoy, however, in the meantime, this consolation — that the end is everlasting blessedness. For the death of Christ is connected with the resurrection. Hence Paul says that he is conformed to Christ's death, in order that he may attain to the glory of the resurrection. Paul's phrase, 'if by any means I may attain ...' does not indicate doubt, but expresses difficulty, with a view to stimulate our earnest endeavour; for it is no easy contest, inasmuch as we must struggle against so many and so serious hindrances.[25]

One can understand why Calvin, in a letter written 10 June 1549, after enduring so much trouble, wrote, 'You must remember ... that wherever we go the cross of Jesus Christ will follow us.'[26] Following a dispute regarding the Lord's Supper and excommunication, Calvin and his fellow Reformer Farel had been expelled from Geneva by the General Council. Calvin went to Bern, then to Zürich, with Farel. Soon he moved on to Basle, hoping to live down his bitter defeat, but he remained there only briefly and then went to Strasbourg. Trouble followed him wherever he went, or so it seemed to him. The troubles he endured for the sake of the truth were, in his view, the cross of Christ.

The cross, Calvin writes, is useful to us in two ways:

It is by the cross that God tries our faith and that we become partakers with Christ... Let us remember that the trial of our faith is most necessary and that we thus ought willingly to obey God who provides for our salvation. The chief consolation, however, is to be derived from *fellowship with Christ.* Hence Peter, in 1 Peter 4:12-14, not only forbids us to think it strange when God sets persecution before us, but also bids us to rejoice. It is, indeed, a cause of joy when God tries our faith by persecution; but the other joy far surpasses it — that is, when the Son of

God allots to us the same course of life with himself, so that he might lead us with himself to a blessed participation in heavenly glory. For we must bear in mind this truth, that we have the dying of Christ in our flesh, in order that his life may be manifested in us.[27]

That sharing Christ's sufferings and having 'the dying of Christ in our flesh' is a cause of joy is demonstrated in Paul's sufferings for the good of the church. Though tested to the utmost by brutal beatings and malicious criticism, Paul could say that he rejoiced in his sufferings for the churches. He was an honourable apostle of Christ, but his detractors considered his imprisonments and persecutions proof that he was an impostor. To Paul, however, suffering on behalf of Christ's body, the church, proved the opposite — that his apostleship was genuine, for he had been appointed not by any human agency but by God himself. And because he saw the fruits of his labour — the Colossians' faith in Christ and their love towards their fellow believers — Paul was able to rejoice in his sufferings for them. Not only so, *but he was sharing in the sufferings of Christ* (Col. 1:24). Calvin writes,

> Paul assigns a reason why he is joyful in his sufferings. It is because he is in this thing a partner with Christ, and nothing can be happier to all the pious than to know that in all tribulations, especially in so far as they suffer anything for the sake of the gospel, they are partakers of the cross of Christ and that they may enjoy fellowship with him in a blessed resurrection.[28]

Paul goes beyond expressing joy in his suffering. He declares that by suffering for the church he is filling up what is lacking in the afflictions of Christ. He states in Colossians 1:24-25: 'I now rejoice in my sufferings for you, and *fill up in my flesh what is lacking in the afflictions of Christ,* for the sake of his body, which is the church, of which I became a minister according to the stewardship from God which was given to me for you, to fulfil the word of God.'

We misinterpret Paul if we understand him to be saying that the sufferings endured by Christ for the redemption of believers were insufficient and needed to be completed by the sufferings of his followers. Paul has already spoken of the all-sufficiency of the redemptive work of Christ, 'in whom we have redemption through his blood, the forgiveness of sins' (Col. 1:14). So it is, of course, impossible to add anything to what Christ has accomplished by his suffering.

Andrew T. Lincoln has given an interpretation which is consonant with Calvin's understanding of what it means to be a partner in suffering with Christ:

> In any case [the verse in question] seems to assert that the sufferings of Christ are not the redemptive sufferings of Christ ... but the subsequent afflictions of Paul for the church in connection with his witness to the gospel. They can be called the afflictions of Christ in the sense that Paul actively participates in the same pattern of suffering that Christ experienced... [Christ's sufferings] are lacking so long as the work of proclamation is incomplete — that is, until the *parousia* [second coming]. Paul, as the suffering apostle to the Gentiles, is depicted, then, as playing a major part in making up the deficiency through his unique missionary role. In this way his share in the afflictions of Christ are not redemptive but missionary in character. He is portrayed as rejoicing in such suffering because it is for the sake of Gentile converts and, therefore, by no means meaningless. Instead, his suffering is part of the fulfilment of God's plan in bringing in the consummation through the worldwide proclamation of the gospel.[29]

Calvin understands the 'deficiency' of the afflictions of Christ in the light of the unity between Christ and the members of his body, the church. In Paul's letters to the churches, especially

Romans and 1 Corinthians, the human body is an illustration of the intimate relationship between Christ and believers (1 Cor. 12-27). This being the case, Calvin observes:

> As, therefore, Christ has suffered *once* in his own person, so he suffers *daily* in his members, and in this way there are *filled up* those sufferings which the Father has appointed by his decree. There is here a second consideration, which ought to support our minds and comfort them in afflictions: that it is thus fixed and determined by the providence of God that we must be conformed to Christ in endurance of the cross, and that the fellowship that we have with him extends to this also.
>
> Paul adds a third reason — that his sufferings are advantageous not merely to a few, but to the whole church. He had previously stated that he suffered in behalf of the Colossians, and now he declares still further that the advantage extends to the whole church. What could be clearer, less forced, or simpler than this exposition, which states that Paul is joyful in persecution because he considers, in accordance with what he writes elsewhere, that we must carry about in our body the dying of the Lord Jesus, that his life also may be manifested in us? (2 Corinthians 4:10). Furthermore, he considers that we must not refuse the condition which God has appointed for his church, namely, that the members of Christ may have a suitable correspondence with the head (i.e., Christ), and that afflictions must be cheerfully endured, inasmuch as they are profitable to all the pious and promote the welfare of the whole church by adorning the teaching of the gospel.[30]

Calvin concludes his exposition regarding Paul's filling up what is lacking in the afflictions of Christ with a further clarifying statement: 'We know that the ministry was committed to him, not of *redeeming* the church but of *edifying* it; and he immediately afterwards expressly acknowledges this. This also is what he writes to Timothy, that he endures all things for the sake of the elect, that they may obtain the salvation which is in Christ Jesus (2 Tim. 2:10)... Notice under what character Paul suffers for the church — not to *give* the price of redemption, but to *proclaim* it.' [31]

Paul's filling up what is lacking in the afflictions of Christ applies not only to Paul, but also to all of Christ's followers. Individual Christians in many countries are suffering, as we have noted — Chinese Christians Pastor Gong, Philip Xu, and Zhang Yinan; and Vietnamese Christians Ly Chin Sang, Ly Chin Quang, Vang My Ly, and Vang Chin Sang, who 'organ-ized and led weekly worship services in a house church and were sentenced to prison for disturbing public order'. But inasmuch as they, as well as we, are all members of one body, we share not only in the fellowship of Christ's sufferings, but in the sufferings of all believers. Paul tells the Corinthians that the church is one body and, consequently, 'The members should have the same care for one another. And if one member suffers, all the members suffer with it' (1 Cor.12:25-26). The fellowship of Christ's sufferings extends beyond the local congregation, however; it is the burden — and the privilege — of the whole church of Jesus Christ throughout the world.

Paul exhorts the churches of Galatia to 'Bear one another's burdens, and so fulfil the law of Christ' (Gal. 6:2). Calvin limits those burdens of fellow believers to 'the weaknesses or sins under which we groan' and he states that the members of Christ's body ought to relieve those burdens by 'mild and friendly correction' if any one has been 'overtaken in any trespass'. Calvin rightly understands mutual burden-bearing in terms of its context in Galatians 6, regarding any member who has fallen into sin. But surely the law of Christ, which requires that we love one another as Christ has loved us (John 13:34), includes praying for those who suffer afflictions — especially those who suffer for their Christian faith — and reaching out to them with loving regard and kindly support.

Congregations in North America and Britain, and in the 'Christian West' generally, have not been well informed regarding the vicious persecution of individual Christians and whole congregations in places like Beijing and Lisoning province in China, Ha Gong Province in Vietnam, in northern Nigeria, and in many other regions of Africa and Southeast Asia. And the aid sent to beleaguered Christians by the churches has been sporadic and minimal. Much more needs to be done to heighten awareness of the persecution of Christians today. An abundance of information is available online (keyword: persecution), and if pastors were informed about the plight of Christians in Asia, Africa, and the Middle East, then the Holy Spirit might induce church members to open their hearts and share in the sufferings of fellow Christians, which are the sufferings of Christ.

## The church is 'the communion of saints'

'The sacred Supper of Christ', to use Calvin's term, is a sacrament of the whole church. 'The cup of blessing which we bless, is it not the communion of the blood of Christ? The bread which we break, is it not the communion of the body of Christ?' Paul raises those questions in order to make the point that in the Lord's Supper Christians together share in the sufferings and death of Christ. The word *communion* in the verse just cited (1 Cor. 10:16) is *koinonia;* its meaning is participation, sharing, fellowship, communion. Calvin understands the blessed cup and the broken bread as a sign that 'Believers are united together in Christ's blood, so as to become one body.'[32] The church the world over is one body because its members, though separate congregations, are partakers of the same cup and the same bread. 'But from where', Calvin asks, 'comes that *koinonia* (communion) between us, but from this, that we are united to Christ in such a way that "We are flesh of his flesh and bone of his bones" (Eph. 5:30). For we must first be incorporated (so to speak) into Christ in order that we may be united to each other... We may conclude, therefore, that the communion of the blood is that connection which we have with the blood of Christ, when he engrafts all of us together into his body, that he may live in us and we in him.'[33]

The communion of the saints has far-reaching implications for our responsibility to relieve the afflictions of the suffering church. This responsibility is implicit in the *Heidelberg catechism*'s answer to the question, 'What do you understand by "the communion of saints"? First, that believers, all and every one, as members of Christ, have communion with him and share all his treasures and gifts. Second, that everyone is duty-bound to use his gifts readily and cheerfully for the benefit and well being of the other members.'

This understanding of the communal nature of the church reflects Calvin's viewpoint. The term 'communion of saints', he writes, 'ought not to be neglected, because it excellently expresses the character of the church; as though it had been said that the saints are united in the fellowship of Christ on this condition, that whatever benefits God confers upon them, they should mutually communicate to each other'.[34]

It is clear from everything Calvin has to say regarding the suffering church that in the New Testament Christ is the focal point of everything. All human suffering and relief from its misery converge in him. As we consider Christ's experience of suffering, we know that his primary mission was to proclaim the nearness of the kingdom of heaven and to liberate suffering people from the pain and misery of their afflictions. In the gospels we witness Jesus going from village to village teaching and healing the sick and raising the dead to life. His entire ministry from beginning to end was committed to making whole the bodies and spirits of people whom he touched and taught.

The gospels portray a world that knew suffering and desperately needed a physician who could heal and restore those who were afflicted. The sick and suffering crowds that gathered about Jesus cry out in their misery for his help. In the midst of

this world of suffering in its many forms, Jesus stands in solidar-
ity with the afflicted, the poor, and the humble. His ministry to
the sick and suffering of his day is a sign of his ultimate triumph
over sickness and sorrow and death. In his passion Jesus
identifies with those who suffer. Even in his triumph, the risen
Christ still bears his wounds, which are a sign of his fellowship
with all who suffer. And when his triumph over sin and death
results in new heavens and a new earth, 'God will wipe away
every tear from their eyes; there shall be no more death, nor
sorrow, nor crying. There shall be no more pain, for the former
things have passed away' (Rev. 21:4).

*Suffering — understanding the love of God*

Selections from the writings of John Calvin

---

## Chapter 11

## The hope of glory

---

'Faith is the foundation
on which hope rests; hope
nourishes and sustains
faith.'

# II.

# The hope of glory

*O glorious resurrection! O God of Abraham and of all our fathers, in thee have the faithful trusted during so many past ages, and none of them have trusted in vain. I also will hope.*

Idelette de Bure[1]

Shortly before midnight on 14 April 1912, the British luxury liner *Titanic*, weighing 46,000 gross tons, was steaming in the Atlantic on its maiden voyage from Southampton to New York, when it struck an iceberg about ninety-five miles south of the Grand Banks of Newfoundland. The massive ship sustained severe damage in the collision and sank in less than three hours. More than 1,500 of the 2,220 passengers died as the ship slowly came to rest on the ocean floor, about 12,000 feet below the surface. There were only about half enough lifeboats on board to accommodate the passengers and crew — probably because the ship had been proclaimed unsinkable and more lifeboats were deemed unnecessary.

One can only imagine the panic felt by the terror-stricken people aboard the ill-fated ship. As they scrambled on deck and below deck to search for a place of safety, a grim mixture of fear and hope churned within them. Fear and hope are often mingled when disaster strikes and there seems to be no place to turn for safety or rescue.

Life situations are indeed hopeless sometimes. When death, fearsome and inevitable, is imminent, dread can overshadow hope for survival as life ebbs away. Still, there is hope for those whose faith is anchored in Christ. 'The hope of glory', he is called, and those whose lives are bound up with him have hope that looks beyond the shores of the present life and envisions by faith 'a better, that is, a heavenly country' (Heb. 11:16). The writer of the book of Hebrews cites the promise of God as the basis of Christian hope, and he desires that every believer will possess 'the full assurance of hope until the end' (Heb. 6:11). God, he states, gave his word and confirmed it with an oath, so that 'by [these] two immutable things, in which it is impossible for God to lie, we might have strong consolation, who have fled for refuge to lay hold of the hope set before us. This hope we have as an anchor for the soul, both sure and steadfast...' (Heb. 6:11, 18-19). Calvin writes:

> It is a striking likeness when the writer of Hebrews com-pares faith leaning on God's Word to an anchor. Doubt-less, as long as we sojourn in this world we do not stand on firm ground, but are tossed here and there as it were in the midst of the sea, which is indeed very turbulent, for Satan is incessantly stirring up innumerable storms which would immediately upset and sink our vessel, were we not to cast our anchor fast in the deep. For nowhere does a haven appear to our eyes, but wherever we look water alone is in view. Waves also threaten us; but in the same way that the anchor is cast through the waters into a dark and unseen place and, lying there, keeps the vessel, beaten by the waves, from being overwhelmed, so must our hope be fixed on the invisible God. There is this dif-ference: the anchor is cast downward into the sea, which has the earth as its bottom; but our hope rises upwards and soars aloft, for in the world it finds nothing on which it can stand — nor ought it to cleave to created things, but to rest on God alone.
>
> As the cable by which the anchor is suspended joins the vessel with the earth through a long and dark inter-

mediate space, so the truth of God is a bond to connect us with him, so that no distance of place and no darkness can prevent us from cleaving to him. Thus when united to God, though we must struggle with continual storms, we are yet beyond the peril of shipwreck. Hence the writer of Hebrews says that this anchor is sure and steadfast, or safe and firm. It may indeed be that by the violence of the waves the anchor may be plucked off, or the cable be broken, or the beaten ship be torn to pieces. This happens on the sea, but the power of God to sustain us is wholly different, and so also is the strength of hope and the firmness of his Word.[2]

## Christ, the hope of glory

How is Christ our hope of glory? The answer is not difficult. Adam's sin is the sin of all. With Adam as our representative, all humankind 'sinned in him, and fell with him, in his first transgression'.[3] Thus Paul can say that 'All have sinned and fall short of the glory of God' (Rom. 3:23). The glory of God is his image, in which all were made. Since all have sinned, that image, or glory, of God is blemished. Through Christ, whose glory is the image of God (2 Cor. 4:4), sinners are renewed according to the image of their Creator (Col. 3:10). 'And we, who ... reflect the Lord's glory, are being transformed into his likeness, with ever-increasing glory, which comes from the Lord, who is the Spirit' (2 Cor. 3:18, NIV). Christ then is our hope of salvation, our hope of heaven, our hope of glory, as Paul states in Colossians 1:27. When we have Christ as our hope of glory, Calvin writes, we are assured that 'Nothing is lacking to us for complete blessedness when we have obtained Christ. This, however, is a wonderful work of God that in earthen and frail vessels (2 Cor. 4:7) the hope of heavenly glory resides.'[4]

The hope we have in Christ is totally reliable, a fact which should be comforting when we are facing surgery or any trouble with which we cannot cope. When we have been justified by faith, that is, forgiven and accounted righteous, 'We have peace with God through our Lord Jesus Christ ... and rejoice in hope of the glory of God. And not only that, but we also glory in tribulations, knowing that tribulation produces perseverance; and perseverance, character; and character, hope. Now hope does not disappoint, because the love of God has been poured out in our hearts by the Holy Spirit who was given to us' (Rom. 5:1-5).

We have many disappointments in life: our carefully laid plans don't work out; the job we hoped for is given to someone else; the money we invested has diminished; a son we have reared hoping he would commit his life to Christ did not turn out the way we had hoped. Hopes are not always realized. But hope linked with faith in Christ — hope for salvation — can never be disappointed, because nothing can separate us from the love of God, which has been poured out in our hearts. Calvin says,

> Hope in Christ does not disappoint; that is, it regards sal-
> vation as most certain. It therefore appears that the Lord
> tries us by adversities for this end — that our salvation
> may thereby be gradually advanced. Those evils cannot
> then render us miserable which do in some way promote
> our happiness. And thus is proved what Paul had said,
> that the godly have reasons for glorying in the midst of
> their afflictions.[5]

## Christian hope rests upon faith in Christ

Hope is indissolubly linked to faith, not only because faith and hope share a strong element of confidence, but because faith is focused specifically on Christ. That is why Christ can be called the hope of glory. In many different ways Paul joins hope with faith and knowledge, and faith and love, which together give expression to the Christian life as lived 'in Christ'. Hope, then, rests on Christ (Gal. 5:5); it is the hope revealed in the gospel (Col. 1:23), the hope of the Lord's calling (Eph. 1:18), and, together with one Spirit, one body, one faith, one baptism, it is linked as 'one hope of your calling' (Eph. 4:4), and as such 'It represents the new life given in Christ and wrought by the Spirit.'[6]

Without faith there can be no hope, and, conversely, where there is faith, hope is bound to be joined to it. Calvin insists on the close relationship of faith and hope:

> Now, wherever living faith shall be found, it must neces-sarily be joined with the hope of eternal salvation as an inseparable concomitant, or rather, faith must originate and produce it, since the lack of this hope would prove us to be utterly destitute of faith, however eloquently and beautifully we might discourse concerning it. For if faith is ... a certain persuasion of the truth of God, that it can neither lie nor deceive us, nor be frustrated, then they who have felt this assurance likewise expect a time to arrive when God will accomplish his promises. According to their persuasion, God's promises cannot be anything but true; so, in short, hope is nothing other than expecta-tion of those things which faith has believed to be truly promised by God. Thus faith believes in the veracity of God; hope expects the manifestation of it in due time. Faith believes him to be our Father; hope expects him always to act towards us in this character. Faith believes that eternal life is given to us; hope expects it one day to be revealed. Faith is the foundation on which hope rests; hope nourishes and sustains faith.
>
> As no one can have any expectation from God, unless one has first believed his promises, so also the weakness of our faith must be sustained and cherished by patient hope and expectation, lest it grow weary and faint. Hope, while it is silently expecting the Lord, restrains faith, so

that it will not be so impatient; it also confirms faith, so that it may not waver in the divine promises or begin to doubt the truth of them. Hope refreshes faith, that it may not grow weary; it extends faith to the farthest goal, so that it may not fail in mid-course, or even at the entrance of it. Finally, hope, by continually renewing and restoring faith, causes it frequently to persevere with more vigour than hope itself.[7]

The prayer of David in Psalm 57, uttered with confidence that God will protect him from vicious enemies, is an expression both of trust and of hope: 'Be merciful to me, O God, be merciful to me! For my soul trusts in you; and in the shadow of your wings I will make my refuge, until these calamities have passed away' (v. 1). Calvin observes,

There are seasons when we are privileged to enjoy the calm sunshine of prosperity; but there is not a day of our lives in which we may not suddenly be overtaken by storms of affliction, and it is necessary that we are per-suaded that God will cover us with his wings. To hope the psalmist adds prayer. Those, indeed, who have placed their trust in God will always direct their prayers to him, and David gives here a practical proof of his hope — by showing that he appealed to God in his emergencies. In addressing God, he applies to him an honourable title ('God Most High', v. 2), commending him as the God who performs whatever he has promised, or (as we may understand the expression) who carries forward to perfection the work which he has begun.[8]

Thus the apostle Peter assures his readers that through the trial of their faith, which is more precious than gold that is tested by fire, they will in the end receive, through faith, the salvation of their souls. Tied to their faith, he states, is 'a living hope

through the resurrection of Jesus Christ from the dead'
(1 Peter 1:3, 5, 7, 9). Calvin's comment on verse 9 follows:

> Peter reminds the faithful that they ought to direct all their
> thoughts to eternal salvation. This world holds all our
> affections ensnared by its allurements; this life and all
> things belonging to the body are great impediments
> which prevent us from applying our minds to the con-
> templation of the future and spiritual life. Hence the apos-
> tle sets before us this future life as a subject of deep medi-
> tation, and he implies that the loss of all other things is to
> be deemed as nothing, provided our souls are saved. By
> saying that they are receiving the end, or goal, of their
> faith, he takes away all doubt, in order that they might
> more cheerfully go on, being certain of obtaining salva-
> tion. In the meantime, however, he shows what the 'end'
> of faith is, lest they should become over-anxious because
> it is as yet deferred... We learn from the apostle's words
> that salvation is not otherwise obtained than by faith, and
> we know that faith leans solely on the promise of unwar-
> ranted adoption. If that is so, doubtless salvation is not
> owing to the merits of works, nor can it be hoped for on
> account of works.
>
> But why does he mention salvation of *souls* only,
> when the glory of a resurrection is promised to our bod-
> ies? As the soul is immortal, salvation is properly ascribed
> to it, as Paul says: 'that the soul may be saved in the day
> of the Lord' (1 Cor. 5:5). So it is the same as if Peter had
> said 'eternal salvation', for there is an implied comparison
> between it and the fading life which belongs to the body.
> At the same time, the body is not excluded from a par-
> ticipation in glory, since it is annexed to the soul.[9]

The connection between faith and hope and between hope
and eternal glory frequently appears in Calvin's writings and in
his preaching. The following excerpt from one of his commen-

taries should be encouraging to anyone who lacks assurance of salvation.

> Our understanding of the divine favour to which faith is said to refer includes the possession of salvation and eternal life... Faith does not promise us length of days, riches, and honours (unless the Lord is pleased that any of these should be appointed us), but is contented with the assurance that God will never fail us, however poor we may be in regard to present comforts. The chief security lies in the expectation of future life, which is placed beyond doubt by the Word of God. Whatever are the miseries and calamities which await the children of God in this world, they cannot cause his favour to stop bringing complete happiness.

Calvin thinks that 'The most remarkable passage of all of Scripture is that of Job', who has unshakeable hope of immortality and assurance of faith: 'I know that my Redeemer lives, and that he shall stand at last on the earth; and after my skin is destroyed, this I know, that in my flesh I shall see God, whom I shall see for myself, and my eyes shall behold, and not another' (Job 19:25-27).

> Those who would make a display of the acuteness of their intellect pretend that these words of Job are to be understood to mean the day when Job expected that God would deal more gently with him, and not the last resurrection. Granting that this is partly meant, we shall, however, compel them, whether they will or not, to admit that Job never could have attained to such fullness of hope if his thoughts had risen no higher than the earth. It must, therefore, be confessed that he who saw that the Redeemer would be present with him when lying in the grave must have raised his eyes to a future immortality. To those who think only of the present life, death is the

extremity of despair; but it could not destroy the hope of
Job. 'Though he should slay me', said Job, 'yet will I trust
him' (Job 13:15).[10]

## Waiting and hoping for the coming of Christ

In 1555, when Calvin was a pastor of the church of St Pierre in
Geneva, he preached seventeen sermons on Titus. His sermon
on Titus 2:11-14 is about grace, godliness, and glory. The text
reads, 'For the grace of God that brings salvation has appeared
to all men, teaching us that, denying ungodliness and worldly
lusts, we should live soberly, righteously, and godly in the
present age, looking for the blessed hope and glorious appear-
ing of our great God and Saviour Jesus Christ, who gave
himself for us, that he might redeem us from every lawless
deed.' In the sermon Calvin reminds his hearers that the
church, as it waits for Christ's coming, will be put to the test, but
must continue to wait and hope for Christ's coming to judge the
world.

> Here Paul declares that there are good reasons why we
> should occupy ourselves in God's service throughout our
> lives, and why God should test us regarding our service to
> him. Nevertheless, since we are grieved by the length of
> time that we must continue to endure trials, he also
> teaches us that our service must be marked by waiting
> and hoping for the coming of our Lord Jesus Christ. He
> shows us that we must not muse upon the present state of
> the world if we intend to be steadfast and constant in
> serving God. On the contrary, we must give close atten-
> tion to the hope we have been given, that the Son of
> God will come to judge the world.
>     Let us bear in mind accordingly that God intends to
> test his faithful ones. He permits and ordains their grief
> and vexation during this earthly life. They pass through

many troubles, and things do not fall out as they would like them to… But we must understand that he has good reason for doing all this and that we need to be exercised in this way. If a man were to deliver silver or gold to us, we would want to know whether it was good or not; and if we doubted its genuineness, we would test it by fire. Is not our faith more precious (as Peter says) than all the corruptible metals that are tested so carefully?[11]

Calvin exhorts his congregation regarding the need to continue in diligence and hope. In view of the shortness and swiftness of life, he says, 'We will soon have finished our race and therefore we ought not to faint. We must also have an eye to the hope to which we are called.'[12]

Romans 8:17-18 is a testimony of hope that has encouraged many of God's children. It puts their suffering in a perspective that sees beyond our life in the world to our life in glory. Inasmuch as God's children are joint heirs with Christ, we are destined to suffer with him that we may also be glorified with him: 'For I consider that the sufferings of this present time are not worthy to be compared with the glory which shall be revealed in us' (v. 18). Calvin comments,

It ought not to be grievous to us if we must pass through various afflictions into celestial glory, since these, when compared with the greatness of that glory, are of the least importance. Paul implies that the afflictions of the world are such as pass away quickly. The comparison of suffering with the greatness of glory lightens the heaviness of the cross, in order to confirm the minds of the faithful in patience.[13]

The salvation which God's children obtain, Paul says, is 'in Jesus Christ with eternal glory' (2 Tim. 2:10). One of my friends, a former associate, is seriously ill with cancer. His physicians have not given him encouragement for recovery. He recently told me that of late he has been thinking much about heaven and the glory that awaits all believers. He knows, even in a time of suffering, that eternal glory is the reward for a life lived in faith and hope. Calvin had a similar view of eternal glory:

> This is the end of the salvation which we obtain in Christ; for our salvation is to live to God. This salvation begins with our regeneration and is completed by our perfect deliverance, when God takes us away from the miseries of this mortal life and gathers us into his kingdom. To this salvation is added participation in heavenly — that is, divine — glory. Therefore, in order to magnify the grace of Christ, the apostle gave to salvation the name *eternal glory*.[14]

Paul, as we have noted, states that for those who have been justified by faith, hope does not disappoint, because grace reigns 'through righteousness to eternal life through Jesus Christ our Lord' (Rom. 5:5, 21). Calvin's comments on Psalm 61:5 should encourage God's children in a time of serious illness to trust in God's promises and to hope for eternal blessedness:

> God never disappoints his servants, but crowns with everlasting happiness the struggles and the distresses which may have exercised their faith... The people of God enjoy a species of prosperity more solid and enduring than that of 'the wicked', their momentary and short-lived troubles having only the effect of promoting their eternal welfare. The psalmist praises God that those who fear his name are not left to the poor privilege of rejoicing for a few days, but are secured in a permanent heritage of happiness.[15]

In both sickness and health, the prospect of heavenly glory is an incentive to perseverance in the Christian life, as well as a

consolation in times of affliction and distress. It was this prospect
that enabled Paul to say, 'Therefore we do not lose heart. Even
though our outward man is perishing, yet the inward man is
being renewed day by day. For our light affliction, which is but
for a moment, is working for us a far more exceeding and
eternal weight of glory' (2 Cor. 4:16-17).

In April 1549, Calvin wrote to Madame de Cany, the wife of
a ranking peson in Picardy, Calvin's home province in France,
giving an account of the death of Madame Laurent de Nor-
mandie. In his letter he refers to her as 'a good woman', whose
faith was exceedingly strong. Calvin was by her side early in the
morning of her death. His words of hope comforted her, and
her response was a testimony of faith and assurance. She said
to those gathered about her, 'The hour draws near that I must
needs depart from the world; this flesh asks only to go away
into corruption, but I feel certain that God is withdrawing my
soul into his kingdom… My confidence is in his goodness, and
in the death and passion of his Son. Therefore, I do not doubt
of my salvation, since he has assured me of it…' [16]

## Looking beyond the sunset

Although Calvin does not disparage the temporary earthly life,
he would have us meditate on the eternal heavenly life:

> As we are too much taken up with the present life, so
> long as everything goes on as suits us, the Lord, by taking
> away from us little by little the things that we are en-
> grossed with, calls us back to meditate on a better life.
> Thus it is necessary that the condition of the present life
> should decay, in order that the inward man may be in a
> flourishing state — in proportion as the *earthly* life de-
> clines, the *heavenly* life advances.[17]

Calvin does not disapprove of the distressed feelings of suffering people. Even to the most devout Christian, pain is pain, and pain hurts. But when we are hurting, we are likely to be 'influenced much more by present feeling than by the hope of heavenly blessings'. In a pastoral tone, Calvin writes,

> Paul on that account admonishes us that the afflictions and vexations of the pious have little or no bitterness if compared with the boundless blessings of everlasting glory... Paul, with the view of shaking us off from a carnal attachment to the present life, draws a comparison between present miseries and future happiness.[18]

The remedy for vexation in a time of suffering is to remember what Paul says about present suffering — it is only for a moment — and to fix one's attention on the prospect of future glory. Things that are seen are temporary, Paul says; things that are not seen are eternal. And it is the latter that gives consolation and hope (2 Cor. 4:17-18). Calvin states the case with eloquence:

> Mark what it is that will make all miseries of this world easy to endure — if we carry forward our thoughts to the eternity of the heavenly kingdom. For a moment is long if we look around us on this side and on that; but when we have raised our minds heavenward, a thousand years begin to appear to us to be like a moment. Further, the apostle's words imply that we are imposed upon by the view of present things, because there is nothing there that is not temporary, and, consequently, that there is nothing for us to rest upon with confidence in a future life. Observe the expression, *look at the things which are unseen:* the eye penetrates beyond all our natural senses, and faith is also on that account represented as *the evidence of things not seen* (Heb. 11:1).[19]

When Paul speaks of the Christian life, he never loses sight of things eternal. Our life, he says, is 'hidden with Christ in God', and 'When Christ, who is our life, appears, then you also will appear with him in glory' (Col. 3:3-4). Since the end of life is glory, Paul lays down a rule of life for Christians: 'Seek those things which are above, where Christ is... Set your mind on things above, not on things on the earth' (Col 3:1-2). Such a heavenly focus is difficult to maintain, for we are necessarily preoccupied with earthly things, earthly tasks, and earthly associations. Paul does not minimize the importance of the present life; he does, however, suggest that we should view our present life in a heavenly perspective. Jesus laid the same demand on his followers: 'Seek first the kingdom of God and his righteousness, and all these things [food and clothing and other necessities] shall be added to you' (Matt. 6:33).

Paul does not deviate from either his own or Jesus' admonition: seek the things that are above; seek the kingdom above all else. Calvin's comment on Psalm 88:47 are quite to the point:

Here it may be said that the saints take too much upon them in prescribing to God a time in which to work, and that God afflicts us with continual distresses, so long as we are in our state of earthly pilgrimage. There is no ground to conclude from this that we have been created in vain, since there is reserved for us a better life in heaven, to the hope of which we have been adopted, and, therefore, that it is not surprising though now our life is hidden from us on earth. I answer: It is by the permission of God that the saints take this liberty of urging him in their prayers to make haste; and there is no impropriety in doing so, provided that they, at the same time, keep themselves within the bounds of modesty and, restraining the impetuosity of their affections, yield themselves wholly to his will... Although we must continue to drag out our life amid continual distresses, we have abundant consolation to aid us in bearing all our afflictions, *provided we lift up our minds to heaven.*[20]

In the *Golden booklet of the true Christian life,* the same focus on 'the life to come' is on Calvin's mind. Contemplating our mortality may be depressing, but meditation on relevant passages of Scripture will not only uplift one's spirit but give joy and hope. Following are some of Calvin's pastoral remarks from the *Golden booklet:*

Calvin mentions our inordinate attachment to life in this world. To counteract this tendency, 'The Lord by various and severe lessons of misery teaches his children the vanity of the present life.'[21]

Suffering, whatever form it may take, should turn our eyes heavenward towards 'the life to come', anticipating 'the glory of the heavenly kingdom'.[22]

Calvin sets before us the prospect of future glory, which, amid our various afflictions, should fill us with joy, since we know that 'Christ shall come to us as a Saviour to deliver us from this bottomless maelstrom of all evils and miseries, and shall guide us into the blessed inheritance of his life and glory.' When God's children suffer abuse, or poverty, or disease, 'Let them lift up their eyes above this world, and they will not have any difficulty to maintain their peace of heart under such calamities.'[23]

Even those Christians whose situation is hopeless may find comfort in the prospect of heavenly glory. Conscious of the uncertainty of his own life, Calvin wrote a pastoral letter to one of the prisoners, a faithful and courageous Christian who was facing martyrdom. In his letter he stated that, although he was speaking 'outside the battle, but not far', he suspected that his own turn was near.[24] But Calvin lived his life with a view to the eternal kingdom and encouraged the faithful to lift their eyes towards heaven, even in the face of imminent death. God, says

Calvin with the conviction born of faith and hope, promises a better life beyond the sunset of life in this world. Commenting on Psalm 49:15, he asks, 'How could the psalmist have arrived at an assured promise of the redemption of his soul, except by the general fact known to him of the future glory awaiting the children of God, and by including himself among their number?'

To those Christians who expect rewards for their Christian service and become annoyed at the delay of those rewards, Calvin says, 'Let us first learn to consider the consolations with which the Lord reduces the bitterness of the cross in this world, and then let us raise our spirits to the hope of heavenly life.'[25] And to those who suffer for the gospel — Christians in countries where there is conflict over religious faith, for example — he gives this encouragement, based upon Paul's admonitions, which include 'rejoicing in hope, patient in tribulation, continuing steadfastly in prayer' (Rom. 12:12):

Paul forbids us to acquiesce in present blessings and to ground our joy on earth and on earthly things, as though our happiness were based on them; and he bids us raise our minds up to heaven, that we may possess solid and full joy. If our joy is derived from the hope of a future life, then patience will grow up in adversities; for no kind of sorrow will be able to overwhelm this joy. Hence these two things are closely connected together — that is, joy derived from hope and patience in adversities. No one will calmly and quietly submit to bear the cross except those who have learned to seek their happiness beyond this world, so as to mitigate and allay the bitterness of the cross with consolation and hope.

But as both these things (joy and patience) are far above our strength, we must persevere in prayer, continually calling on God, that he may not permit our hearts to faint and to be pressed down or broken by these adverse events. Paul not only stimulates us to prayer but

also expressly requires perseverance. We have a continual warfare: new conflicts arise daily, and even the
strongest are not equal to sustain the fight, unless they
frequently gather new rigour. That we may not then be
wearied, the best remedy is diligence in prayer.[26]

Calvin did not advocate courting martyrdom, but neither did
he approve of renouncing one's faith in order to avoid it. A far
better life, he believed, awaits those who suffer death because
of their Christian witness. In July 1553 he corresponded with
several scholars who had been imprisoned because they had
faithfully and courageously adhered to the 'sacred truth', as
Calvin called the gospel. Calvin encouraged them to hold fast
their confession, even in the face of death, for, he said, that
sacred truth 'should be more precious to you than your own
lives'. God sustained you in your earlier conflicts, he said, and
'It remains to entreat him to strengthen you more and more in
the midst of your further conflict. And seeing that he has
promised victory in the end, you will have more ample evidence in future that he does not make a beginning only to leave
his work imperfect.'[27]
   The hope of glory gives us a glimpse of the eternal kingdom
which lies beyond the sunset, beyond the struggles of the
present life, beyond pain and suffering, and beyond our sweet-
est dreams of a happier life in this world. This, in a nutshell, is
the Reformer's view of the Christian's hope.

## The triumph of grace

Grief is one of the most acute forms of suffering. Those who
grieve may also experience guilt, anger, fear, loneliness, and
hopelessness. The old saying, 'Time heals all wounds', is only
partly true. Time and grace together heal the wounds of sorrow
and renew the spirit. The scars will remain but the pain will be

made bearable, provided we find consolation in God's promise
that his love will abide with us despite our loss.

Scripture records a number of persons who grieved, and
some allowed grief to consume them — at least, Calvin thought
so. He cites the case of Jacob, whose sorrow is recorded in
Genesis 37:35 concerning his son Joseph, whom he thought to
be dead: 'And all his sons and daughters arose to comfort him;
but he refused to be comforted, and he said, "For I shall go
down into the grave to my son in mourning." Thus [Joseph's]
father wept for him.' Calvin speaks of Jacob's 'excess of grief'
when he concluded that Joseph had been 'torn to pieces' by a
wild beast. He states, 'From this we learn the blindness of
immoderate grief, which almost quenches the light of faith in
the saints. So much the more diligent, then, ought we to be in
our endeavour to restrain it.'

Recalling the example of Job, whose grief over the loss of
sons and daughters was certainly justified, Calvin thinks that
Job, so to speak, went 'over the edge'.

> Job greatly excelled in piety, yet, after he had been op-
> pressed by the magnitude of his grief, in what a profane
> manner he mixes men with beasts in death (Job 12:7;
> 18:3). If the angelic minds of holy men were thus dark-
> ened by sadness, how much deeper gloom will rest upon
> us, unless God, by the shining of his Word and Spirit,
> should scatter it, and we also, with suitable anxiety, meet
> the temptation before it overwhelms us? The principal
> mitigation of sorrow is the consolation of the future life;
> whoever applies himself to this need not fear lest he
> should be absorbed by excess of grief.[28]

Calvin himself experienced grief. While struggling with
opponents of the Reformation in Geneva — a sufficient cause
for grief — he suffered a more grievous blow to his already
wounded spirit: his beloved wife Idelette, whom he called 'the
excellent companion of my life', died. Calvin grieved deeply,

and expressed his sorrow to his friends; but he went on, by
God's unfailing grace, fulfilling his calling as God's servant.

Many, if not most, people — even those with strong Christian faith — fear death, especially when struggling with life-
threatening illness. Christ came into the world to be the Saviour
of all who hope in him; he took on human nature, 'that through
death he might destroy him who had the power of death, that
is, the devil, and release those who through fear of death were
all their lifetime subject to bondage' (Heb. 2:14-15). Calvin
writes:

> He put on our nature that he might thus make himself
> capable of dying, for as God he could not undergo death.
> And though Hebrews refers only briefly to the benefits of
> his death, yet there is in this brevity of words a singularly
> striking and powerful representation: that he has so deliv-
> ered us from the tyranny of the devil that we are rendered
> safe, and that he has so redeemed us from death that it is
> no longer to be dreaded.[29]

Regarding the statement of Hebrews 2:15, that Christ
assumed human nature in order to deliver us from fear of death
and death itself, Calvin writes,

> This passage expresses in a striking manner how miser-
> able is the life of those who fear death. They must feel it
> to be dreadful, because they look on it apart from Christ;
> for then nothing but a curse appears in it — for from
> where does death come but from God's wrath against
> sin? Hence is that bondage throughout life even perpet-
> ual anxiety by which unhappy souls are tormented; for
> through a consciousness of sin the judgement of God is
> ever presented to the view. From this fear Christ has de-
> livered us, who by undergoing our curse has taken away
> what is dreadful in death. For though we are not now

freed from death, yet in life and in death we have peace
and safety when we have Christ going before us.[30]

It was hope in Christ that inspired John Donne to write his
oft-quoted lines,

Death, be not proud, though some have called thee
Mighty and dreadful, for thou art not so.

When the Philistines captured David, they might have killed
him, and David was aware of the danger he was facing. Yet he
said, 'Whenever I am afraid, I will trust in [God]... In God I
have put my trust; I will not fear' (Ps. 56:3-4). David, Calvin's
model of trust and hope, brought forth from Calvin's pen a
pastoral note:

David acknowledges his weakness, insofar as he was sen-
sible of fear, but denies having yielded to it. Dangers
might distress him, but he could not induce himself to
surrender his hope. He makes no pretensions to that lofty
heroism which holds danger in contempt, yet, while he
admits that he felt fear, he declares his fixed resolution to
persist in a confident expectation of the divine favour.
The proof of faith consists in this, that when we feel the
solicitations of natural fear, we can resist them and prevent them from obtaining an undue ascendancy. Fear
and hope may seem to be opposite and incompatible
affections, yet it is proved by observation that the latter
never comes into full sway unless there exists some
measure of the former. In a tranquil state of mind, there is
no scope for the exercise of hope. At such times it lies
dormant, and its power is only displayed to advantage
when we see it elevating the soul under dejection, calm-
ing its agitations or soothing its distractions. This was the
manner in which it manifested itself in David, who feared

and yet trusted; who sensed the greatness of the danger he faced, and yet quieted his mind with confident hope.[31]

If, as Paul declares, those who trust in Christ are 'more than conquerors' over all the troubles of life and over death itself (Rom. 8:37), then eternal blessedness is assured and the hope of glory is confirmed to us. But salvation, which is the 'end' of our faith and the realization of our hope, is not attained without our perseverance by God's grace. The triumph of Christ over all the powers of darkness guarantees our victory over fear, grief, and even death. Calvin is sure that God will not let us down in the midst of life's troubles, but he also knows that we cannot share in Christ's victory unless we persevere in faith and hope:

> In one word, he only is a true believer who, firmly persuaded that God is reconciled and is a kind Father to him, hopes everything from his kindness, and who, trusting in the promises of divine favour with undoubting confidence, anticipates salvation — as Hebrews shows in these words, 'We have become partakers of Christ if we hold fast the confidence we had at the beginning, steadfast to the end' (Heb. 3:14). The writer of Hebrews thus holds that no one hopes well in the Lord except those who confidently glory in being the heirs of the heavenly kingdom. No one, I say, is a believer but he who, trusting in the security of his salvation, triumphs over the devil and death, as we are taught by the noble exclamation of Paul: 'I am persuaded that neither death nor life, nor angels nor principalities nor powers nor things present nor things to come, nor height nor depth, nor any other created thing shall be able to separate us from the love of God which is in Christ Jesus our Lord.' In like manner, the same apostle does not consider that the eyes of our understanding are enlightened unless we know what is the hope of the eternal inheritance to which we are called (Eph. 1:18).[32]

The hope of glory for God's children is assured by the triumph of Christ over spiritual enemies, those 'principalities and powers' which act as agencies of evil in the world and, together with the chief agent of evil, Satan, will be crushed at the return of Christ (Col. 2:15; Rom. 16:20; Jude 6; Rev. 20:10). Believers in Christ will share in his victory, 'For whatever is born of God overcomes the world. And this is the victory that has overcome the world — our faith' (1 John 5:4). Meanwhile, there are many reasons for sorrow, weeping, and lamenting. But, said Jesus to his disciples, 'You will be sorrowful, but your sorrow will be turned to joy' (John 16:20). Calvin writes:

> We know that the apostles, as long as they lived, sustained a severe warfare, that they endured reproaches, that they had many reasons for weeping and lamenting; but renewed by the Spirit, they had laid aside their former consciousness of weakness, so that with lofty heroism they nobly trampled under foot all the evils that they had endured. Here then is a comparison between their present weakness and the power of the Spirit, which would soon be given to them; though they were overwhelmed for a time, yet afterwards they not only fought bravely but also obtained a glorious triumph in the midst of their struggles. Yet it ought to be observed that he points out not only the interval that elapsed between the resurrection of Christ and the death of the apostles, but also the period which followed afterwards — as if Christ had said, 'You will lie prostrate, as it were, then will begin a new joy, which will continue to increase until, having been received into the heavenly glory, you shall have perfect joy.'[33]

We have many enemies, many of them spiritual, during our lifetime. Christ has disarmed them, though they still war against us (Col. 2:15; Eph. 6:12). The last enemy that we shall encoun-

ter is death, and that too will be destroyed. So writes Paul in 1
Corinthians 15:26. In his resurrection Christ triumphed over
death, and his resurrection is the ground of our hope in the
resurrection of our own bodies.

Let believers, therefore, be of good courage and not give
up hope until everything that must precede the resurrection shall have been accomplished. However, in what
sense does Paul affirm that death shall be the last enemy
that will be destroyed, when it has already been destroyed by Christ's death, or at least by his resurrection,
which is the victory over death and the attainment of life?
I answer that it was destroyed in such a way as to be no
longer deadly to believers, but not in such a way as to
occasion them no uneasiness. The Spirit of God dwelling
is us is life, it is true; but we still carry about with us a
mortal body (1 Peter 1:24). The substance of death in us
will one day be drained off, but it has not been so yet.
We are 'born again of incorruptible seed' (1 Peter 1:23),
but we have not yet removed all imperfection. Or to sum
up the matter briefly in an illustration: The sword of death
which could penetrate into our very hearts has been
blunted. It nevertheless still wounds, but without any
danger, for we die, but by dying we enter into life. Simply
stated, as Paul teaches elsewhere in regard to sin
(Rom. 6:12), such must be our view of death — it dwells
in us, indeed, but it does not *reign*.[34]

Musing upon Paul's vision of the believer's final triumph over sin and death, Alexander Pope penned the following lines:

> The world recedes; it disappears!
> Heaven opens on my eyes! My ears
>     With sounds seraphic ring:
>     Lend, lend your wings! I mount! I fly!
> O Grave! Where is thy victory?
> O Death! Where is thy sting?

## Received at last to glory

'We know', writes Calvin, 'that supreme sovereignty, both in heaven and earth, has been given to Christ (Matt. 28:18) in order that he may defend his people not only from temporal dangers, but especially from all the harassing annoyances of Satan, until, having delivered them at length from all trouble, he gathers them into the everlasting rest of his heavenly kingdom'.[35]

'My heart was grieved, and I was vexed in my mind' — so a psalmist confessed. His inner turmoil was caused by envy; he saw that the wicked were at ease and happy in their prosperity, while the righteous were poor and distressed (Ps. 73:3, 21). But behind his grief was also lack of trust in God's goodness — until he experienced, in the midst of worship, a renewal of trust in God. Looking back upon his distress, he exclaimed, 'Truly God is good to Israel, to such as are pure in heart' (Ps. 73:1). And once his trust was renewed, 'The psalmist assured himself that, since the Lord had brought him back into the right way, the Lord would continue from that point on to guide him, until at length he received him into his glorious presence in heaven':[36] 'You will guide me with your counsel, and afterward receive me to glory' (Ps. 73:24).

Calvin writes,

> To *counsel* there is added *glory,* which I think ought not
> to be limited to eternal life, as some are inclined to do. It
> comprehends the whole course of our happiness from the
> commencement, which is seen here upon earth, even to
> the consummation, which we expect to realize in heaven.
> David, then, assures himself of eternal glory through the
> free and unmerited favour of God. Yet he does not ex-
> clude the blessings which God bestows upon his people
> here below, with the view to affording them, even in this
> life, some foretaste of that happiness.[37]

Scripture's meditation on the future does not centre on
man's attainment of eternal happiness, however, but on the
glory of God, on salvation by grace, and, ultimately, on the
marriage of the Lamb:

> Worthy is the Lamb who was slain
> To receive power and riches and wisdom,
> And strength and honour and glory and blessing!

This is the standard for all of the church's doxologies: they
are directed to Christ's redemptive work and are full of honour
and glory and blessing.[38]

*Suffering — understanding the love of God*

Selections from the writings of John Calvin

---

## Chapter 12

## A place where gold is refined

---

'But he knows the way that I
take; when he has tested me,
I shall come forth as gold'
(Job 23:10).

# 12.

# A place where gold is refined

*Having been disciplined a little, they will receive great good,*
*because God tested them and found them worthy of himself;*
*like gold in the furnace he tried them, and like a sacrificial burnt*
*offering he accepted them. In the time of their visitation they will*
*shine forth, and will run like sparks through the stubble.*

Wisdom 3:5-7

When we ponder the problems of evil and suffering, our understanding is very limited; we can find meaning in suffering only in so far as Scripture provides glimpses of God's design. Now and then we learn of a case of unspeakably heartbreaking suffering, which strikes us as terribly cruel and unfair.

In the fall of 2004, the evening news broke the tragic story of charity worker Margaret Hassan, who devoted twenty-five years of her life to the care of the poor in Iraq. A native of Dublin, she moved to Iraq, married an Iraqi and held joint British and Iraqi citizenship. For twelve years she worked for CARE International, the world's largest humanitarian relief agency, with organizations in seventy-two countries. Wherever Ms Hassan went, she was a friend to the needy and a helper to the helpless. Felicity Arbuthnot, a film-maker who went to Iraq to document Ms Hassan's work, described her as 'an extraordinary woman'. Once, at a water sanitation plant in a poor area, a crowd gathered and small children threw their arms round her legs. They knew her as their friend, calling her 'Madam Hassan'.

Whatever her religious beliefs were, her work of benevolence was undoubtedly a divine calling.

On 19 October 2004, Ms Hassan was snatched from her car during one of her assignments and taken to a secret location, where she was subjected to brutal treatment by her kidnappers. After a month of psychological torture, her captors released to Arab television network Al-Jazeera a videotape showing a masked militant holding a handgun, shooting a blindfolded woman, purportedly Margaret Hassan, in the head. The video shows her suffering intense physical pain and emotional distress. Sitting blindfolded and bound in her cell, she pleaded for her life, but in vain. Her family members, hearing that she had been murdered, were, needless to say, heartbroken.[1]

The nagging questions which are raised by undeserved suffering are addressed in the book of Job and are answered in different ways by three friends who came to comfort Job. Their answers, though commonly accepted, are simplistic: suffering is God's punishment for sin. Job has committed some grievous transgression, for which he has been justly punished. Their well-meaning explanations are all variations of the same theme, but none penetrates to the heart of the problem of why 'innocent' people suffer.

Of course, theologically speaking, no one is innocent, for 'All have sinned and fall short of the glory of God' (Rom. 3:23). One thing becomes clear, however, when the book of Job is read: suffering is not always punishment. Job is called 'a blameless and upright man, one who fears God and shuns evil' (Job 1:8); yet he suffered the loss of his seven sons and three daughters and all his property (he was enormously wealthy).

John Calvin's sermons on the book of Job do not attempt to solve the riddle of evil and suffering as they relate to God's 'eternal purpose'. Again and again, Calvin insists on the incomprehensibility of God's ways and encourages Job-like trust in God's goodness. During 1554-55, Calvin preached 159 sermons on the book of Job; this chapter comprises excerpts from some of these sermons which deal with suffering and faith.

Calvin himself suffered many afflictions, especially in his later years. He did not catalogue his ailments, but from a biography by his colleague Theodore Beza we learn that Calvin was often in very poor health. He suffered migraine headaches, stomach cramps, and chronic diarrhoea. Haemorrhoids also caused him a great deal of discomfort, and he was troubled with excruciating pain from kidney stones. He never expressed concern about his health, Beza tells us, except when the pain became unbearable. Towards the end of his life, he was racked with abdominal pain and, because of his frugal diet, gout, an arthritic inflammation of the joints in the foot, set in.[2]

Calvin does not attempt to solve the problem raised by Job's suffering — why God permits Satan to inflict devastating loss and pain on his servant Job — but rather to point to the incomprehensibility of the divine purpose. God has secrets which cannot be known; his inscrutable purpose is behind Job's suffering. How then could *Job* 'figure it out'? There are no glib solutions to the problem of 'undeserved suffering'. Job at times complains bitterly and answers his counsellors scornfully. He knows that he is suffering innocently and so he indulges in self-justification and even contends with the Almighty.

God allows Job and his friends to have their heated debate, and then God himself speaks while Job listens. God reminds Job that his wisdom and power are infinitely greater than Job's; how then can he know God's secrets? 'Shall the one who contends with the Almighty correct him?' (Job 40:2). 'Would you indeed annul my judgement? Would you condemn me that you may be justified?' (Job 40:8). This interrogation brings Job up short, and he replies, 'I am vile; what shall I answer you? I lay my hand over my mouth' (Job 40:4).

It is interesting that when God condescends to answer Job 'out of the whirlwind' he does not charge Job with sins that caused his suffering. God does not rebuke Job for asserting his own integrity, nor does he respond to Job's whining by telling him why he has suffered. The bone that God has to pick with Job is not Job's self-justification, but Job's audacious condemn-

ing of God in order to justify himself. God does not answer all
of Job's questions — I am innocent; why then have I suffered
like this? Why have you dealt unjustly with me? Instead, God
reveals Job's weakness and ignorance in comparison with
God's power and wisdom. This revelation brings Job to his
knees in humble repentance and reverent respect in the presence of his Creator.[3]

Job, however, denies that he has tried to justify himself.
Although his friends have tormented him with false accusations,
he has not responded 'after the manner of hypocrites in
smoothing his case before men to justify himself, but knew that
he had to do with God'. With full confidence in God's justice,
Job believes that God will ultimately vindicate him. He declares,
'I know that my Redeemer lives, and he shall stand at last on
the earth.' In Job's view, a Redeemer is *gaal,* an advocate who
pleads the cause of one accused and proves his innocence.
Most people, says Calvin, will labour to excuse themselves,
because they don't think of God as the one with whom they
have to do. 'It is enough that the world thinks well of them and
that they are taken for honest men.'

> If I do not know God [Job continues], it is enough for me
> that others hold me in good repute. What do I gain from
> that? Nothing at all. Is it not shameful that — although
> my own conscience accuses me and I am convinced that
> I have done wrong — I will stick my nose in the air and
> say, 'Of what can any man accuse me? What I have
> done? Do I not have a good case?' ... As men boldly
> defend their own case, they have no regard for God. Job,
> on the other hand, says, 'I know that my God is alive,
> and that in the end I will rise up from the dust.' It is as if
> he says, 'I am mistaken for a wicked man and a desper-
> ate person, as though I had blasphemed God in trying to
> justify myself against him. No, I want nothing except to
> humble myself before him and to rest wholly in his grace.
> Yet for all that, I am obliged to maintain my uprightness

against you... My defence, then, is to look to God and
have my eyes fixed on him...' Let all of us, then, come
before the heavenly judge of both great and small, and let
every one of us present himself there to beg pardon for
his sins. Let us not doubt that if we come in genuine repentance that he will acquit us, not for any worthiness in
us, but of his own grace and mercy.[4]

In the end, Job *was* vindicated when he acknowledged his
own lack of understanding of God's ways and humbled himself,
repenting in dust and ashes. After the Lord had taught Job
'things too wonderful' for him, the Lord turned to Job's friend
Eliphaz and said, 'My wrath is aroused against you and your
two friends [Bildad and Zophar], for you have not spoken of
me what is right, and my servant Job has.' There is more: After
Job's three accusers went to him and offered a sacrifice, and
Job prayed for them, the Lord restored Job's losses. 'Indeed the
Lord gave Job twice as much as he had before.' Then all his
brothers and sisters and former acquaintances came to his
house to celebrate with him, and 'Each one gave him a piece of
silver and a gold ring.' The Lord doubled his former livestock
holdings and gave him seven sons and three daughters. Thus
Job's vindication was complete: 'The Lord blessed the latter
days of Job more than the beginning' (Job 42:1-17).
     Calvin's sermons on the book of Job cover a broad range of
issues related to suffering and faith, including God's goodness,
purposes, and promises; God's wrath and punishment; prayer,
the sufferer's recourse; the necessity of patience; pastoral
concerns for those who suffer; and, above all, the incomprehensibility of God's providence.

## God's ways are incomprehensible

*Surely there is a mine for silver, and a place where gold is
refined* (Job 28:1).

There are many things in the world that are secret and in
which there seems to be no reason. Even so, men will
find reason in them in the end and also will find the
things that are hidden. But men will never attain to God's
wisdom or reach so high as the wisdom of God. This
comparison holds true from smallest to greatest, as if Job
were to say to his friends, it is a hard thing for a man to
seek out the means of finding gold and silver and precious stones. While it is true that men do find them, still it
may well be called a secret of nature. There are other
things at which men are perplexed and can do no more
than wonder at them. Sometimes rivers run out of some
place where no river was ever thought to be, depending
upon water levels which sometimes rise and sometimes
fall; a man may go through such a place with dry feet,
and shortly afterward the water may rise as high as his
chin, or one may cross when the brooks are dry, while
another crosses when they are full of water. Certainly
there seems to be no great secret in this; brooks increase
by melting snow and by great rain. But you will sometimes see springs that are dried up, and shortly afterwards
so much water gushes out that a man can only say that
God chose to show his power in such changes. These are
examples of things that are seen in the world and serve
for this present life; yet they also are obscure. It is also
true that man's reason may well inquire after these things
and study them so that he finds reason in them.

But God's wisdom is another matter. When we come
to God's judgements, let us not think that we can contain
them in our brains or encompass them with our wits, but
let us reverence the things we do not know. Let us confess that the majesty of God is too high for us and that it
becomes us not to belittle God's majesty by thinking of it
just as we choose. Let us be content with what God reveals to us, assuring ourselves of the overlong distance
between God and us; God must be willing to come to us,

or else we will never come to him. In coming to us, however, God does not reveal all his mysteries; he does not mean for us to know now those things that he will show us at the last day.

Thus you see what Job means. That meaning notwithstanding, it is not now necessary to stand upon all the things that are spoken here. The intent of the Holy Spirit is not to show us how to find the mines of which Job speaks. It would be of very little profit if I were to preach three or four sermons to teach you to seek out mines of gold and silver. That is not the thing we must seek, and every man would not occupy himself in that trade. So then, we must not stand upon every piece when we find mention of mines of gold and silver, or when it is said that gold or grains of metal are to be found in the sand or in some river. It should be enough for us to see that God has put secrets or mysteries in his creation in order that we might magnify him. Thus we ought to acknowledge God's infinite power and wisdom — even in the least things in the world. We ought to give much more thought to those secrets that are so strange to us — gold and silver and such things — for then we should be more moved and our minds more awakened to better perceive and understand the inestimable power of God. Our Lord would not have us be dullards, like blocks of wood, but he would have us behold the works of his hands. So it is good for us to know his works and to think on them in such a way that we give him the glory due to him.[5]

Job's friends insisted that God had forsaken him and that he deceived himself in believing that God would be merciful to him. Calvin says:

Job maintains a good case... He knows that God never punishes men according to the measure of their sins but has his secret judgements, to which he does not make us

privy. Therefore it behoves us to wait till he reveals to us
for what cause he does this or that. In this whole dis-
course, Job is persuaded that God does not always punish men according to the measure of their sins; and on
that ground he assures himself that he is not a man re-
jected by God, as his friends would make him believe.[6]

It behoves us to humble ourselves and to wait till the
day comes that we may better comprehend God's secrets, which are incomprehensible to us at this day.
Therefore we must learn to magnify them and to honour
God's judgements, holding them in reverence and admiration until they are better known to us. Therefore we
must walk in humility, contenting ourselves to know only
in part, until full knowledge is disclosed to us at the latter
day.[7]

Let us boldly have recourse to God, not only in one
kind of adversity, but in as many as come upon us, assuring ourselves that his power extends even to all the
deaths that can threaten us, according as it is said that he
not only has a way to deliver us from death, but also has
ways which are incomprehensible to us. When we are
afflicted on the one side, God will, on the other side,
make us feel that we are helped. When we are locked up
so that there seems no way for us to hope, God will find a
way for us — yes, after his own fashion, that is to say,
beyond our understanding and opinion... We are hereby
warned to prepare ourselves to be patient ... according as
we see how many are born to various afflictions. What
shall we do regarding his incomparable secrets and pri-
vate determinations, when both generally and particularly
he works in such a way as seems strange to us and far
outreaches our capacity to understand? Does it become
us to presume to judge in any case and to give our ver-
dict upon it as though we were able to comprehend the
things that he does beyond our wit and capacity? He
sends many adversities and miseries: one man loses his

goods, another is smitten with sickness; another falls into reproach and slander, and another is wronged and beaten.

It might be thought that God is mistaken in handling men so roughly. No, not so. In all these things it behoves us to learn to confess that God is always righteous, and that he knows a reason why he handles us so, and that the same reason is good and right, though it is unknown to us. And if we do not acknowledge this, yet we are still in his hand, and we gain nothing by all our grumbling. Do we see the wicked and ungodly receiving all their desire in this world? Do we see those who despise God living at their ease? Do we see them in honour and authority, the masters and lords of the world? Do we see that they regard God with contempt and yet are not immediately punished? Do we see on the other hand that we are obliged to endure shame and trouble and treason while God does not help us as soon as we would have him do? Let us wait patiently till God delivers us, since he knows what is expedient for us. And besides that, let us understand that if we wonder at the things that we may see as it were before our own feet, how much more do we have reason to wonder at — yes, and honour — the secrecy that surpasses even the angels. Therefore let these lower things teach us to settle ourselves to the magnifying and glorifying of our God; and so long as we shall be in this world, let us permit ourselves to be guided and governed by his Holy Spirit, to the end that he may order our lives after his good pleasure.[8]

Job, says Calvin, 'pressed too far into God's secrets'. In the end, however, 'To correct himself, he says that those things were too wonderful for him.' Calvin then goes on to give pastoral counsel regarding attempts to pry into God's secrets:

Let us note well that when we come to God and begin talking of his works, we ought to consider that his mysteries are too high for our weak wits and understanding. It behoves us to be similarly persuaded about God's providence in general as about the things that belong to his spiritual kingdom.

Since God orders all things, and nothing is done in this world without his will, it behoves us to note that secret well. Although every man should grant that God is a sovereign Lord and governor, nevertheless, when we come to this point, the things which we see as so troublesome and out of order do not cease to be guided by the secret providence of God, who holds the throne above and turns things to such an end as he thinks good.[9]

## Let us be silent before God

God's works surpass us, so that we do not know why he so disposes the things we see. What is to be done? We must lay our hand upon our mouth; that is to say, we must not be so bold as to prattle about them… We need to know no more than what is given us… It is true that we must always have our mouth open after one sort: that is, to glorify God. But we presume to bring him under the compass of our understanding and would have him reserve nothing to himself. Where do we go then? Is it not an open despising of God? He intends to hide things from us. And why? It is so that we should know our own ignorance, and yet not cease to acknowledge him to be righteous and to honour his wonderful and incomprehensible ordinances … But if God hides the reason for his works from us, and if he is too high for us to reach, let us shut our mouths; that is to say, let us not be talkative, babbling after our own imagination, but let us glorify God and not be ashamed to be ignorant. The true wisdom of the faithful is to know no more than it has pleased God to show them. Therefore, let us keep silence before God regarding whatever he does, till the last day comes, when he reveals himself and when we see him face to face in his glory and majesty.[10]

Elihu, a young visitor who speaks to Job just before God speaks from the whirlwind, shares his 'wisdom' with Job. Claiming to be divinely inspired, he merely repeats in his own words the views of Job's three friends: God has his secrets, which he does not share with us. Calvin says, 'Elihu meant to indicate that God will not always make us privy as to why he executes his judgements, but that we shall be blind in respect to that.'[11]

## Both the righteous and the wicked suffer

We know that God's justice and uprightness consists of two parts: the punishing of evil people and the relieving of good people and maintaining them in their righteous and sound conduct. Therefore, if God punishes the wicked, he must also maintain the good, for he keeps them under his care and does not permit them to be troubled or tormented; they feel his help as soon as they cry out to him. However, in our view, the good are punished not for a day or two but with lingering pains all their life long, so that, instead of showing any sign that he is inclined to help them, it seems that God takes vengeance on them and is determined to plunge them into the bottomless pit... The one of these points cannot be separated from the other: that is, if God is righteous and intends to show it perfectly in this world, on the one side he must have his eye upon all that do wrong and not allow them to escape his hand, but make them come to a reckoning. On the other side, when good men are disquieted or have any wrong or violence done to them, he must pity them and show how he has them in his hand... I have declared before now ... that God's righteousness is not always apparent and that we must not take it for a general rule that as soon as men have sinned, God has his hand bent to punish them. On the other hand, he will at the first blow show himself to be a preserver of the good by ridding them of all their miseries. And why? It is not God's will that his righteousness should always be known to us, but rather to show how it is not for us to enter at any time into his judgements. It behoves us to humble ourselves whenever he deals with us in a manner not to our liking. We must not presume to murmur against him for it, but we must reverence these great secrets which are far above our capacity to understand, until that time when we may comprehend that which is hidden from us now... You see, then, what Job's meaning is. It is true that he did not cease to be tormented with an excessive passion. Let us learn from his example that it behoves us to humble ourselves before God and that, although he deals with us in such a mysterious way that we do not perceive either equity or uprightness in it, we must, notwithstanding, cast down our eyes. But if we have any inclination to murmur against God when he does things that we do not comprehend by our own reason — the same will then especially show itself when he forgives us.[12]

## Am I being punished?

Elihu asserts that God cannot be unjust; therefore Job has grievously sinned against God, and his suffering is punishment. He accuses Job of self-righteousness: 'Job has said, "I am righteous, but God has taken away my justice; should I lie concerning my right? My wound is incurable, though I am without transgression"' (Job 34:5-6). Calvin says:

> When Job spoke of his righteousness, it was only in order to show that he was not punished for his offences and that he ought not to be judged wicked because God afflicted him so grievously above all other men. When God afflicts men, it is not always with the purpose of punishing their sins; he sometimes intends to test their patience — as happened with Job when God gave Satan permission. It was not because Job was of low or worthless character and had provoked God's wrath by great offences. No, although Satan found no fault in him, yet Satan obtained permission to torment him. So then, the reason God afflicted Job in that way was not that he was angry with him, but that he intended to try his obedience, so that it might be a mirror to us. Therefore Job contended very well in saying that he was not punished for his offences, but that there was some other purpose.[13]

The wrath of Elihu was aroused against Job because Job justified himself rather than God. Job was punished, then, because 'he was righteous in his own eyes' (Job 32:1-2). Calvin gives pastoral counsel regarding such an assumption:

> Let us bear in mind what I have touched upon before now. We should behave ourselves carefully when God afflicts men and not venture to judge them by assuming that he whom God punishes is forthwith to be condemned, and that his sins are to be measured by his afflictions. It would be rash and unwise to make a general rule of that... Let us understand that God has diverse reasons for afflicting men. It is true that it is his ordinary justice to punish sins. Nevertheless, sometimes it is his will to try the obedience of good men, and of such as have served him and applied their whole endeavour to follow

his commandments. In fact, those will be handled with greater rigour than the wicked. And why? God intends to teach them what it is to be humble and obedient. Seeing that the case stands so, it behoves us to refrain from hasty judgement when any man is afflicted. For God will also preserve his servants from the temptation that he sends them.[14]


## Satan is not in charge

*And the Lord said to Satan, 'Behold, he is in your hand, but spare his life'* (Job 2:6).

By this God shows us that we must not be afraid, although Satan has such a power that he is called the prince of the world. I say, we need not be afraid that he will overwhelm us, so long as we are armed with faith. For we will have strength enough and we will be sure of the victory if we rest upon God and lean on the grace of our Lord Jesus Christ, which is mentioned in John 10. The Father (Jesus says), who has put you into my hand, is stronger than all. Do not fear that Satan will overcome his maker. God has put us into the hands of our Lord Jesus Christ, to the intent that he should be the good and faithful keeper both of our souls and of our bodies. Therefore let us rest ourselves upon him; but let us not cease to be wary and careful. Those who are negligent will find themselves overtaken at every blow. The sureness which we have in God does not make us dull or forgetful of the dangers in which we find ourselves, but only upholds us that we do not faint in fighting.[15]

*May the day perish on which I was born, and the night in which it was said, 'A male child is conceived'* (Job 3:3).

Notice how the faithful withstand temptations, namely, that at some point they may chance to stoop — yes, even in such a way that God humbles them all the days of their life, in order that they may have occasion to know their own infirmities till they groan again. Yet, for all that, they get the upper hand in encountering adversity, and God does not permit them to be utterly oppressed... When God sends them any affliction, they may well feel such inward heaviness of mind that they do not know where to turn. Yet they always have some good affection, and even though their legs fail them, still their heart holds its own.[16]

## God is our strength in trouble

*How have you helped him who is without power? How have you saved the arm that has no strength?* (Job's answer to Bildad, Job 26:2). Calvin says:

Now look to yourselves: When any of you sees himself weak, or cold, and set back by difficulties and overly fearful in serving God and his neighbour, let him exert himself, let him gather his strength, and let him come and seek courage in the Word of God. Do not flatter yourselves in your sins. When you feel yourselves weak, do not say, 'I am weak', but seek the remedy for it in God's Word. Go read and give ear to the promises that are contained there. Notice how God tells you he will maintain those that are his, and that if they faint his Spirit is strong enough to recover them. Wait for such help at his hand, and with your waiting walk on still in the same trust.[17]

Calvin believed that repetition in his sermons would drive a point home, and often he repeated important ideas in virtually the same words. The need to gather strength from God's Word was important to Calvin. In the following passage from Sermon 95 he repeats what he had said earlier in the sermon:

> Now then, if I am weak and need to gather strength, it behoves me to pay careful attention in order to receive the remedy which God's Word gives me. In short, according to the diseases which every man suffers, let him learn to do whatever God has ordained, and let him embrace God's promises for the remedy.[18]

We note, however, that we must not imagine more than God promises us. It is a vain and fond presumption when men assure themselves of that thing of which God leaves them in doubt... Therefore, whenever men presume upon themselves, that is nothing but vanity and wishing, and it is no wonder that they are disappointed as to their purpose... So we must hold this as a general rule: our trust must be settled wholly upon God's promises... And now let us consider what God promises. He says that if he has thought upon us today he will not forget us anymore tomorrow, but we will be helped by his hand all the time of our life. Consider what his promise is, and then we may well assure ourselves that God will always keep us and that we will not be in danger of falling into decay. But we must make our account to be subject to many considerations. For our Lord does not say that he will keep us shut up in a cage in continual joy and happiness, so that we see no adversity or are not acquainted with any trouble. He promises us no such thing, but only that he will hide and help us in all our necessities. Therefore it behoves us to understand that God will exercise us with many adversities and that we are subject to the common afflictions of this present life; in the meantime we ought to be satisfied to know that we will be aided by him and that we will not be utterly forsaken.[19]

*Where then is my hope? As for my hope, who can see it?*
(Job 17:15).

> The desire of the faithful, in effect, is this: that they shall
> never be without many trials, and especially that they
> shall not be subject to so many miseries during their
> earthly wayfaring. But those who endeavour to fear God
> best cease not to be overly pressed with many inconven-
> iences and many afflictions... When we are astonished by
> the suffering of the faithful, it can only be that we must
> think it strange at the outset. Let us fight against such
> temptations and let us hold on to the right way without
> starting to go out of it. And although we find many hard
> things in our own lives, let us pray God to give us such
> invincible strength that we may continue in his service
> even to the end, notwithstanding Satan's labours to thrust
> us out of it.[20]

## Job: a model of self-control and patience?

Sorrow and trouble are not painless, and we should not dismiss
them as if we felt no pain; after all, says Calvin, we are not
blocks of wood or a stone! Take Job for example, who felt
intense pain, yet was submissive to God in his trial (Job 1:21-
22).

> If there is any adversity, it must be assuaged by consider-
> ing that God never stops procuring our welfare. We ought
> to be subject to him and consider that he governs us ac-
> cording to his good pleasure. Here is where patience
> shows itself. We have seen that Job might have been
> overwhelmed with the report of so many evil tidings. But
> he rose up and tore his clothes and shaved his head and
> cast himself upon the ground to humble himself before
> God. Here we see that those who are patient will surely

be subject to some grief, so that they feel great sorrow
and anguish of heart; for if we were like a block of wood
or a stone, it would not be a virtue. Is that man worthy to
be prayed for who has no feeling at all of his adversity?

Here we see, first of all, that those who are patient are
sure of some grief, so that they feel great sorrow and anguish of heart; for if we were like a block of wood or a
stone, it would produce no virtue at all in us... So then,
let us observe that this word *patient* or *patience* does not
mean that men should become blockish, so that they
have no heaviness at all or are not faced with any grief
when they experience adversities. The virtue is when they
can control themselves and hold such moderation that
they do not cease to glorify God in the midst of all their
miseries. The virtue is when they are not excessively burdened and so swallowed up with sorrow and anguish as
to faint altogether. Rather they fight against their own
passions until they are able to come to terms with the
good will of God, to reach the same conclusion that Job
does here, and finally to say that God is righteous in all
respects.[21]

We have here in Job chapter one a godly record that
afflictions are not always signs that God hates us. If we do
not have this belief, it is impossible that we should be
patient in adversity. It is not for nothing that Paul says we
ought to have comfort through patience. If a man does
not comfort himself in God, though he shows ever so
great and invincible courage, still, that is not to be called
patience, for he is not patient as he ought to be. It is but
the patience of a lummox, as we say in the proverb: that
is to say, it is patience born of necessity and against our
will, like a mule chewing against his bit... But God will
have us to be patient after another manner: he will have
us to be ready to endure all things, assuring us that good
and evil proceed from his hand. He will have us abide his
chastisement, desiring nothing but to be governed by him

and renouncing all our own affections... It behoves us to be well assured that when God scourges us he does not intend our destruction, but rather procures our welfare.

Can we love God when we persuade ourselves that he seeks nothing but to undo us and to destroy us? So then, it is very necessary for us to be fully resolved that when God punishes us, it is not a token that he hates us, nor that he holds us as his enemies, but rather that he by that means procures our salvation. And here we see how (as Paul says) our victory consists in taking hold of this love of God, so that we are fully persuaded that God has adopted us to be his children. If we have that principle, we shall not be dismayed with any affliction.[22]

It behoves us to say, O my God, your judgements are incomprehensible, and to the extent that I am not able now to know any more because of my ignorance and lack of understanding, I will wait patiently till you make me to perceive the cause of my suffering. So Lord, when I have tarried in this way like a poor blind soul, you will open my eyes and make me perceive to what these things tend and what is the purpose of them, and I will profit better by them than I do now.[23]

## The virtue of simplicity

Above all things, when we are in such difficulties that we can bear no more, let us then appeal unto God, that it may please him to help us and to have pity on us. We see, then, that God looks with favour on those who are, as it were, the outcasts of the world, to the end that he might help them... We see here yet one more comfort, which it behoves us to mark well, in spite of the fact that our enemies assail us on all sides. It is true that God spares us sometimes... But it is impossible that God's children should live in this world and not be in many perils continually. And why so? It is because they must walk in simplicity. It is true that they ought to be wise, and our Lord has given them as much wisdom as is requisite for them. But however the world goes, they must not maintain themselves by craftiness and deceit or by wicked practices. Although they are among wolves, yet they must be as lambs and sheep; and although they are among foxes, yet they must continue as doves, and they must keep the same simplicity which God commands them.[24]

## Cast your burden on the Lord

*Cast your burden on the Lord, and he will sustain you* (Ps. 55:22).

So long as we have such heart-burning that we chew on our bridle, it is impossible for us to comfort ourselves in his goodness, which he is ready to make us feel. Therefore we must pray to him to hold us in awe, if we are to have our minds abide quiet and peaceful in the midst of troubles that befall us. And this also cannot be done unless Jesus Christ is at hand with us, so that we may have some solace in him, according as he himself says, 'Come unto me all who labour and are heavily burdened, and I will refresh you, and you shall find rest for your souls.' As often, then, as God scourges us, let us determine to pray to him that we may turn our heart and mind to our Lord Jesus Christ, so that in him we may have the rest of which he speaks.[25]

*Set your minds on things above, not on things on the earth. For you died, and your life is hidden with Christ in God* (Eph. 3:2-3).

Let us not esteem our life or our welfare by that which we see and that which may be discerned by eyesight or by our native intelligence, but let us understand that God intends to preserve us by means which we are not able to comprehend. Our life (says Paul) is hidden with our Lord Jesus Christ. And therefore let us wait upon that good God and pray to him to give us the grace to look always to him, till the time comes when he will reveal that which is now unknown... We may feel here on earth some taste of his grace, and he may well give us experience of it. Yet, if we do not feel it at times, we must pray to him to waken us and to make us know the love that he bears towards us.[26]

*For affliction does not come from the dust, nor does trouble spring from the ground; yet man is born to trouble, as the sparks fly upward* (Eliphaz to Job, Job 5:6-7).

When there happen to be any afflictions in the world, let us be sure it is the hand of God which lights upon us for our sins, and that all the mischief comes of ourselves, and that we have the very wellspring and groundwork thereof within us. Let us, I say, acknowledge this, to the end that we may dislike ourselves in our vices and immediately pray to God to draw us to himself. Let us also pray to God to make his graces, which he has put in us, available for our salvation, so that being maintained by his power — which he has openly showed towards us in the name of our Lord Jesus Christ — we may be able to prosper through his blessing.

And let us cast ourselves down before the presence of our good God, with acknowledgement of our faults, praying to him to make us feel in such a way that we may return to him in true repentance and offer ourselves to be governed from this point forward by his hand; yes, in such a manner that his holy name may be glorified by us throughout our entire life.[27]

*Call out now; is there anyone who will answer you? And to which of the holy ones will you turn?* (Eliphaz challenges Job, Job 5:1).

We see how they who have some good outward appearance become like beasts. Therefore let us be sure that God visits us with whips because of our sins. Yet in spite of his discipline, let us not stop trusting him continually and calling upon him, praying him to bury our former faults and to guide us in such a way from this point forward as may serve to draw us unto himself. And to the intent that he may have pity upon us, let us come to him with a humble mind, so that we do not have the envy and heart-burning that is mentioned here. We may assure ourselves that if we have such faults, it will only further stir up and inflame God's vengeance against us ... as is said in the eighteenth Psalm: 'With the devious you will show yourself shrewd.'[28]

*The peace of God, which surpasses all understanding, will guard your hearts and minds through Jesus Christ* (Phil. 4:7).

When we trust God and call upon him, it is not so much as to say that we should never have any bickerings in ourselves. But faith must get the upper hand. The peace of which Paul speaks must win the victory; it must get the mastery in our hearts. Although Paul attributes victory to it, he shows clearly that we will have turmoil within us and that we will be tossed to and fro. What remedy is there for it? This peace of God must be of such power that it may gain the mastery in the end.[29]

Prayer does not always change things, Calvin observes; we must learn patience.

> Let us compare our miseries with Job's. If we consider well the afflictions that he endured, they were so strange that he might well have said, 'I do not know how I can take them, for God so sorely oppresses me.'
> So much the more, therefore, it behoves us to know that we have learned to take patiently all the corrections that he sends us, seeing that they tend to our welfare... Among other things, let us note that it is a hard and very dangerous temptation when God does not hear our cries and complaints. And why? It is said that God's name is a sure stronghold for all who flee to enter into it. Whoever calls upon the name of the Lord shall be saved. Yes, and although heaven and earth were melded together and the whole order of nature confounded, we would still be preserved by calling upon the name of God, as Job says. God has promised that he will hear us before we open our mouth, and that he will reach out his hand to help us as we speak. You see, then, that God shows himself so bountiful that you marvel when assured that he will help our necessity. And yet, for all that, when we have called upon him more than once or twice, and when we have persisted in praying him to have pity on us, we continue still in the same state; and (which is worse) it seems to us that God sharpens himself against us to torment us the more when we have called upon him... But here we note that although God has promised to be near to all them who call upon him, and to help them even before they open their mouths to desire him, yet that does not mean that he always makes it apparent to the eye. How then? After his own manner he does it.
> It is certain that before we call upon God he is willing and ready to help us. The proof of this is: from where comes the desire to pray? Does it not come from the Holy

Spirit? For a man would never of his own mind resort to
God. So it is because God looks upon us with pity —
when we think he has turned his back on us. Again, if we
have stood up under testing at any time, it must be that
his helping us with his hand made us to be patient and
humble in our adversities.[30]

Even though God does not seem to hear our prayers, we
must continue calling upon him.

God's children must continue in prayer and must have
perseverance or holding out. Although God afflicts them
and seems to turn his back to them and to be deaf to
their requests, yet nevertheless they hold on still and
never completely give up.
    On the contrary, if God does not grant the faithful
their request as soon as they pray to him — if he does not
please them by and by, if he does not perform their desires without delay — they think they have wasted their
time. And so we see that the manner of praying properly
is, first, not to wait till extremity compels us, but rather to
be doing so beforehand, as there is need to be praying
God to anticipate our prayers with his gracious goodness… Again, if we should be in trouble and difficulty, let
us not cease to pray — as well as if we were in prosperity.[31]
    It is a hard and burdensome temptation when our
prayers are not heard at the first. When we are in adversity, truly our last remaining comfort is that God should
receive us if we desire him to have pity upon us, and that
we might feel that our resorting to him for help has not
been in vain. This (I say) is the welfare and comfort of all
the faithful. But if it seems that we have wasted our time
in running to God to be aided at his hand, what will become of it? Will we not be as good as in despair? Yet it is
God's good pleasure to exercise his children in that

way — by hiding himself from them and by giving no appearance of hearing them or of taking notice of the miseries they endure. True it is that he has promised to be ready to help us as soon as we desire it of him; yes, and that he will not delay when appealed to, but will already know our requests. And that is what makes the temptation much more grievous, namely, that when God seems to have dallied with us and to have given us a vain and futile hope. Let us understand that, seeing he has previously exercised his children so, we must not marvel that he does so now. Therefore let us wait patiently, and we will see in the end that he has not forgotten us, nor ceased to hear us, although he does not show immediately in the open sight of the world that he has his hand stretched out over us. And without doubt, if we are patient and able to continue in prayer — that is a token that God has heard already.[32]

## Christ's priesthood our certainty

When Job prayed for his friends, God was favourable towards Job and accepted his prayer, inasmuch as he had appointed him to be a priest. I urge you, do we not have much better certainty, seeing that our everlasting advocate who has entered into the sanctuary of heaven — that is, our Lord Jesus Christ — is never refused? Nor will we be refused either, if we come to God the Father by his means — that is, through Christ our mediator — holding evermore the way and furtherance of our interest that he has given us.[33]

## Christ our hope of heaven

I have told you already that we need not look to live so
long in order to take knowledge of God's fatherly love
thereby; for if we lived but three days in this world, it
would be enough to give us a taste of God's goodness
and mercy and to confirm our faith. For seeing that our
Lord Jesus Christ has died and is risen again, we do not
need a long time in this world to know that God is our
Father and that we are sure of our salvation. Therefore,
as soon as he gives us knowledge of the truth of his gospel, let us always be ready to die, assuring ourselves that
he has adopted us as his children and that he will show
himself our Father both in life and in death. You see,
then, that we must always be satisfied with life, seeing
that God has given us a good pledge of his love in our
Lord Jesus Christ, and we must not desire to have our life
prolonged here, to the end that we might have confirmation of his love.[34]

So then, let us learn not to put our trust in this world,
or in any of the inferior means here below. But let us lean
upon God, seeing that he has given us our Lord Jesus
Christ, to the end that being grafted into him we may
drain such strength and sap from him that, although our
life is hidden so that we are even as it were in death, we
may not cease to continue still. And we may be maintained in a good and sure state, waiting till this good God
has delivered us out of all worldly miseries and out of all
the troubles which we are obliged to suffer here, until he
calls us and brings us into the kingdom of heaven and
into the glory which he has purchased by the precious
blood of our Lord Jesus Christ.[35] 'So Job died, old and
full of days' (Job 42:17).

## 'Death, be not proud'

*For we were born yesterday, and know nothing, because our days on earth are a shadow* (Bildad, Job 8:9).

> God has wonderful and incomprehensible means to deliver us from affliction ... and notwithstanding that we were as good as at death's door, so that it might seem we should never be plucked out of our miseries, yet God will find some good way out of them. This cannot be perceived at the first glance, since his intention is also to bring us low, in order that we may learn to flee to him for refuge.[36]

*Though he slay me, yet will I trust him* (Job 13:15).

> Naturally we desire to live and, consequently, we shun death. Death is horrible to us because it is contrary to our nature. It is a thing that dismays a man. But on the other part we see that we are held here as in a prison: so long as this body of ours compasses us about, we are in bondage to sin, and therefore we are forced to sigh and be sorry. And besides, we long for the everlastingness which is promised us after the time that God takes us out of this world. When we draw near towards death (then we come to it, and death is the very gate of life), we assure ourselves that inasmuch as Jesus Christ has passed the same way, we do not need to be afraid that death will have any power over us; it is a dulled or blunted sword of which the point is broken off, so that it cannot hurt us. And although it will draw some blood from us, the same sword will serve only to rid us of all diseases.[37]

## Tested as gold in a furnace

*Look, I go forward, but he is not there,*
*And backward, but I cannot perceive him;*
*When he works on the left hand, I cannot behold him;*
*When he turns to the right hand, I cannot see him.*
*But he knows the way that I take;*
*When he has tested me, I shall come forth as gold.*

(Job 23:8-10)

Let us consider well that when we have trudged up and
down we will never be a whit nearer to finding out the
end of all things. Our Lord will show us that our wit is too
weak and ignorant to attain to such height. Our knowing,
therefore, must be only in part, and it must be sufficient
for us to taste in some certain measure the things that are
for our welfare, waiting for the latter day when we shall
have them fully revealed to us... Now Job adds immediately, 'But he knows the way that I take; when he has
tested me, I shall come forth as gold.' By this Job indi-
cates that God has a great advantage over him. I cannot
know *him* (says Job), but he knows *me;* I do not understand his works, and he judges mine to fall short. He tries
me as gold in the furnace, so that there is not so much as
a piece of dross or infirmity in me, except that he sees
and discerns it; and therefore it is to no purpose for me to
go to law with him... Now this saying of his is very true
— that God knows our ways and he tries and proves us
as gold in the furnace; yet notwithstanding his testing us,
have we any reason to complain that we are not his
equal? ... Though God does not make us hail-fellow with
himself, ought we to say that he does us wrong or injury?
Therefore, whenever it comes to our mind that God
knows all our ways and that he tries us and purges and
sifts out all the sinful affections and superfluous thoughts
that are in us, let us understand that the same must teach

us humility and reverence, and not to provoke us to make any complaint, as Job does.[38]

## From John Calvin's final sermon on Job

When we are suffering, it must not grieve us as if we are meanly afflicted and that God chastises us according to our infirmity... We must not think it strange; but let us resort to this story of Job, which is written for our learning, and therefore have an eye to the end. If we look no further than the extremity in which Job was during the time that God persecuted him — alas, we will be utterly dismayed, and there is none who will not be utterly afraid, saying, 'What does it profit a man to fear God, seeing that those who have walked in his fear are most unfortunate?' But when we look upon the end, that is the thing in which we have to comfort ourselves: first of all (as I have said), the afflictions of God's children last only a while; and secondly, afflictions serve as salves and medicines. Moreover, the end of them is always happy, inasmuch as they have every reason to glorify God, not only when he delivers them, but also because he mortifies their wicked faults. In this also they have a better confirmation of the doctrine that, where our Lord Jesus Christ is the living image of all the faithful children of God, they are made to conform to him. As Paul declares in the eighth chapter of Romans, in all our adversities we are shaped like the image of our Lord Jesus Christ, who is the eldest Son in the house of God. And truly, if we look only upon the cross of Jesus Christ — it is cursed by God's own wrath — we see nothing there but shame and terror and, to be short, it will seem that the very gate of hell is open to swallow up Jesus Christ. But when we join his resurrection to his death — behold it to comfort us, behold it to assuage all our sorrows, so that we shall not be over-sorrowful whenever it pleases God to afflict us. This was purposely fulfilled in our Lord Jesus Christ, to the intent that we should know that this was not written for any one person only, but that all of us should understand that the Son of God will make us partners of his life if we die with him, and partakers of his glory, if we bear all the shame and adversities which it shall please God to lay upon our shoulders.[39]

## The prayer that John Calvin ordinarily made at the end of his sermons

Let us fall down before the face of our good God ... that it may please him to grant this grace, not only to us but to all people and nations of the earth, bringing back poor ignorant souls from the miserable bondage of error and darkness to the right way of salvation. For the doing thereof it may please him to raise up true and faithful ministers of the Word, who seek not their own profit and glory but only the advancement of his holy name and the welfare of his flock, and to root out all sects, errors, and heresies, which are seeds of trouble and division among his people, to the end that we may live in good brotherly accord altogether. May it please him to guide with his Holy Spirit all kings, princes, and magistrates, who have the rule of the sword, to the end that their reign will not be marked by covetousness, cruelty, tyranny, or any other evil and disordered affection, but in all justice and uprightness; and that we also living under them may yield them their due honour and obedience, so that by means of good peace and quietness we may fear God in all holiness and honesty. May it please him to comfort afflicted persons whom he visits in diverse manners with crosses and tribulations, all people whom he afflicts with plague, war, or famine, or other of his rods; and all persons who

are smitten with poverty, imprisonment, sickness, banishment, or other calamity or vexation of mind, giving
them good patience, till he sends them full discharge of
their miseries. May it especially please him to have pity
upon all his poor faithful ones who are dispersed in the
captivity of Babylon under the tyranny of Antichrist,
chiefly those who suffer persecution for the witnessing of
his truth, strengthening them with true confidence and
comforting them, and not allowing the wicked and raven-
ing wolves to execute their rage against them, but giving
them such a true steadfastness that his holy name may be
glorified by them, both in life and death. Finally, may it
please him to enlighten all churches that are nowadays in
danger and assaulted for the quarrel of his holy name,
and overthrow and destroy all the devices, practices, and
attempts of all his adversaries, to the intent that his glory
may shine over all and the kingdom of our Lord Jesus
Christ may be increased and advanced more and more.
Let us pray to him for all the said things in such a way
that our good Master and Lord Jesus Christ has taught us
to pray, saying, Our Father, etc.

'When he has tested me, I shall come forth as gold' (Job 23:10).

Let thy gold be cast into the furnace,
    The red gold, precious and bright;
Do not fear the hungry fire,
    With its caverns of burning light;
And thy gold shall return more precious,
    Free from every spot and stain;
For gold must be tried by fire,
    As a heart must be tried by pain!

In the cruel fire of sorrow
    Cast thy heart, do not faint or wail;
Let thy hand be firm and steady,
    Do not let thy spirit quail;
But wait till the trial is over
    And take thy heart again;
For as gold is tried by fire,
    So a heart must be tried by pain!

I shall know by the gleam and the glitter
    Of the golden chain you wear,
By your heart's calm strength in loving,
    Of the fire they have had to bear.
Beat on, true heart, forever!
    Shine bright, strong golden chain!
And bless the cleansing fire,
    And the furnace of living pain!

                          Adelaide Anne Proctor

# Endnotes

## Preface

[1] Lt Carey H. Cash, *A table in the presence,* W Publishing Group, a Division of Thomas Nelson Publishers, 2004.

## Chapter 1

[1] John Calvin, Commentary on Jeremiah 36:3; translated by Calvin Translation Society, Christian Classics Ethereal Library; hereafter, Calvin's Commentaries are abbreviated: Comm.

[2] Comm., Ps. 41:1.

[3] Comm., Ps. 25:18.

[4] John Calvin, *Golden booklet of the true Christian life,* tr. Henry Van Andel, Baker Books, 1952, p.66.

[5] Calvin, *Institutes of the Christian religion,* tr. John Allen, Wm. B. Eerdmans, 1949, III.8.2.

[6] *Golden booklet,* p.51.

[7] As above.

[8] *Institutes,* III.8.2.

[9] *Institutes,* III.8.3.

[10] Seneca, *De Vit Beata* ('Concerning the blessed life'), 15, quoted in *Institutes* III.8.4.

[11] *Institutes,* III.8.5.

[12] *Institutes,* III.8.6.

[13] Comm., Ps. 37:25.

[14] Comm., Zech. 13:9.

[15] As above.

[16] Calvin, comment on 1 Peter 1:17 in his correspondence, source unknown.

[17] Comm., Ps. 66:10.

[18] Comm. IV, 'The Christian life' 3. Calvin's comments on 1 Peter 1:7 express the same dual purpose of trial by the fire of affliction.

[19] Comm., 1 Peter 1:7

[20] As above.

[21] Comm., James 1:2-3.

[22] From Calvin's correspondence; source unknown.
[23] Comm., Rom. 5:3.
[24] Comm., Rom. 5:5.
[25] Comm., 2 Cor. 12:7.
[26] Comm., Ps. 119:71.
[27] Comm., Ps. 142:4.
[28] Comm., Isa. 25:4.
[29] Comm., Ps. 138:7.
[30] *Institutes,* III.9.3.
[31] Herman Bavinck, *Our reasonable faith,* tr. Henry Zylstra, Wm. B. Eerdmans Publishing Co., 1956, p.28.
[32] *Psalter hymnal,* CRC Publications, 1987, p. 500.

## Chapter 2

[1] *The Belgic confession,* Article 13. During the sixteenth century the churches in the Netherlands were suffering fierce persecution by the Roman Catholic Church-state; the *Belgic confession of faith* was drafted as a witness that the adherents of the Reformed faith were law-abiding citizens who professed the true Christian doctrine according to the holy Scriptures.
[2] Comm. on Ps. 29:10-11.
[3] As above.
[4] *Institutes,* I.17.11.
[5] Comm. on Ps. 11:4.
[6] *Institutes,* I.16.2.
[7] Benjamin B. Warfield, 'The theology of John Calvin', Presbyterian board of publication, 1909.
[8] Comm. on Ps.138:6; includes a comment on Ps. 113:6.
[9] Comm. on Ps. 35:22.
[10] Comm. on Ps. 22, introduction.
[11] Comm. on Ps. 37:18.
[12] Comm. on Ps. 11:4.
[13] Comm. on Ps. 61:7.
[14] Comm. on Ps. 135:6.
[15] Comm. on Ps. 93:1-2.
[16] Comm. on Ps. 11:4.
[17] Calvin, *Lettres françaises, 1:16-17; 1:14.*
[18] Comm. on Ps. 135:6.
[19] Comm. on Ps. 73:2.
[20] *Institutes,* I.17.7.
[21] *Institutes,* I.16.2.
[22] *Institutes,* I.17.11.
[23] *Institutes,* I.17.8.
[24] Calvin, Sermon 79 on Job.
[25] Comm. on Ps. 37:1.

26  Comm. on Ps. 37:19.

27  Comm. on Ps. 37:24.

28  Comm. on Ps. 88:6.

29  Comm. on Ps. 37:23-24.

30  *Institutes,* II.15.4.

31  Comm. on Ps. 39:9.

32  Comm. on Ps. 71:20-21.

33  As above.

34  *Supplementa Calviana,* 1:726; quoted in Bernard Cottrett, *Calvin: a biography,* translated from the French by M. Wallace McDonald, Wm. B. Eerdmans Publishing Co./ T. & T. Clark, 1955/2000, p.307.

35  Comm. on 1 Peter 3:17.

36  Comm. on Ps. 91:8.

37  Comm. on Ps. 36:6.

38  As above.

39  Alan Paton, *Cry, the beloved country,* Macmillan Publishing Co., a Scribner Classic/Collier edition, 1948, p.108. Reprinted with permission of Scribner, an imprint of Simon & Schuster Adult Publishing Group from *Cry, the beloved country* by Alan Paton. Copyright 1948 by Alan Paton; copyright renewed 1976 by Alan Paton.

40  Comm. on Ps. 88:5.

41  *The Presbyterian hymnal,* Westminster/John Knox Press, 1990, p. 270.

42  Comm. on Ps. 56:8.

43  G. C. Berkouwer, *The providence of God,* translated from the Dutch by Lewis B. Smedes, Wm. B. Eerdmans Publishing Co., 1952, pp.46-47.

## Chapter 3

1   G. C. Berkouwer, *The providence of God,* Wm. B. Eerdmans Publishing Co., 1952, p.232.

2   Berkouwer, *Providence,* p.233.

3   John Calvin, Comm. on Jer. 44:13.

4   Comm. on Hab.1:13.

5   Hab. 3:17-18.

6   Elihu Root (1845-1937), 'Experiments in government and the essentials of the constitution', The Stafford Little Lectures, p.13. Root was one of America's notable statesmen. His lecture was delivered in 1913 at Princeton University.

7   John Calvin, 157th Sermon on Deuteronomy, quoted in Bernard Cottrett, *Calvin: a biography,* translated from the French edition, 1955, by M. Wallace McDonald, Wm. B. Eerdmans Publishing Co., 2000, p.306.

8   Source: CARE Newsroom, online report.

9   Comm. on Rom. 1:24.

10  As above.

11  Comm. on Ps. 6:1, emphasis added.

[12] Comm. on Ps. 66:10-12, emphasis added.
[13] Comm. on Ps. 66:10.
[14] As above.
[15] Comm. on Ps.74:1
[16] *Institutes,* III.2.20-21.
[17] Comm. on Heb. 12:4.
[18] Comm. on Heb. 12:6.
[19] Comm. on Heb. 12:11.
[20] Comm. on Ps. 119:67.
[21] Comm. on Ps. 51:3.
[22] Comm. on Ps. 38:1, 2.
[23] Comm. on Ps. 38:3.
[24] Comm. on Ps. 38:6.
[25] Comm. on Ps. 137:1
[26] Comm. on Ps. 130:3
[27] Comm. on John 9:2
[28] Comm. on 1 Peter 3:17, emphasis added.
[29] Comm. on John 9:3.
[30] Joni Eareckson Tada, 'Suffering and the sovereignty of God', Gospel-com.net, n/d.
[31] Comm. on Ps. 88:15.
[32] Comm. on Ps. 103:4.
[33] Comm. on Ps. 74:9-12.
[34] Comm. on Ps. 79:10-13.
[35] Comm. on Ps. 89:30-37.
[36] As above.
[37] Comm. on Isa. 48:9.
[38] *Institutes,* III.8.6.
[39] Berkouwer, *Providence,* p.266.
[40] Rev. 15:3.
[41] Berkouwer, *Providence,* pp.269-70.

## Chapter 4

[1] Comm. on Ps. 12:6.
[2] *Institutes,* III.2.28.
[3] *Institutes,* III.2.29.
[4] *Institutes,* III.2.32.
[5] Comm. on 2 Cor. 1:20.
[6] *Institutes,* III.2.41.
[7] Comm. on Ps. 43:3.
[8] Calvin, *Golden booklet,* p.52.
[9] *Institutes,* III.2.17.
[10] Comm. on Ps. 42:5.
[11] Calvin, *Golden booklet,* p.52.

12 Comm. on Ps. 145:18.
13 Comm. on Ps. 119:28.
14 Comm. on Ps. 27:13.
15 Comm. on Ps. 27:1.
16 *Institutes*, III.8.3.
17 Comm. on Ps. 11:1.
18 As above.
19 Comm. on Ps. 119:107.
20 Comm. on Hab. 3:17-18.
21 Comm. on Ps. 62:1.
22 Comm. on Ps. 13:1-2.
23 Comm. on Ps. 37:4.
24 Comm. on Ps. 37:9.
25 As above.
26 John Donne, 'Death, be not proud'.
27 Comm. on Hosea 13:14.

## Chapter 5

1 Augustine, *The confessions of St Augustine*, Book XI; John B. Alden, Publisher, 1891, p. 348.
2 *Heidelberg catechism*, 1563, Q. & A. 117.
3 Comm. on Ps. 13:1.
4 Comm. on Ps. 62:8.
5 Comm. on Ps. 25:6.
6 Comm. on Ps. 102, prefatory synopsis.
7 Comm. on Ps. 102:1
8 Comm. on Ps. 22:19.
9 Comm. on Ps. 22:17.
10 Comm. on Ps. 88:14.
11 Comm. on Ps. 142:1-4.
12 Comm. on Ps. 38:9.
13 Comm. on Hab. 1:2-3.
14 As above.
15 Comm. on Ps. 34:17.
16 Comm. on John 14:14.
17 Comm. on 1 John 5:14.
18 Comm. on 1 John 5:15.
19 Comm. on 1 John 3:22.
20 *Institutes*, II.16.16.
21 Sermon on 1 Tim. 2:5-6, John Calvin, *Grace and its fruits*, prepared by Joseph Hill, Evangelical Press, 2000. p.52.
22 As above.
23 Comm. on Rom. 8:26.
24 As above.

25  Comm. on Rom. 8:27.
26  Comm. on Ps. 119:153, emphasis added.
27  Comm. on Ps. 13:3.
28  Comm. on Ps. 13:4. Such comments by Calvin have application especially to persecuted Christians.
29  Comm. on Ps. 22:1.
30  Comm. on Ps. 9:18.
31  As above.
32  Comm. on Ps. 86:5.
33  Comm. on Ps. 86:6-7.
34  Comm. on 2 Cor. 12:8.
35  *Institutes,* III.20.51.
36  Comm. on Ps. 143:6.
37  Comm. on Ps. 34:6-7, emphasis added.
38  Comm. on Ps. 88:7, emphasis added.
39  Comm. on Ps. 86:2.
40  Comm. on Ps. 65:2.
41  Comm. on Ps. 74:12, emphasis added.
42  Comm. on Ps. 6:6, emphasis added.
43  *Institutes,* III.20.52.
44  Comm. on Ps. 55:16-17.
45  Comm. on Rom. 12:12.
46  Comm. on Ps. 39:5, emphasis added.
47  Comm. on Ps. 131:1.
48  As above.
49  Comm. on Ps. 91:15.
50  Comm. on 1 John 5:14.
51  Comm. on Ps. 143:10.
52  Comm. on Ps. 25:4-5, emphasis added.
53  Comm. on Ps. 25:19.
54  *Heidelberg catechism,* Q. & A. 116.
55  *Institutes,* III.20.28.
56  Comm. on Phil. 4:6
57  Comm. on 1 Thess. 5:16-18.

## Chapter 6

1   William Shakespeare, *Othello,* Act II, Scene 3.
2   Comm. on 2 Thess. 1:4.
3   Comm. on Ps. 40:1, emphasis added.
4   Ps. 63:5, *Today's English Version* (TEV).
5   Comm. on Ps. 63:5.
6   Ps. 119:81, emphasis added.
7   Comm. on James 1:3, emphasis added.
8   As above.

[9]  Comm. on James 1:4.
[10] John Milton, *Paradise lost,* Book II, line 568; 'obdur'd', from obdurate, stubborn.
[11] 'Keen', a loud wailing lamentation.
[12] Comm. on Ps. 31:9.
[13] Comm. on Ps. 39:3.
[14] Comm. on Heb. 10:36.
[15] Comm. on 1 Peter 3:14.
[16] Comm. on Ps. 94:12-13.
[17] François, *Moral maxims and reflections,* No. 420, F. A. Stokes Co., 1930.
[18] Comm. on Ps. 94:13.
[19] *Institutes,* III.7.10.
[20] *Institutes,* III.8.11.
[21] *Institutes,* III.8.10.
[22] *Institutes,* III.8.9.
[23] *Institutes,* III.8.10.
[24] Comm. on Col. 1:11.
[25] *Golden booklet,* p.60.
[26] Comm. on Ps. 94:12-13.
[27] Comm. on Rom. 15:4.
[28] Comm. on Ps. 27:14.
[29] Comm. on Ps. 130:5.
[30] Comm. on Jer. 20:17-18.
[31] As above.
[32] Comm. on James 5:10-11.
[33] As above.
[34] Comm. on Ps. 116:7, emphasis added.

## Chapter 7

[1]  *Golden booklet,* pp.52-53.
[2]  J. Calvin, twenty-sixth sermon on 1 Timothy; in Bernard Cottrett, *Calvin: a Biography,* p.194.
[3]  Sermon on 2 Tim. 4:7-8, *Grace and its fruits,* pp.244-245.
[4]  *Grace and its fruits,* p.246.
[5]  Comm. on Heb. 12:2.
[6]  Comm. on 2 Cor. 12:9, emphasis added.
[7]  Comm. on Ps. 16:8, emphasis added.
[8]  *Institutes,* III.8.3.
[9]  Comm. on Ps. 143:4.
[10] As above.
[11] Comm. on Ps. 63:8, emphasis added.
[12] William Walters, *The life and labours of Robert Moffat,* Walter Scott, 1887, p.113.
[13] Comm. on Hab. 3:19.

14  Comm. on 2 Thess. 2:16-17, emphasis added.
15  Comm. on Ps. 69:3.
16  Comm. on Ps. 48:14, emphasis added.
17  As above.
18  *Grace and its fruits*, p.135.
19  Comm. on Isaiah 40:31.

## Chapter 8

1  John Calvin, *Letters of John Calvin, selected from the Bonnet edition,* Banner of Truth Trust, 1980, p.182; used by permission.
2  *Letters,* p.186.
3  Comm. on Ps. 91:5.
4  In the time of the prophet Elisha, the army of Syria, or Aram, made repeated raids on Israel and was seemingly invincible. But another army was standing by to do battle with Syria — the 'horses and chariots' of God. This army was not only invincible, but *invisible* (2 Kings 6:8-23).
5  Comm. on Ps. 112:7-8.
6  Comm. on Ps. 37:3, emphasis added.
7  As above.
8  *Letters,* p.90.
9  Comm. on Ps. 121:3
10  Comm. on Ps. 121:8.
11  Comm. on Ps. 121:6.
12  'Felix of Nola', *Catholic Encyclopedia,* E. Knight, online editor.
13  Comm. on Acts 16:23-28.
14  Comm. on Ps. 63:6-7, emphasis added.
15  As above.
16  Comm. on Ps. 83:2-3, emphasis added.
17  Comm. on Ps. 119:114, emphasis added.
18  Comm. on Ps. 27:5.
19  Comm. on Ps. 91:4.
20  Comm. on Ps. 17:8.
21  Comm. on Ps.61:3-4.
22  *Institutes,* I.14.7.
23  Comm. on Ps. 91, introduction.
24  Comm. on Ps. 91:11.
25  Comm. on Ps. 34:7.
26  Comm. on Acts 12:7, 11.
27  Persecuted church news, online: worldevangelical.org.
28  *Letters,* p.225.
29  Comm. on Matt. 16:18.
30  Comm. on Isa. 54:17.
31  Comm. on Ps. 68:7.
32  Comm. on Ps. 46:1.

33 As above.
34 Comm. on Ps. 31:1-5.
35 As above.
36 Comm. on Ps. 36:1-2.
37 *Institutes,* III.2.21.
38 Comm. on Ps. 49:15, emphasis added.
39 Comm. on Isa. 11:4.
40 As above.

## Chapter 9
1 John Dryden (1631-1700), *Brittania Rediviva.*
2 Rich Miller, 'Park branches', newsletter of Park Presbyterian Church, April 2004; used by permission.
3 Comm. on Ps. 30:4.
4 Comm. on Phil. 4:4. Paul acknowledges the difficulty of finding joy in a time of trial. See also comments on 1 Peter 4:13: 'For it is not suitable in the midst of afflictions to think of joy, which can free us from all trouble; but the consolations of God moderate evils, so that we can rejoice at the same time.'
5 Comm. on Ps. 32:7.
6 Comm. on Ps. 40:3.
7 Comm. on Ps. 13:5-6.
8 Jer. 20:14.
9 Comm. on Jer. 20:14-16, emphasis added.
10 Comm. on Ps. 66:13-15. See also Ps. 54:6, 'I will freely sacrifice to you; I will praise your name, O LORD...'
11 Comm. on Ps. 17:7, emphasis added.
12 *Institutes,* III.8.11.
13 Comm. on Ps. 56:4.
14 Comm. on Ps. 126:2.
15 Comm. on Ps. 34:3.
16 Comm. on Jer. 20:13.
17 Comm. on 1 Thess. 5:16-18.
18 As above.
19 As above.
20 Comm. on Ps. 140:13.
21 Comm. on Ps. 30:11-12.
22 Comm. on Ps. 34:1-2.
23 Comm. on Ps. 35, Introduction.
24 Comm. on Ps. 104:33.
25 Comm. on Ps. 66:13-16, emphasis added.
26 Comm. on Heb. 2:12, emphasis added.
27 Comm. on Acts 16:25.
28 Comm. on Ps. 37:6.

## Chapter 10

[1]  Calvin, *Letters,* p.76.
[2]  Comm. on Acts 14:22.
[3]  Comm. on Matt. 24:9.
[4]  As above, emphasis added.
[5]  Ann Coulter, *How to talk to a liberal (if you must),* 2004, online excerpts.
[6]  Comm. on Ps. 44:22.
[7]  Courtney Anderson, *To the golden shore: the life of Adoniram Judson,* Judson Press, 1987, p.257.
[8]  Comm. on 1 Peter 4:12.
[9]  Comm. on 2 Tim. 3:12.
[10] Calvin, *Letters,* p.197.
[11] Comm. on Matt. 16:24.
[12] Calvin, 'On suffering persecution', *The world's famous orations,* Continental Europe, Bartleby.com, 1906.
[13] Comm. on 1 Peter 2:21.
[14] Comm. on Heb. 2:10.
[15] J. Hudson Taylor, biography, Bethany House, n. d., pp.68-71.
[16] Comm. on Acts 5:46.
[17] Comm. on Gal. 6:17.
[18] Calvin, 'The Christian warfare', comm. on Matt. 19:27-29.
[19] Calvin, *Letters.*
[20] Calvin, *Golden booklet,* pp.48, 49.
[21] 'Christian persecution in China', online report, Pesecution.org.
[22] *Institutes,* III.8.1, emphasis added.
[23] *Institutes,* III.18.7.
[24] *Institutes,* III.15.8.
[25] Comm. on Phil. 3:10-11.
[26] *Lettres françaises,* ed. J. Bonnet, Meyrueis, 1854, vol. 1, p.303.
[27] Comm. on 1 Peter 4:12-14.
[28] Comm. on Col. 1:24.
[29] Andrew T. Lincoln, Colossians, *New interpreter's Bible,* Leander Keck, editor, Abingdon, 2000, vol. XI, used by permission.
[30] Comm. on Col. 1:24-29.
[31] As above.
[32] Comm. on 1 Cor. 10:16.
[33] As above.
[34] *Institutes,* IV.1.3.

## Chapter 11

[1]  Calvin, *Letters,* p.107. On 11 April 1559, Calvin wrote to his friend William Farel informing him of the death of Idelette de Bure, Calvin's wife. He

relates that, on her deathbed, shortly before her departure, she offered a prayer as best she could. This prayer serves as the epigraph to the chapter.
2 Comm. on Heb. 6:19.
3 *Westminster Shorter Catechism,* Q & A 16.
4 Comm. on Col.1:27.
5 Comm. on Rom. 5:5.
6 Herman Ridderbos, *Paul: an outline of his theology,* tr. John Richard DeWitt, Wm. B. Eerdmans Publishing Co., 1975, p.248.
7 *Institutes,* III.3.42.
8 Comm. on Ps. 57:1-2.
9 Comm. on 1 Peter 1:9.
10 *Institutes,* II.10.19.
11 *Grace and its fruits,* pp.309-310.
12 *Grace and its fruits,* p. 311.
13 Comm. on Rom. 8:18.
14 Comm. on 2 Tim. 2:10.
15 Comm. on Ps. 61:5.
16 *Letters,* p.110.
17 Comm. on 2 Cor. 4:16-17.
18 As above.
19 As above.
20 Comm. on Ps. 89:47, emphasis added.
21 John Calvin, *Golden booklet,* p.68.
22 As above, p.73.
23 As above, pp.79-80.
24 Calvin, *Lettres françaises,* 2:310, quoted in Cotrett, *Calvin: a biography.*
25 Calvin, 'The Christian warfare', comments on Matt. 19:27-29.
26 Comm. on Rom.12:12.
27 *Letters,* p.153.
28 Comm. on Gen. 37:35.
29 Comm. on Heb. 2:14.
30 Comm. on Heb. 2:15.
31 Comm. on Ps. 56:3-4.
32 *Institutes,* III.2.16.
33 Comm. on John 16:20.
34 Comm. on 1 Cor. 15:26.
35 Comm. on Ps. 72:12.
36 Comm. on Ps. 73:24
37 As above.
38 Rev. 5:12. See G. C. Berkouwer, *The providence of God,* pp.265-269, for a treatment of 'doxology'.

## Chapter 12
1 Sources: BBC News, 20 October 2004; CNN News, 16 November 2004.

[2] Theodore Beza, *The life of John Calvin,* Evangelical Press, 1997, p.95

[3] For an excellent treatment of Job and the problem of suffering and evil, see D. A. Carson, *How long, O Lord,* Baker Books and Intervarsity Press, 1990, pp.153-178.

[4] John Calvin, *Sermons on Job,* Facsimile 1574 Edition, Banner of Truth Trust, 1994, Sermon 71, p.335.b.49.

[5] John Calvin, Sermon 101 (Job 28:1-9), p.476.a.7. Hereafter, sermon number, text, and page of first line.

[6] 1 (Job 1:1), p.1.b.38.

[7] 5 (Job 1:9-12), p.22.b.2.

[8] 22 (Job 5:19-27), p.100.a.24.

[9] 157 (Job 42:4-5), p.739.a.35.

[10] 78 (Job 21:1-6), p.369.b.4.

[11] 131 (Job 34:21-26), p.623.b.13.

[12] 36 (Job 9:23-28), p.165.b.58.

[13] 135 (Job 35:2-7), p.639.a.14.

[14] 121 (Job 32:11-22), p.569.b.47.

[15] 8 (Job 2:1-6), p.36.a.14.

[16] 11 (Job 3:2-10), p.48.a.39.

[17] 95 (Job 26:1-7), p.445.a.61.

[18] As above, p.445.b.25.

[19] 14 (Job 3:1-6), p.61.a.44.

[20] 66 (Job 17:6-16), p.310.b.6.

[21] 7 (Job 1:20-22), p.29.a.2.

[22] 6 (Job 1:13-19), p.26.a.20.

[23] 123 (Job 33:8-14), p.579.b.16.

[24] 20 (Job 5:11-16), p.89.a.64.

[25] 27 (Job 7:1-6), p.127.a.30.

[26] 70 (Job 19: 13-16), p.330.a.1

[27] 18 (Job 5:1-7), p.83.b.41.

[28] 17 (Job 4:20—5:2), p.79.a.4.

[29] 50 (Job 13:11-15), p.236.b.47.

[30] 69 (Job 19:1-12), p.326.a.38 and a.56.

[31] 99 (Job 27:8-12), p.466.a.11.

[32] 70 (Job 19:13-16), p.327.a.21.

[33] 159 (Job 42:9-17), p.748.a.10.

[34] As above, p.750.b.50.

[35] 32 (Job 8:13-22), p.150.b.47.

[36] 31 (Job 13:11-15), p.142.b30.

[37] 50 (Job 13:11-15), p.236.a.24.

[38] 90 (Job 23:8-12), p.418.b.55.

[39] 159 (Job 42:9-17), p.749.a.60.

[40] John Calvin, *Sermons,* pp.751-52.